ANTHEM OF MISOGYNY

ANTHEM OF MISOGYNY

The War on Women in North Africa and the Middle East

IBTISSAM BOUACHRINE

ROWMAN & LITTLEFIELD
Lanham • Boulder • New York • London

Published by Rowman & Littlefield
An imprint of The Rowman & Littlefield Publishing Group, Inc.
4501 Forbes Boulevard, Suite 200, Lanham, Maryland 20706
www.rowman.com

86-90 Paul Street, London EC2A 4NE

British Library Cataloguing in Publication Information Available

Library of Congress Cataloging-in-Publication Data
Names: Bouachrine, Ibtissam, author.
   Title: Anthem of misogyny : the war on women in North Africa and the Middle
      East / Ibtissam Bouachrine.
   Description: Lanham, Maryland : Rowman & Littlefield Publishers, 2022. |
      Includes bibliographical references and index. | Summary: "This book
      investigates experiences and practices of misogyny in North Africa and
      the Middle East"-- Provided by publisher.
   Identifiers: LCCN 2022021208 (print) | LCCN 2022021209 (ebook) | ISBN
      9781538160893 (cloth) | ISBN 9781538198827 (paper) | ISBN 9781538160909 (ebook)
   Subjects: LCSH: Misogyny--Africa, North. | Misogyny--Middle East. |
      Women--Violence against--Africa, North. | Women--Violence
      against--Middle East. | Women--Africa, North--Social conditions. |
      Women--Middle East--Social conditions.
   Classification: LCC HQ1790.5 .B68 2022 (print) | LCC HQ1790.5 (ebook) |
      DDC 305.40961--dc23/eng/20220521
   LC record available at https://lccn.loc.gov/2022021208
   LC ebook record available at https://lccn.loc.gov/2022021209

To all the women and girls whose pain is unseen

This is a trigger warning for the entire book. It contains discussions of rape and different forms of violence and abuse against women and girls both offline and online.

Contents

PREFACE

This book is about the persistence of misogyny in North Africa and the Middle East, the various forms and articulations of violence that women and girls in the region endure because of men's attitudes toward their bodies, and a construction of masculinity that is intimately tied to having and maintaining supremacy over women. It takes as a point of departure that the only reason human beings abuse others is because they can.

For many, this book is akin to heresy as it is written against a dominant orthodoxy in Western feminism. "Gendered orientalism," "savior complex," and even "Islamophobia": these are the accusations made against critics who dare to bring up misogyny and gender-based violence in North Africa and the Middle East in contexts other than blaming the West. Rather than exaggerate Western agency, I am invested in making visible Muslim agency. This cannot be done through celebratory narratives about Muslim women's resistance and resilience alone, for not all stories about Muslim women are soothing and uplifting. There are narratives of violence and injustice that produce discomfort, anger, and even despair. Those stories merit being told, and those behind the injustices are entitled to an unapologetic portrayal, because the non-West, too, is deserving of critique.

My aim is to bring misogyny to the center of the debate about women in North Africa and the Middle East and to retrace existing power relations, social practices, and cultural norms that have normalized the abuse of women and girls in the region. Misogyny here is understood both in its simple and basic definition of hatred against women with the aim of keeping them under patriarchy's control and as a complex moral system of legitimacy that uses religion and tradition to secure a supply of transgressions, which, in turn, reinforce the need to sustain misogyny.

Through this understanding, I seek to shift the perception of misogyny in the region from a consequence to a cause of women's condition. Often, in a hierarchical order of priorities, misogyny is viewed as an involuntary side effect of more important injustices, such as unemployment, poverty, and lack of resources, that impact the entire society, women and men alike. First comes employment, or first comes education, or first comes access to water, the argument goes, and then women's rights will follow. Moreover, as new academic trends and global concerns emerge, the most recent of which is the COVID-19 pandemic, women find themselves, once again, further down the list of priorities.

In this book, I argue that misogyny, which operates through an interconnected network of ideologies, institutions, beliefs, aesthetics, and cultural trends, is too complex and too deep-rooted to eradicate with superficial changes. Like a national anthem, misogyny in North Africa and the Middle East has come to acquire a sacred status that leaves it accepted uncritically and is woven effortlessly into daily practices, to create a community of men of different ages, educational levels, and socioeconomic backgrounds who are united in their sense of entitlement to evaluate, scrutinize, deter, question, and expose women, who, for their part, are ever-vigilant. For them, it is as if they are in a state of perpetual war, forever on the verge of being accused of deviating from the norms and then of being punished. These norms, however, are neither clear nor predictable. The misogyny studied in this book continuously evolves, as well as creates and innovates.

Too often, it is only after violence has reached a high threshold and is visually documented and made public that the suffering inflicted on a woman in the region comes to the forefront of national and international discussion. Therefore, an additional goal is to interrogate the limited understanding of what constitutes legitimate suffering when one is a woman. This book seeks to expand the debate about women in North Africa and the Middle East to include injustices that do not necessarily leave black, blue, and bloody marks on women's bodies. The injustices are committed both in private and public, on Facebook, Instagram, and YouTube. Though the scars are at times invisible to the naked eye, they are just as damaging and long lasting. Most often, these injustices serve as prologue to the final injustice: death.

OVERVIEW

This book is anchored in the story of Hanan, a Moroccan woman who was subjected to rape and torture that resulted in her death. The six chapters around which this book is organized are an attempt to reconstruct the larger context that led to the violence that Hanan endured. The first chapter begins by telling Hanan's story and the reactions it triggered. It then explores the subject of critics' positionality and how it affects feminist silence and counter-silence about misogyny in North Africa and the Middle East. Chapter 2 delves into the medieval context of present-day misogyny in Muslim-majority societies. It concludes with a discussion of the Taliban regime's misogynistic laws and practices as an example that complicates understandings of progress and allegiance in the region.

Chapter 3 focuses on what I term "isolatory narratives" of gender-based violence. These narratives seek to construct violence against women as a series of isolated phenomena, thus denying or minimizing the central place misogyny occupies in Muslim-majority societies. The chapter illustrates how, far from isolated events, violence in the region has become banalized, affecting all women and girls regardless of age, education, ability, privilege, or socioeconomic status. This violence, however, is not limited to the offline world. The next chapter turns to misogyny online. North Africa and the Middle East have one of the world's largest communities of "digital natives," prolific in consuming and creating online content. The chapter examines various forms of cyber violence and their potentially devastating impact on women's lives online and offline.

Chapter 5 analyzes further the intimate relationship between trends, technology, and misogyny. It looks at how hatred for women has turned into "spoken truth" through a genre of popular songs that combines hip hop, rap, and reggaeton with other indigenous African genres including chaabi, raï, and gnawa. Although produced primarily in Morocco, and mainly in Darija (Moroccan Arabic vernacular), these songs, all of which are released on YouTube, have achieved success throughout North Africa, the Middle East, and beyond. The summer following the release of Saad Lamjarred's "Enty" ("You feminine") (2014), I heard it played in a shop on Jerusalem's Salah ad-Din Street and sung by a street performer in Istanbul's Istiqlal Street. These songs and their singers, the chapter argues, have come to serve as the anthem of the new Muslim *rujula* (masculinity): global in its aesthetics and local in its allegiances.

The prevalence of violence against women and girls throughout North Africa and the Middle East at home, on the street, online, and in popular culture coincides with the increasing engagement of Muslim-majority societies with various aspects of Western modernity. The final chapter, therefore, explores the persistence of misogyny in the context of the coexistence of the values of local traditions and Western modernity. It argues that a selective engagement with Western modernity has enabled societies in the region to choose which aspects of modernity to adopt or reject, thus making it difficult to achieve lasting feminist reforms if unsanctioned by religion and tradition.

Methodology

This book is not intended primarily for an academic readership. I am far less interested in advancing a particular academic thesis than in making visible misogyny and its centrality in North Africa and the Middle East. This book's methodological considerations reflect this agenda. It relies on a variety of sources to allow for a divergent style of thinking about women and gender issues in the region. These texts include scholarship by feminists, philosophers, artists, sociologists, and political scientists from the West and Muslim-majority countries, as well as those who occupy both spaces. Publications on the various social media platforms have also been privileged in this study, though the focus is not social media. Instead, I rely on the most popular texts produced, disseminated, and consumed in North Africa and the Middle East, and these texts happen to be content videos, images, and commentary published online. In this sense, it is my belief that no study of the region today can ignore social media, regardless of whether the digital is part of its scope.

Furthermore, including social media and breaking academia's textual hierarchy allows for the inclusion of voices often marginalized in more conventional academic studies, which, at best, tend to privilege texts in modern standard Arabic. At worst, scholars rely exclusively on knowledge of European colonial languages to think about and analyze the societies and cultural practices of the region, even as they, ironically, seek to give voice to the subaltern. This is especially true for studies of the Maghreb in which it is often assumed that knowledge of French is sufficient to think and write about Moroccan, Algerian, or Tunisian societies. Rather than ignore the many dialects spoken throughout the region, this book gives them center stage, paying attention to the linguistic trends and tools used to simultaneously articulate and dissimulate misogyny. It is also with inclusion in mind that, overall, this book relies on texts and lived experiences from the Maghreb. The two decades since 9/11 saw a growing number of feminist publications about Muslim women. Most of them, however, focus almost exclusively on the Middle East. It is in large part due to the political relevance of many Middle Eastern countries to the West, which in turn influences a linguistic academic training that marginalizes the native dialects and languages of the Maghreb. It is worth repeating that French is not the native language of the majority of people in the Maghreb.

A final methodological consideration is the language in which I choose to write this book. Whenever possible, I have avoided the academic jargon as much of it came to replace dialogue and privilege immediate consensus over debate. Women's lived oppression can be told in simple language and need not be obscured in inaccessible jargon. Moreover, even in discussions of violence, I have avoided euphemisms and other discursive tools often used to attenuate the intensity of trauma. Instead, I have opted for explicit and direct language. This approach will inevitably produce discomfort since most will find it difficult to remain indifferent to other beings' suffering. Nevertheless, although this book is not prescriptive, one of its goals is to articulate misogyny in clear and direct language in order to shake it out of normality and make it visible.

ANTICIPATION

As discussions about Muslim women that deviate from celebrated resilience and the rhetoric of empowerment can trigger skepticism, even rejection, this book is likely to anger more than a few readers, including those who care about justice and women's welfare. Nonetheless, choosing not to focus on resistance does not mean to reduce Muslim women's lived experience to "single stories" of trauma, nor does it imply that women are passive victims. One could declare with certainty that there never is a passive victim in any circumstance. There cannot be anything passive about a body enduring pain and injustice, whether it is a knife's cut or an insult's scar. However, it is deeply unsettling to glorify the strategies women use to survive and cope with oppression, when it is the oppressor that ought to be the center of critique.

It merits saying, however, that there is a valid concern that voicing critique of misogyny in Muslim-majority societies may be used to validate hateful narratives, especially when such a critique comes from a non-white native of the region. All things considered, it is a risk worth taking. Narratives of oppression may serve unintended political and ideological purposes, but by silencing or censoring critique, one is also responsible for the other narratives that fill the void. Rather than let this happen, this book seeks to shift the critical gaze from women who are burdened with expectations of resistance and resilience to the agents of oppression. It intentionally wants to redirect the discourse from empowering women to disempowering misogyny.

***

This book would not have been possible without the support and guidance of countless individuals, a few of whom are named here. I owe special thanks to Hind Bouachrine for her expert knowledge of the politics of North Africa and the Middle East, for our ongoing conversations about the region's dynamic cultural developments, and for her illuminating comments on the manuscript. I am much indebted to the friends and colleagues who read drafts of all or parts of the chapters at various stages of this project. I particularly would like to acknowledge Matthew Wright,

James Lindsay, Inna Naroditskaya, Idelber Avelar, Larry Simpson, Daho Djerbal, Donna Divine, Kenneth Stow, Marc Lendler, Nancy Whittier, Martine Gantrel, and the anonymous reviewers. I would especially like to thank my editor at Rowman & Littlefield, Katelyn Turner, for her help, encouragement, and for supporting a project she knows would generate strong reactions among readers. Additional thanks to Anne Cushman for her editorial assistance. Thanks also go to all my students at Smith College. They inspire me with their intellectual curiosity, doubt, and challenges.

Whatever merits this book may have would not exist without my family's support. I am grateful to my parents, Hayat al-Noufous el-Hajjali and Bouchaib Bouachrine, for the videos they sent me through WhatsApp, many of which I cite throughout this book. Hind, Matt, Béatrice, Kiki, Stella, Joujou, and Tito—thank you for the laughter, food, and music.

Finally, the war on women and girls described in *Anthem of Misogyny* takes place predominantly in cities. Yet, there is more to these spaces than violence. I am grateful to the cities that housed me while I was writing this book. Thank you, Casablanca, Paris, and New York.

CHAPTER 1

Feminist Silence

FAILING HANAN

On the evening of Monday, July 15, 2019, a two-minute video in Moroccan Darija was published on Facebook and later disseminated within Morocco and beyond via the various social media platforms including YouTube, Instagram, and the most widely used instant messaging application, WhatsApp. In a dimly lit room, a woman is laying on her back, bruises covering her naked body. A man is sitting between her legs sodomizing her with a plastic bottle. As the woman screams in pain calling her tormentor by his name, Abdelwahed, the rapist explains that he is about to insert a glass bottle in her vagina. The man filming the scene responds: "Wow, one in the vagina and the other in the anus. That's too much." Beyond that, he does not show any concern. The filming is uninterrupted and the image is stable enough indicating that he never stood up or attempted to intervene and stop the rape. Abdelwahed is not concerned either. He responds with clinical detachment: "she is wide."

In the meantime, the woman continues to beg for mercy. In an attempt to appeal to his compassion, she evokes his mother. He replies that if she were to show up, he would rape her, and if her mother were to come, he would take her to the bathroom and sodomize her as well. She begs the man filming the scene to intervene. Feigning helplessness, he explains: "I asked until I got tired. He doesn't want to stop." To escalate his victim's pain, Abdelwahed picks up a hammer. "The hammer, no" she yells, imploring him to "curse Satan" to say *a'udu billah mina shaytan ar-rajim* (I seek protection in Allah from the accursed Satan.) In spite of the fear and pain, the woman weighs in her words, shifts the blame to Satan, careful not to anger her tormentor further. Abdelwahed hits the bottle once, then twice, then it breaks inside the woman's uterus. She continues to beg in an increasingly weaker voice over the sound of shattering glass. The video ends.

Following the release and rapid dissemination of the video, Rabat's court of appeal issued a statement in which it explained that the rape and torture took place over a month earlier and that the rapist has been arrested along with eight other men.[1] According to the various media outlets, on June 10, the victim, a thirty-four-year-old woman by the name of Hanan, was found in a Rabat street barely alive. In an interview, Moroccan lawyer and human rights activist Mohammed Ziyan revealed that Hanan's torture that night, prior to and after the filming of the video, lasted for hours. He shared details from the medical report filed by the emergency department of the hospital Ibn Sina where the police took Hanan.[2] Following the rape, Abdelwahed used a screwdriver to dig holes in his victim's body and a hammer to hit her head before he dropped her in the street. According to the report, Hanan was in the ICU until she was declared dead on June 11. In another interview, Ziyan shared the police report from the day Hanan was found: she is described as "a girl" (*bent*) of "thick composition" (*ghalidat al-binya*), "white skinned" (*bayda' al-bashra*), "completely naked" (*'ariya tamaman*), and "completely unconscious" (*faqidat al-wa'y tamaman*). The wounds were "bleeding and deep" (*jourouh damiya wa gha'ira*), some as deep as twelve centimeters. Her body, which was covered with blue marks, had traces of "severe beating" (*darb mubarrih*), "scars" (*nudub*), and "torture" (*ta'dib*).[3] In both interviews, Ziyan asked repeatedly: Why would the Public Prosecutor's Office regard torture, the use of weapons, and murder a "misdemeanor" (*junha*) and send the case to the Court of First Instance (*al-mahkama al-ibtida'iya*)?

Indeed, were it not for the video and the social media platforms, the killing of Hanan would have been just another crime on Abdelwahed's long record. At fifty-six, Abdelwahed has served multiple prison sentences for drug trafficking and other offenses, but not rape, even though his neighbors insisted that he had been accused of rape on several occasions. Yet, as with many crimes against women, the victims and their families end up dropping the charges, fearing the criminal's retaliation. Even after his arrest, Abdelwahed continued to terrorize his neighbors. Hanan's mother confessed in an interview that she worried he would send a member of his family to attack her.[4]

Of all his victims, Hanan suffered the most, and the longest. She had been at his mercy since she was a fourteen-year-old child. First, he was her "lover," then her pimp. According to her own mother, whenever Hanan tried to escape his sexual and physical abuse, Abdelwahed kidnapped and imprisoned her before pimping her body again in the streets of Rabat.[5] Allegedly, it was her last attempt to escape him and the lifestyle he imposed on her that led to her death. It is said that while he was serving yet another prison sentence, Hanan met a man who was going to save her from the cycle of abuse and prostitution. Hanan's neighbors as well as YouTubers who never met her confirmed the story. Indeed, she was at a turning point, on the verge of rebirth. She was preparing for marriage and perhaps even children. Finally, she was about to become a "respectable" woman. When Abdelwahed was released from prison, he was not pleased with Hanan's transformation and decided to teach her a lesson that was going to be her last.

Judging from her life trajectory until the moment of her death, as well as the trajectory of the many women in similar circumstances, Hanan's radical transformation and rebirth are highly unlikely. It is more of a trope at the service of those who sought to reconcile their pity for the victim with the lifestyle choices she had made/were imposed on her, which continued to cast a shadow even posthumously. Anyone who grows up in a Muslim household is likely to hear a version of the story of the two women attributed to Muhammad, the Prophet of Islam. One woman, despite having led a pious life, was sent to hell for the death of a cat she locked up and did not feed. The other woman, a prostitute, was sent to paradise for giving water to a dog dying of thirst. From an early age, one is taught that a woman who has sex with multiple men outside marriage stands as an example of the worst possible character. Hanan was such a woman. She was a *zaniya*, or woman who has sex with a man to whom she is not married. In a few Muslim-majority countries, she would have been stoned. In Morocco, if caught, she would have been jailed. To make matters worse, Hanan displayed too much audacity. In a context in which a woman's body is *'awra*, or "shame," which must be covered lest it trigger men's temptation and cause *fina*, or "chaos," Hanan's photo, the only one of her circulating online, shows a woman who takes great pride in how she looks. Her symmetrically drawn eyebrows bring out dark shiny eyes. Jet-black layers of hair frame her face. Everything in the photograph is aesthetically intentional. In the neighborhood she was known as *f'rmaja*, or "piece of cheese," in reference to her white skin.

In the eyes of many men *and* women in her society, Hanan was, therefore, a *mutabarrija*, a woman who disregards the veil and puts herself on display. This view is evident in the videos of YouTubers who, while condemning Abdelwahed for his crimes, at the same time express their disapproval of Hanan's looks and lifestyle. Many warn other women against following her example, asking them to preserve their virginity and offer it to their husbands alone. Yet, because of the conditions under which she died, one can sense something more than condemnation. There is a genuine attempt at saving her, even after her death, as if desperately searching on her behalf for a dog dying of thirst in the desert. They found her a man instead. It was said over and over in news outlets and YouTube videos that she was about to leave behind a life of drugs, alcohol, and illicit sex in order to marry and bear children. The intended husband owned a store; what he sold was irrelevant. He sounded honest. But then again, anybody would when compared to Abdelwahed. Unfortunately, she died too soon, which, ironically, works even better for the salvation narrative being constructed on her behalf. In Islam, *niyyah*, or "intention," holds an important place. Indeed, it is said that intention counts even more than the action itself. Hanan's life was cut short, never given the time to pass to the act. Imagining that she had the *niyyah* to repent is a way of securing her a spot in Paradise, perhaps in the company of the prostitute who took pity on the thirsty dog fourteen centuries ago, on one burning-hot day in Arabia.

However, no matter how elaborate, fabricated stories of redemption could not succeed in appeasing the misogynistic discomfort with Hanan's body. In fact, Hanan's body is never mentioned in the press and social media comments. Instead, there is an excessive use of euphemisms. He inserted the bottles in the "front" and the "back." Vague terms are employed to talk about the rape without bringing up a woman's body. As "uncomfortable" as Abdelwahed's crime is, it is still not as bad as the discomfort that a woman's body provokes. Indeed, in the vocabulary of Darija, words that relate to a woman's body are reserved for profanities. When one must use them in proper company outside the context of jokes or insults, the word is often followed by the idiom *hashak*. In Maghribi Arabic, *hashak* is used to apologize to one's interlocutor for using a term or bringing up beings considered inappropriate in the context of a polite conversation. Dogs, donkeys, prostitutes, Jews, parts of a woman's body, and the word "woman" itself can be followed with *hashak*, a request for pardon for bringing up the unclean.

Today, qualifying the word "woman" with the apologetic *hashak* might not be as common among educated urban Moroccan men. However, the linguistic discomfort in articulating what a woman's body endured persists even among the highly educated elite, both men and women, as seen in the way Hanan's rape was reported in the various print and online outlets. In an article published in *Maroc Diplomatique*, the feminist scholar Souad Mekkaoui asks: "Comment pourrait-on qualifier cette horreur?" (How could one qualify such a horror?) Her answer is that "c'est un crime odieux, inqualifiable" (it's an odious crime, unspeakable).[6] Words used throughout the article include "barbarie," "sauvageries," and "jungle." The rapists are "des creatures ignobles." They are monsters whose "impulsion bestiale" commands "les actes innommables" (unnamable acts). Mekkaoui calls for severe punishment for the rapist in order to deter "toute âme pétrie de mal" (souls full of evil). One could attribute the vocabulary to the language and a certain style of writing more dominant in the context of Francophone academic training, except that one finds a similar trend in articles written in Arabic as well. Abdelwahed is a *wahsh* (monster), a *haywan* (an animal), and a *wahsh adami* (human monster).[7] He is the perpetrator of a *jarima bashi'a* (heinous crime) and *sadiyya* (sadistic).[8] Even the court of appeal's statement refers to Abdelwahed's "monstrous acts" (*a'mal wahshiyya*).[9] In all these elaborate and verbose narratives, Hanan's body is never named.

On YouTube, Hanan's story was trending throughout July 2019. Numerous YouTubers, both women and men, made videos sharing their views about the rape. Common terms used to refer to Abdelwahed include "animal" (*hayawan*), "not human" (*mashi bnadem*), "crazy" (*hmeq*), and "sick" (*mrid*). A video titled "Hanan and the Beast" (*Hanan wa'l wahsh*) has close to one million views.[10] Part of the recycling of the vocabulary and ideas, especially on YouTube, has to do with economics. Uploading content videos on YouTube has become the sole profession of many women and men throughout North Africa and the Middle East. As a marketing strategy, monetized content therefore caters to the expectations of the audience by focusing on "buzz" topics and popular perspectives that generate the largest number of views. For example, trending responses had to do with "bringing back" the death penalty, as well as the application of retributive justice (*qisas*), which in Islamic criminal jurisprudence grants the victim and family in the case of specific offenses, such as murder, the right to request a punishment equivalent to the crime, or "eye-for-eye" retribution.[11]

Unfortunately, whether it is a highly educated feminist or a YouTuber who generates income from views, the deliberate obfuscation of what Hanan went through by relegating Abdelwahed to the realm of monsters and supernatural beings adds yet another injustice to the many she has already endured. Such discourse is primarily concerned with distancing oneself from the rapist by securing humanity for the "self" and excluding the rapist as an exception to said humanity. Indeed, the use of exceptionalism, or what I term "isolatory narratives" (see chapter 3), as a strategy is not uncommon in the region, though the subject of exception is negotiated depending on the argument and situation. When the matter being evaluated is positive, it is the "self" who is the exception. This is often used in discussions of rights and freedoms when nations in North Africa and the Middle East self-designate as "tolerant" of difference and respectful of human rights, particularly those of women, sexual and religious minorities. When what is being evaluated is negative, however, then it is the other who is categorized as the exception. One example is the discussions that follow a terrorist act committed by a person who identifies as Muslim. Often out of context, commentators in official and unofficial platforms in Muslim-majority countries and in the West, as well, are quick to insist that the terrorist does not represent "true" Islam. Convenient categories such as "Wahhabism," "Islamist," and even "lone wolf terrorist," to go back to the nonhuman animal vocabulary, are employed to construct the criminal once again as an exception, an outlier that is radically different and clearly distinguishable from the "true" Muslim self.

To be sure, as an escapist strategy, exceptionalism or isolatory narratives offer the luxury of engaging in a discussion and sharing an opinion safely without compromising the self. The exceptionalism case can be pulled out of one's bag of already-made arguments to make sense of tragedies, performatively, in an always already rehearsed manner that echoes the many voices around, confirming one's belonging to a community of those who are on the *right side*. Unfortunately, whether it is to mark a positive or negative exception, the discourse of exceptionalism caters primarily to a narcissism that is more invested in the self than it is in investigating the injustice at hand. Declaring that a terrorist is not Muslim with the intention of protecting Islam, when the terrorist himself insists that he is Muslim, does not do much for advancing a critique whose primary beneficiaries would be Muslims. Similarly, wasting energy on discussions about the inhumanity of Abdelwahed, and obscuring the debate with supernatural jargon does not do much for Hanan and the many women like her.

Any discussion about the rape and torture to which Abdelwahed and his companions subjected Hanan needs to take as a given that Abdelwahed is a human. He is a man, and so is the man who recorded the rape and torture, and so are the men who were in the room to delight in Hanan's pain. At one point in the video, the music in the background becomes louder for a few seconds only. Perhaps it was the favorite song of one of the men in attendance triggering the urge to turn up the volume. Perhaps he then realized, or was reminded, that his favorite song interfered with the video's sound quality, so he turned off the device. These are not the acts of monsters or beasts, but rather they are the intentional doings of a group of misogynists, who hated a woman so much that they saw nothing wrong with the rape and torture they inflicted and witnessed. As such, there is nothing "unspeakable" or "indescribable" about their acts. It is very much describable, using a human language. Indeed, should not any human language be able to refer to Hanan's body and Hanan's sexual organs, one by one, without evoking embarrassment or shame, bringing to the surface, instead, the misogyny that united a group of men and entitled them merely because they were born men to a woman's body merely because she was born a woman?

With this purpose in mind, insisting on the nonnegotiability of Abdelwahed's humanity and documenting his acts in an unambiguous and understandable language grounded in the realm of humans is not meant as an apology for his crimes or as some twisted and perverse invitation to pathologize misogyny or to understand the rapist under the pretense that he, too, is a victim of his socioeconomic circumstances. On the contrary, insisting on the humanity of Abdelwahed, and all misogynists for that matter, is about holding them fully responsible for their actions and breaking the narcissistic divide that constructs the violence they commit as exceptional. Abdelwahed, like the many men discussed throughout this book, discloses a larger reality in which violence against women has been normalized and weaponized to uphold men's supremacy over women and girls' bodies. Indeed, as seen in the remaining chapters, throughout North Africa and the Middle East there are many Abdelwaheds, many more Hanans, and too many videos depicting various degrees of violent abuse that are published on a daily basis.

MUSLIM WOMEN AND FEMINIST CRITIQUE

At a time when Western feminist scholarship grows increasingly unapologetic in denouncing misogynistic beliefs and practices in the West, increasingly, and rightly so, inclusive of previously marginalized groups, increasingly attentive to newly emerging forms of misogyny, such as online misogyny, it is disheartening to see that the same scholarship has largely overlooked misogyny in North Africa and the Middle East. This is especially concerning in light of the violence that has come to dominate the lives of women and girls in the region, of which anyone in the West would have caught at least a glimpse through the many cases that received international media coverage, including Hanan's murder. As Irish journalist Carol Hunt put it, "why . . . do liberal, feminist calls for equality stop at borders?"[12]

This silence became even more noticeable following the 9/11 terrorist attacks. American writer and political activist Barbara Ehrenreich commented on the "almost total" absence of analytical discussion of Taliban and Islamic fundamentalist misogyny in the weeks following September 11, 2001. She writes:

> *If the extreme segregation and oppression of women do not stem from the Koran, as non-fundamentalist Muslims insist, if it is in fact something new, then why did it emerge when it did at the end of the twentieth century? Liberal and left-wing commentators have done a thorough job of explaining why fundamentalists hate America, but no one has bothered to figure out why they hate women.[13]*

Along the same lines, Kay S. Hymowitz laments Western feminists' silence. She writes, "You haven't heard a peep from feminists as it has grown clear that the Taliban were exceptional not in their extreme views about women but in their success at embodying those views in law and practice."[14] Hymowitz wonders why American feminists did not organize, write articles, or circulate petitions denouncing the brutality of the Taliban regime toward women, which, she argues, "did more to forge an American consensus about women's rights than thirty years of speeches by Gloria Steinem." Instead, she insists feminists "have averted their eyes from the harsh, blatant oppression of millions of women, even while they have continued to stare into the Western patriarchal abyss, indignant over female executives who cannot join an exclusive golf club and college women who do not have their own lacrosse teams."[15]

Instituting a hierarchy of needs and priorities is not productive from a feminist standpoint. Misogyny does not discriminate by geography or privilege so why not be indignant over misogyny in Morocco, Afghanistan, the United States, and everywhere else? However, Hunt, Ehrenreich, and

Hymowitz are right in critiquing feminists' silence. Instead of denouncing misogyny in Muslim-majority societies, feminists in the West, for the most part, have been preoccupied with educating their Western readers through "corrective" narratives telling us that Muslim women are doing just fine. Countless are the books and scholarly articles that establish as a goal to challenge prevailing assumptions about Muslim women's oppression, to "deconstruct constructions" of Muslim women, to confront "orientalist fantasies," and to denounce "latent" Islamophobia, the accusation with which is slammed any message that deviates from a celebration of Muslim women's resistance and resilience. The author of a book about the everyday lives of Moroccan women writes, "At this moment in history, when images of veiled and 'oppressed' Muslim women crowd the television and are used in support of policy initiatives ranging from economic development to war, public understanding, particularly in the United States, of what it means to be a Muslim woman is limited at best." The book is introduced as an intervention against erroneous constructions of Muslim women, who are imagined as "hooded figure[s] . . . to be subjected to a vindictive, patriarchal religion, tribal mores, and certain abuse from [their] husband." These constructions, the author argues, rely on "sensationalized stories" of women and girls' circumcision, honor killings, and the treatment of women under the Taliban regime. Local traditions, religion, and people, the author insists, are not to blame for these abuses: "There is . . . almost no sense that the difficulties women in the Muslim world experience may not be due to 'Islam,' but to poverty, resulting from seemingly abstract forces such as globalization, structural adjustment programs, and uneven modernization."[16]

In another study that examines Western views of Muslim women in the larger local and global politics and economics, the author writes:

Take the figure of the oppressed, enslaved Muslim woman so familiar to us in the post 9/11 era. This figure can be found as early as the late seventeenth century in the writings of Mary Astell and a century later in Mary Wollstonecraft's work. However, while the US government, with support from some US feminists, used the figure of the oppressed Muslim woman to justify the invasion and occupation of Muslim

lands such as Afghanistan, Wollstonecraft used the Muslim woman
in the harem, whom she depicted as deprived of her soul and her
liberties, as a foil with which to criticize Western male philosophers
like Jean-Jacques Rousseau and to argue for Englishwomen's rights.[17]

In the author's views, the only Western writers who merit redemption are
those who, upon interacting with Muslims, became self-critical, meaning
critical of the West. Eventually, they "dissented from the dominant attitude of their time and society toward Muslims and Muslim women."[18]

Predictably, the veil came to play a central role in these "counter-
narratives." In a book about fashion in Muslim-majority countries, the
author begins with what people in the West allegedly think about the
veil: "Many Westerners view modest clothing as the ultimate sign of
Muslim women's oppression."[19] Her own experience of veiling, however,
revealed otherwise:

During my summer in Iran, I realized that modest dress had a moral
effect on me. It altered how I saw myself and how I interacted with
others, and it influenced my expectations for how Islamic public space
should be organized in terms of gender segregations. It also had an
aesthetic effect on me, shaping what I expected from and admired
about Muslim women's clothing. This is all to say that I found sur-
prise, pleasure, and delight in pious fashion, as well as intellectual
challenge to the neat boxes I had once put things in: modest dress as
imposed on women, fashion as a symptom of patriarchy, and aesthetics
as separate from ethics.[20]

It is difficult to reconcile the denial of Muslim women's oppression with
the many forms of violence women and girls have endured and continue
to endure in North Africa and the Middle East discussed in the coming
chapters. How is Hanan not oppressed? This is not to say that these
authors and others who have written along the same lines are wrong in
denouncing the ways in which women's rights can be instrumentalized
to serve power.[21] What is being criticized here is that while the West and
Westerners' agency is exaggerated, Islam and Muslims' agency is denied.

If Westerners are capable of misogyny without the help or trigger of external forces, then Muslims, too, should be considered as capable of misogyny without the help or trigger of external forces. If feminists are indeed concerned with misogyny and equality, then all agents of misogyny should be unapologetically criticized without allegiance or deference.

Yet, one needs to also be attentive to the ideological context of this scholarship. All the works mentioned so far are written after 9/11, which marked a turning point for feminist thought and research produced in the West about Islam and Muslims. The US invasion of Afghanistan emboldened what could be described as a feminist orthodoxy that is less concerned with misogyny as an oppressive system in Muslim-majority societies. Rather, this feminist orthodoxy mainly views misogyny as an ideologically charged and politically driven allegation whose purpose is to delegitimize Islam and stigmatize Muslims. In other words, many feminists went from exposing misogyny as a system of oppression to weaving tales of Muslim women's empowerment, lest they be accused of ignorance, conservative or neoconservative bias, colonial prejudice, Islamophobia, or whiteness, even when one is not white. Indeed, a recent publication argues that non-white women of Muslim origin who engage in a feminist critique explicitly grounded in a universal understanding of human rights merely "reenact" whiteness.[22] The concern, therefore, is not just the feminist silence but also the silencing of feminists.

Since 9/11, however, no essay has had more influence on feminist research about Muslim women than the piece by Lila Abu-Lughod, the Joseph L. Buttenweiser Professor of Social Science in the Department of Anthropology at Columbia University. Her widely cited 2002 article, "Do Muslim Women Really Need Saving? Anthropological Reflections on Cultural Relativism and Its Others," came out in *American Anthropologist* in response to the United States military invasion of Afghanistan. Abu-Lughod criticizes what she argues is the Bush administration's use of the rhetoric of Muslim women's salvation to justify military invasion in Afghanistan and "the War on Terror" against the Taliban. She refers to the November 17, 2001, radio address by First Lady Laura Bush in which she declared, "the fight against terrorism is also a fight for the dignity of women."[23] In 2013, Abu-Lughod published the book *Do Muslim*

Women Need Saving? in which she expands upon the essay's arguments by looking closely at what she insists is the "moral crusade" to rescue Muslim women. She analyzes various narratives through the critical lens of "gendered orientalism," which she argues "has taken on a new life and new forms in our feminist twenty first century."[24]

To be sure, Abu-Lughod acknowledges that Muslim women in Muslim-majority countries are suffering. She is even willing to concede that religion and tradition can be accomplices in women's oppression. However, she is unwilling to go down that path critically:

> *The suffering of some of these women is not totally unconnected to expectations about gender enshrined in the Qur'an or cultures in the Muslim world, or sometimes justified in terms of interpretations of Islamic law. But in all cases, their suffering has more complex causes. These are the sorts of causes we should explore.*[25]

The "we" in "we should explore" is not rhetorical, as Abu-Lughod finds it inadmissible for critics to focus on local misogyny outside the "West versus Islam" binary mode of thought in which the West always comes out as morally inferior, oppressive, and irredeemable, even if, or perhaps *especially if*, the critic herself is of Muslim descent. In much of the book, Abu-Lughod analyzes what she labels "pulp non-fiction." These are usually firsthand accounts by Muslim, or formerly Muslim, women who share their experiences of oppression in Muslim-majority societies.

Abu-Lughod does not mince her words when writing about these biographies. She dismisses them as "narratives of popular fiction and bad anthropology."[26] Admonishing both the writers and their readers, she asks: "What makes these books so appealing and their authors so celebrated when the writing is often appalling and the stories so extreme?"[27] Somali-born thinker and activist Ayaan Hirsi Ali, who is described as an opportunist who "made a name for herself defending women's rights," stands as the epitome of these writers whose undeserved success baffles Abu-Lughod.[28] Critiquing her memoir *Infidel*, a *New York Times* bestseller, and its sequel, *Nomad*, Abu-Lughod accuses Hirsi Ali of constructing an "IslamLand," or Islam as a "mythical place."[29] She insists that Hirsi Ali "traffics in the ideological certainties of the Right, using the catchphrases they have commandeered."[30] She further condemns her by associating her with intellectuals whom Abu-Lughod had criticized in her previous work: "She [Hirsi Ali] adopts Samuel Huntington's formulation of world politics as a 'clash of civilizations' and Bernard Lewis's most famous sound bite about Muslims: 'What went wrong?'" Ironically, by citing Lewis and Huntington, Abu-Lughod also inscribes Hirsi Ali's thought in the context of an intellectual genealogy that precedes what she alleges is a recent Western trend.

To be sure, Abu-Lughod is far from alone in criticizing Hirsi Ali. Saba Mahmood, who dismisses the writings of women including Iranian-born author Azar Nafisi as "native testimonials," portrays Hirsi Ali as a calculating opportunist who "had no public profile until she decided to capitalize on the anti-Muslim sentiment that swept Europe following the events of 9/11."[31] Similarly, Stephen Sheehi, who mocks Hirsi Ali's autobiography as "self-aggrandizing" (aren't they all?), accuses her of opportunism, like many others who belong to "an uncompromising tradition of positing Islam and Muslims as the inexorable Other."[32] The list in Sheehi's case is quite long. Throughout his book, he refers to opportunist/opportunism sixteen times. There is the "self-promoting opportunist" (Ahmed Chalabi), the "lifelong opportunist" (Thomas Friedman), and the many other types of opportunists including Fareed Zakaria, Bernard Lewis, Fouad Ajami, and others, who, Sheehi insists, take on the form of "the Islamophobic rogue pseudo-scholar, political hack, charlatan native informant, opportunist pundit or activist journalist."[33] In sum, opportunist, like Islamophobe, Orientalist, and neo-Orientalist, is a characteristic shared by all those with whom Sheehi disagrees.

Leaving intellectual and ideological disagreements aside, what makes Hirsi Ali and other women and men like her opportunists? Is it because their work is grounded in personal experience? Or is it the fame, book deals, and speaking engagements? How is this any different from how successful academics make a living? Is their scholarship, which is very much grounded in the personal, any less "nativist"? Have they not used their ideas and publications to earn tenure, promotion, and prestigious titles preceding their names? Have they never taken a trip to the provost's office at their institution to negotiate a salary increase evoking their hard-earned prominence and global recognition? The point here is not to discredit scholars. On the contrary, their voices are crucial for the telling and contesting of narratives, all of which ultimately complicate, and rightly so, the stories of Muslim women. By the same token, other narratives, including those of Hirsi Ali and many other women and men, need to be told as well, for they too tell and contest narratives that ultimately complicate the stories of Muslim women. If they happen to "make a name" for themselves in the process, so what? It would be reductive to assume that just because they endured oppressive misogyny they are no longer entitled to ambition and even the most trivial of aspirations and pursuits. Suffice it to say, oppressed or not, Muslim and formerly Muslim women, too, have bills to pay.

The accusation of opportunism, however, is not just about money. It is also about morality, for to speak about Hirsi Ali and other women's opportunism, to accuse them of exaggerating or even fabricating the abuse they endured has as a goal delegitimizing them morally, and feminist orthodoxy regales in "exposing" these women's moral shortcomings.[34] For example, Abu-Lughod dedicates exaggerated attention to show that Norma Khouri's 2003 memoir *Honor Lost* is a hoax, a point that has already been proven by numerous others including an investigative journalist. This led Khouri's publishers, Random House Australia, to withdraw the book. Abu-Lughod writes that the book, which is based on the alleged honor killing of Khouri's friend in Jordan, "is structured as a classic romance novel, complete with a tall, dark, and handsome love object who is not a sexist brute. It pulses with chaste but throbbing mutual attraction. . . . And there is an Orientalist difference; the gripping plot is interlaced . . . with pedantic lectures on Islam. We are not allowed to forget that we are in IslamLand."[35] Abu-Lughod describes Khouri as "a troubled woman (and compulsive liar) who had grown up in Chicago, had a police record, and was wanted for fraud."[36] One only hopes that the scholar is not insinuating that being "a troubled woman" with a rap sheet says anything about the abuse one may or may not have endured or witnessed.

Khouri's memoir, however, is merely a conduit to criticize the West or the "new imperialism" that allegedly politicizes honor crimes in order to portray Muslim communities as "backward and prone to violence."[37] In other words, Abu-Lughod discredits narratives that bring up honor crimes because of their impact on the balance between the West and the non-West. She insists, "we must be wary—this category [honor crime] risks consolidating the stigmatization of the Muslim world and does not do justice to women."[38] This point illustrates, once again, that the driving concern is not so much Muslim women, or even Islam for that matter. Instead, it is the West that is the object of critique, while Muslim women are mere justifications for such critique. For example, "misogyny" is not mentioned once in Abu-Lughod's book. "Misogynistic" is mentioned three times but never to be analyzed or condemned. One of the uses of "misogynistic" is when quoting the question *New York Times* columnist Nicholas Kristof poses in *Half the Sky: Turning Oppression into Opportunity for Women Worldwide*: "Is Islam Misogynistic?" A question Abu-Lughod finds absurd since, she argues, one would not ask the same about Christianity or Judaism. On the other hand, whenever the West/Western is mentioned (over one hundred times), it is to point to its shortcomings and failures.

To deflect criticisms of misogyny in Muslim society by pointing to the West is a common strategy of Western feminism. For example, political theorist Wendy Brown writes in her critique of liberal democracies that "the idea that Western women choose while Islamic women are coerced ignores the extent to which all choice is conditioned by as well as imbricated with power, and the extent to which all choice itself is an impoverished account of freedom, especially political freedom."[39] Brown is right to problematize the question of choice when it comes to non-Muslim women in the West. However, why does she not extend the same critique to Muslim women and what they claim (or what is claimed on their behalf) to be their choice? Why doesn't Brown denounce the violence and injustices that women and girls endure in the region and to which the majority of women in the West are immune such as honor crimes, FGM, child marriage, and other human rights abuses discussed in the next chapters? Indeed, what would Brown, Abu-Lughod and other scholars make of the statistics and testimonies cited in the coming chapters? In reference to honor crimes in particular, which Abu-Lughod dismisses as a fantasy, what would she make of a 2019 survey conducted in North Africa and the Middle East that reveals that despite legal reforms, and despite consciousness-raising campaigns, honor crimes continue to garner considerable approval throughout the region. Algeria has the highest approval response to whether honor killings are acceptable. Of Algerian respondents, 27 percent believe that honor killing should be acceptable, followed by 25 percent from Morocco, and 21 percent from Jordan.[40] In all the countries represented in the survey, approval for honor killings exceeds acceptability of homosexuality, which remains socially and legally unacceptable in most Muslim-majority countries.

Abu-Lughod does not address the region's present-day reality. Instead, she invites her readers to look at the Islamic past: "In the literature on honor crimes, there is a striking absence of any mention of Arab literary culture, which is renowned for its artistic elaboration on the themes of love."[41] The next chapter does just that but arrives at a radically different conclusion: today's misogyny is very much grounded in medieval Islamic texts, from which it claims its legitimacy. Nevertheless, if one were to entertain the idea that medieval texts reveal an age before misogyny, thus absolving Islamic traditions of it, why does she not extend the same courtesy to the West, which she reduces to a long history of exploitation, invasions, and abuse of Muslims? Why don't feminists make room for a discussion of Western civilization including Western philosophy, art, and humanism? Why do they not dedicate a section to Voltaire's playful irreverence or Kant's take on the enlightenment? The answer is simple: Voltaire and other Western intellectuals who liberated thought from the grasp of the sacred have left in the West a legacy of critical thinking that allows for no gods, at least for those who struggle with them. As scholars living and working in the West, Abu-Lughod and others are the privileged inheritors of such a legacy. They do not feel the need to apologize for the West or sing its past glories because they are more confident in its future. Indeed, their critique betrays an optimism about the West. They know that with their writings, condemnations, and anger they are contributing to making a better West. They, however, will never be satisfied because no matter how much conditions improve and how many injustices are redressed, their dissatisfaction will continue because they are certain that the West and those who inhabit it are always capable of more and deserving of better. In other words, feminist orthodoxy holds double standards. The West is unapologetically held to the highest standards, thus constantly improving the existence of its inhabitants. On the other hand, Muslim women, and Muslims in general, living outside the West are condemned to an eternal resuscitation of their medieval "golden age." They are afflicted with the burden of allegiance to civilizations from more than one thousand years ago in order to camouflage present-day injustices.

MULTI-SITED FEMINIST DOUBLE CRITIQUE

To be sure, there are feminists who have taken on the more challenging task of criticizing both Islam and the West, with reverence to neither. For example, New Zealand-born feminist philosopher Susan Moller Okin has criticized misogyny in the West, including sexism in the canon of Western political theory. As she observes in *Women in Western Political Thought*, "the great tradition of political philosophy consists, generally speaking, of writings by men, for men, and about men."[42] At the same time, Okin was just as critical of non-Western misogyny. For instance, in "Is Multiculturalism Bad for Women?" she addressed the concept of group rights:

> *Most cultures are suffused with practices and ideologies concerning gender. Suppose, then, that a culture endorses and facilitates the control of men over women in various ways (even if informally, in the private sphere of domestic life). Suppose, too, that there are fairly clear disparities of power between the sexes, such that the more powerful, male members are those who are generally in a position to determine and articulate the group's beliefs, practices, and interests. Under such conditions, group rights are potentially, and in many cases actually, antifeminist. They substantially limit the capacities of women and*

girls of that culture to live with human dignity equal to that of men and boys, and the live as freely chosen lives as they can.[43]

It is important to remember that Islam and Muslims are not Okin's point of departure. In other words, she is neither anti- nor pro-Islam. Her point of departure is feminism, which she defines as "the beliefs that women should not be disadvantaged by their sex, that they should be recognized as having human dignity equally with men, and that they should have the opportunity to live as fulfilling and as freely chosen lives as men can."[44] As a feminist, she is engaged in criticizing cultures everywhere that do not conform to these beliefs about women's rights and entitlements. In this sense, Okin, unlike many feminists, does not discriminate against Muslims, and Muslim women in particular, since she envisions them as equally entitled to human rights, against the cost of being accused of promoting "cultural imperialism." Indeed, Okin's arguments about the incompatibility of feminism and multiculturalism have exposed her to various degrees of criticism. For example, while Sudanese-American legal philosopher Abdullahi An-Na'im agrees with Okin's view that all cultures are misogynistic, "especially many of the minority cultures on whose behalf claims of group rights are being made in Western societies," he also calls for "comprehensive strategies" that are more inclusive in their fight against all forms of discrimination, not just that based on sex.[45] An-Na'im's refusal to entirely reject Okin's argument makes sense given his own personal trajectory. He was exposed from an early age to the limitations imposed on women and girls in his native Sudan. Moreover, in his work on Islam, he has stressed the importance of heretics. He himself was denounced as a heretic after giving a lecture in Mauritius. It is not surprising, therefore, that even as he analyzes the shortcomings of Okin's work he remains sensitive to her role as a heretic in the view of the implied feminist orthodoxy against which she writes.

Nonetheless, not all criticism has been grounded in a sensibility to the core concerns of Okin's humanist feminism. She has been accused of being "paternalistic" and of exemplifying the "contemporary feminism accomplice to the state coercion against Muslim minorities in the West."[46] Others have argued that her views on multiculturalism serve to fuel Islamophobia and anti-immigration discourse.[47] However, at the heart of the critique of Okin's arguments against non-Western patriarchy is legitimacy. As an "outsider," what gives Okin the right to criticize cultural practices as misogynistic? Okin addressed the outsider critique, arguing that "committed outsiders" can be effective critics thanks to their critical distance.[48] Indeed, from a human rights standpoint, an outsider critic can make visible or shed light on persistent abuse that has been normalized in other cultures.

Okin also refers to another effective feminist critic, the "inside-outside" critic, one whose analysis is enunciated from belonging to more than one group.[49] Along similar lines, political scientist Brooke Ackerly uses the term "multi-sited critic," whom she defines as one who "has the unique perspective of an individual who has been an insider or outsider vis-à-vis more than one group: she has acquired local knowledge about more than one group. And she is generally self-conscious about her perspective."[50] Moroccan scholar Raja Rhouni argues in the context of feminists positioned between Islam and the West that this multi-sited positioning "is enabling, since it ensures at the same time a theoretical distance and an empirical anchoring."[51] Algerian-born Marnia Lazreg and Iranian-born Haideh Moghissi, both professors of sociology at Western universities, fit the definition of multi-sited feminist critics well, both distanced and anchored in their study of misogyny in Western and Muslim contexts.

In Lazreg's case, while she has published extensively on gender in the colonial context, her critique is just as sharp when analyzing Islamic institutions such as the veil. In *Questioning the Veil: Open Letters to Muslim Women*, she writes that the veil "implies that a woman should humble, belittle, and feel sorry for her body—the locus of the self."[52] Lazreg argues that the veil is "a man's affair,"[53] for at the heart of Muslim women's veiling is the Muslim man who has constructed himself against the Muslim woman's body, to hide in domestic space and to veil when in the public sphere. She writes:

> *No country in the Muslim world would be in danger of cultural extinction if all women were to jettison the veil. But it would mean that male advocates of veiling would have to make adjustments to*

their perception of themselves. They would have to understand that they are no less men for accepting women as their social equals—for accepting that a woman's body is hers to live, not a man's prerogative to regulate in its most minute details of grooming, dressing, and (most important) experiencing. Conversely, a woman would have to ask herself why she looks on as a woman arrogates to himself the right to advocate for the veil, speak in the name of God, and use persuasion or coercion to keep a woman in line with his conception of her body.[54]

Lazreg's rejection of the veil stands in stark contrast with some feminists' awe of it (chapter 6). As a misogynistic symbol of men's domination over women's body, the veil, she argues, hinders women's "quest for their humanity."[55] It could therefore never function as a symbol of liberation or resistance, not even against alleged Western prejudice.[56]

This simultaneous engagement with Islamic and Western misogynies can also be understood through the lens of what Moroccan philosopher Abdelkabir Khatibi described in *Maghreb pluriel* as "double critique." It is a critique that targets both the West (or colonizer) and Islam (or the self).[57] To be sure, it is not an easy positioning and could potentially leave one with no allies. Moghissi articulates best this double positioning, the difficulties it entails, and how it is necessary despite the difficulties. In "Women, War and Fundamentalism in the Middle East," an essay Moghissi wrote immediately after September 11, 2001, she offers a reflection on the terrorist attack and its potential impact on the discourse about Muslim women and misogyny in Muslim-majority countries.[58] Moghissi acknowledges the challenges of writing about gender and Islam. As she states in the essay's opening paragraph, one needs "to explain the stubborn survival of traditions and practices hostile to women in Islamic societies without adding to the arsenal of racist imagery about Islam and Muslim women." The second task is how to do so "without resorting to apologetic and self-glorifying accounts of Islam and Muslims." While Moghissi recognizes the effect that the tragedy has had on many people, including Muslims, she also laments the positioning shift in the wake of 9/11 among intellectuals, many of whom produced "mostly justificatory accounts about Islam and its practices." She insists that there are more choices available to intellectuals than apology and the silencing of critique: "We can keep our critical stance against various forms of violence and terrorism that have engulfed Islamic societies, and against foreign interests and policies which in fact nourished and sustained them."[59]

In line with Moghissi's critique, the chapters that follow examine misogyny in North Africa and the Middle East as a system of oppression that acquires its legitimacy from centuries of texts and practices and that secures its persistence through negotiations with various aspects of Western modernity. The approach, however, while always necessarily and inescapably multi-sited, will not be through a double critique. The West has received more than a fair share of criticism. The focus, instead, will be exclusively on women and men in Muslim-majority societies, and on the local misogyny that created a context that made the events that led to Hanan's rape and murder possible. Furthermore, all the arguments made in this book are based on the conviction that, as individuals, Muslim women, their rights and freedom, ought to supersede culture, tradition, religion, and all other allegiances. This universalist position taken on Muslim women's rights here should not be understood as a "concession" but rather as a "claim," for, to borrow the words of Ghanaian political philosopher Ato Sekyi-Otu, "To abjure universalism tout court because it is imperialist . . . is the last word of the imperial act."[60]

NOTES

1. "Balagh al-wakil al-'am lil'malik bikhososs qadiyyat ightisab wa maqtal al-shabba Hanane," *Akhbarona*, July 19, 2019, https://www.akhbarona.com/society/276342.html.
2. CAP24TV, "Al-Muhami Ziyan fi aqwa tasrih fi milaf hanan bent al-mallah," YouTube video, 11:21, February 14, 2020, https://www.youtube.com/watch?v=sjbqZCykbkY.
3. Hibapress, "Al-hukm 'ala al-muttahamin fi qadiyyat Hanan," YouTube, February 14, 2020, https://www.youtube.com/watch?v=LN6o4UY7zxA.
4. Sahifa24, "Hasriy . . . Ziyan yaltaqi bi walidat Hanane li'awwal marra wa hada ma kashafa'h li sahifat 24," YouTube, July 30, 2019, https://www.youtube.com/watch?v=NpNMtMuvJwo.
5. Nabila Kandili, "Le viol et la torture mortelle de Hanane à Rabat suscite l'émotion a travers le Maroc," Actu-Maroc, July 22, 2019, https://www.actu-maroc.com/le-viol-et-la-torture-mortelle-de-hanane-a-rabat-suscite-lemotion-a-travers-le-maroc/.

6. Souad Mekkaoui, "Violer en toute impunité..," *Maroc Diplomatique*, July 18, 2019, https://maroc-diplomatique.net/violer-en-toute-impunite/.

7. Oumaima Labyad, "Ghadab wa horqa wa matalib bil'I'dam . . . tadamon wasi' ma'a dahiyyat al-ightissab b' 'lqra'i,'" *Kifache*, July 17, 2019, https://kifache.com/417171/.

8. "Ightisab wa qatl Hanane dahiyyat 'alqer'a' yukhrij l'hoqoqiyun lil l'htijaj bi'ribat," *Febrayer*, July 2019, https://www.febrayer.com/652679.html.

9. "Balagh al-wakil al-'am lil malik bi khusus qadiyyat ightissab wa qatl al-shaba Hanan," *Akhbarona*, July 19, 2019, https://www.akhbarona.com/society/276342.html.

10. Tanjaoui, "Basha'a wa mashahid sa'dima qissat Hanane wal'wahsh," YouTube, July 21, 2019 https://www.youtube.com/watch?v=p4QnwMyHgJQ.

11. The death penalty is legal in Morocco. However, the last execution was in 1993.

12. Carol Hunt, "Why Is Feminism So Quiet about Muslim Women Who Refuse to Wear the Hijab?" *The Irish Times*, August 21, 2017, https://www.irishtimes.com/life-and-style/people/why-is-feminism-so-quiet-about-muslim-women-who-refuse-to-wear-the-hijab-1.3189620.

13. Barbara Ehrenreich, "The Fundamental Mystery of Repressing Women," in *After Shock: September 11, 2001 Global Feminist Perspectives*, eds. Susan Hawthorne and Bronwyn Winter (Vancouver: Raincoast Books, 2003), 189.

14. Kay S. Hymowitz, "Why Feminism is AWOL on Islam," *City Journal* 13, no. 1 (2003): 293–305, https://www.city-journal.org/html/why-feminism-awol-islam-12395.html.

15. Ibid.

16. Rachel Newcom, *Women of Fes: Ambiguities of Urban Life in Morocco* (Philadelphia: University of Pennsylvania Press, 2009), 3–4.

17. Elora Shehabuddin, *Sisters in the Mirror: A History of Muslim Women and the Global Politics of Feminism* (Oakland: University of California Press, 2021), 4–5.

18. Ibid., 5.

19. Elizabeth Bucar, *Pious Fashion: How Muslim Women Dress* (Cambridge: Harvard University Press, 2017), 1.

20. Ibid., ix.

21. See Sara R. Farris, *In the Name of Women's Rights: The Rise of Femonationalism* (Durham: Duke University Press, 2017).

22. Haneen al-Gharba, *Muslim Women and White Femininity: Reenactment and Resistance* (New York: Peter Lang, 2018)

23. Lila Abu-Lughod, "Do Muslim Women Really Need Saving? Anthropological Reflections on Cultural Relativism and Its Others," *American Anthropologist* 104, no. 3 (2002): 784.

24. Lila Abu-Lughod, *Do Muslim Women Need Saving?* (Cambridge: Harvard University Press, 2013), 202.

25. Ibid., 74.

26. Ibid.,125.

27. Ibid., 96.

28. Ibid., 57.

29. Ibid., 69.

30. Ibid., 68.
31. Saba Mahmood, "Religion, Feminism, and Empire: The New Ambassadors of Islamophobia," in *Feminism, Sexuality, and the Return of Religion*, ed. Linda Alcoff and John D. Caputo (Bloomington: Indiana University Press, 2011), 82.
32. *Islamophobia: The Ideological Campaign Against Muslims* (Atlanta: Clarity Press, 2011), n.p.
33. *Islamophobia: The Ideological Campaign Against Muslims* (Atlanta: Clarity Press, 2011), n.p.
34. Saba Mahmood, "Religion, Feminism, and Empire: The New Ambassadors of Islamophobia," 82.
35. Lila Abu-Lughod, *Do Muslim Women Need Saving?* 122.
36. Ibid., 122–23.
37. Ibid., 114.
38. Ibid., 113.
39. Wendy Brown, "Civilizational Delusions: Secularism, Tolerance, Equality" in *Theory & Event* 15, no. 2 (2012): 10.
40. "The Arab World in Seven Charts: Are Arabs Turning Their Backs on Religion?" BBC News, June 24, 2019, https://www.bbc.com/news/world-middle-east-48703377.
41. Lila Abu-Lughod, *Do Muslim Women Need Saving?* 127.
42. Susan Moller Okin, *Women in Western Political Thought* (Princeton: Princeton University Press, 1979), 5.
43. Susan Moller Okin, "Is Multiculturalism Bad for Women?" *Boston Review* (1997), reprinted in Joshua Cohen, Matthew Howard, and Martha C. Nussbaum, eds., *Is Multiculturalism Bad for Women?* (Princeton: Princeton University Press, 1999).
44. Susan Moller Okin, "Feminism and Multiculturalism: Some Tensions," *Ethics* 108, no. 4 (1998): 661.
45. Abdullahi An-Na'im, "Promises We Should All Keep in Common Cause," in *Is Multiculturalism Bad for Women?* 60
46. Alice Aslan, *Islamophobia in Australia* (Glebe: Agora Press, 2009), 146.
47. See Liz Fekete, *A Suitable Enemy: Racism, Migration and Islamophobia in Europe* (London: Pluto Press, 2009).
48. Susan Okin, "Gender Inequality and Cultural Differences," *Political Theory* 22 no. 1 (1994): 19.
49. Quoted in Brook A. Ackerly, *Political Theory and Feminist Social Criticism* (Cambridge: Cambridge University Press, 2000), 154.
50. Ibid.
51. Raja Rhouni, *Secular and Islamic Feminist Critiques in the Work of Fatima Mernissi* (Leiden: Brill, 2010), 146.
52. Marnia Lazreg, *Questioning the Veil: Open Letters to Muslim Women* (Princeton: Princeton University Press, 2009), 24.
53. Ibid., 57.
54. Ibid., 120–21.
55. Ibid., 112.
56. Ibid., 61.

57. Abdelkebir Khatibi, *Maghreb pluriel* (Paris: Denoel, 1983).

58. Haideh Moghissi, "Women, War and Fundamentalism in the Middle East," *After Sept. 11*, Social Science Research Council online collection of essays, November 1, 2001, Socia https://items.ssrc.org/after-september-11/women-war-and-fundamentalism-in -the-middle-east/.

59. Moghissi reexamines these issues in an essay she wrote ten years after 9/11. See Haideh Moghissi, "What We Have Learned from 9/11," Social Science Research Council online collection of essays, September 3, 2011, https://items.ssrc.org/10-years -after-september-11/what-we-have-learned-from-9-11/.

60. Ato Sekyi-Out, *Left Universalism, Africa Centric Essays* (New York: Routledge, 2019), 14.

CHAPTER 2

How Did We Get Here?

HANAN'S STORY, LIKE THE REST OF THE STORIES TO WHICH THIS BOOK bears witness, is narrated and disseminated through twenty-first-century technologies. Most people, even those living within Morocco, would not have heard about Hanan were it not for WhatsApp, YouTube, Facebook, smartphones, Instagram, and the internet. Yet the violence and injustices Hanan endured all her life up to the moment of her murder are the result of centuries of entrenched misogyny and disgust with the woman's body in North Africa and the Middle East that long preceded new technologies. Certes, this malaise predates even Islam in the region. However, religious and other medieval texts, some of which are discussed in this chapter, came to serve, whether directly or indirectly, legitimately or illegitimately, as the foundational narratives for present everyday patriarchal values and misogynistic practices.

Beginning a discussion about misogyny with medieval texts does not necessarily seek to establish or deny origins, as debates about beginnings often deviate into unproductive exercises in defense of one's ideological allegiances. A case in point is the Islamic feminist scholarship addressed in the first section of this chapter, which seeks to absolve Islam as an origin of misogyny in the region. The goal instead is to highlight the continuity and interconnectedness of misogyny as a system of oppression that relies on a specific understanding of progress. Progress in North Africa and the Middle East in general is not measured by a society's and individual's ability to critically distance themselves from the past. Instead, a society's progress is measured by its ability to incorporate elements of a Western lifestyle and aesthetics, while maintaining that a return to the past is the ultimate ideal. This is particularly salient in the relationship with women's bodies, which serve as the terrain through which patriarchy affirms and reaffirms its allegiance to the past through violence, punishment, and restrictions.

Making Sense of Misogyny in Islam

Where does misogyny in Islam come from? This is a key question in Islamic feminist scholarship. To answer it, Islamic feminists tend to focus on three main issues in Islamic jurisprudence, all connected to the domestic sphere: inheritance (a brother inherits twice as much as his sister), polygyny (a man is allowed to marry up to four wives at a time), and wife beating (men are given permission to beat their wives). To be sure, there are other issues in Islamic law that are not focused directly on the domestic sphere but that use women's household duties as a justification. One example is testimony. According to Islamic law, one man's legal testimony equals that of two women. It has been argued that the reason behind such inequality is to protect women "from the rigor and discomfort of prolonged trials," and to help them "forego distractions" from household duties.[1]

Many Islamic feminists including Moroccan biologist Asma Lamrabet (*Women in the Qur'an: An Emancipatory Reading*, 2016), American theologian Amina Wadud (*Qur'an and Woman: Rereading the Sacred Text from a Woman's Perspective*, 1999), and Pakistani-American scholar Asma Barlas (*Believing Women in Islam: Unreading Patriarchal Interpretations of the Qur'an*, 2002), have insisted that the Qur'an reaffirms women's equality. As to the apparent misogyny of the scriptures, they blame it on patriarchal bias, arguing that men's authority has gone unchallenged for too long, granting them monopoly over the interpretation not only of the Qur'an but also of the hadith (Prophet Muhammad's sayings).[2] For example, Wadud calls for an interpretation of the Qur'an that takes into consideration women's experiences. Not only that, but she insists that women must participate actively in Qur'anic exegesis. As

Hibba Abugideiri puts it, "Wadud shows that a hermeneutical approach to interpreting woman in the Qur'an must include women as active agents."[3] Wadud, who believes that God is inherently just, attributes the misogynistic injustices of the scripture to the male-centered Islamic commentarial tradition.[4]

Barlas concurs. She views the Qur'an as "an egalitarian text,"[5] hence her objective is "to recover the egalitarian aspects of the Qur'an's episteme,"[6] and "to absolve the Qur'an 'itself' of culpability for what Muslims have, or have not, read into it."[7] Reading her work, one soon realizes that absolving the Qur'an of misogyny is a point of departure rather than a conclusion. She argues, without leaving much room for nuance, that "patriarchal readings of Islam collapse the Qur'an with its exegesis . . .; God with the languages used to speak about God . . .; and normative Islam with historical Islam." In a fleeting moment of doubt, she writes: "This does not mean that I did not consider seriously the alternative argument that the problem is not one of reading but of the very nature of some of the Qur'an's teachings."[8] However, she quickly dismisses any reading that allows for such a conclusion as a misreading, even when it comes to one of the scripture's most polemical issues, namely wife beating. She writes that "Contextualizing the Qur'an's teachings (that is, explaining them with reference to the immediate audience and social conditions to which they were addressed) shows that, far from being oppressive, they were profoundly egalitarian; it depends on how we position the Qur'an and also ourselves in relation to it historically."[9] One can concede to Barlas that patriarchy is invested in maintaining male dominance over women through misogynistic exegesis. At the same time, it is necessary to address the question: Why do texts allow so easily for misogynistic readings?

The silences in Barlas's writing are common in most Islamic feminist scholarship. The core question is rarely whether Islamic norms and scriptures are misogynistic or not. Rather, the guiding concern is how to demonstrate that Islamic scripture is egalitarian and just. In certain instances, the scholar's convictions about "true" Islam are so forceful they become more orthodox than the positions articulated in the Qur'an and the hadith. This is most evident in Lamrabet's work. Like Wadud and

Barlas, Lamrabet rejects claims of inequality in Islam. She addresses several controversial verses in the Qur'an that often come up in discussions about gender in Islam, insisting that, when read in their context, these verses are far from misogynistic. On the contrary, what may be perceived as discrimination, she argues throughout her work, is, in fact, empowering to women. For example, when discussing unequal inheritance, she evokes the doctrine of *qiwama*, or men's authority over women. Lamrabet writes:

> *The Qur'an has indeed insisted on this obligation on men to provide for women's needs—whether they be rich or poor—in several verses and has thus delineated the field of action of this responsibility or qiwama, essentially at the heart of the family unit and in a spirit of financial responsibility for the family. This responsibility incumbent upon men should not be understood as a means of subordinating women who would be thus maintained and of seeing in this distinction a discrimination towards women. In fact, one could suggest that the Qur'an offers women an additional security in a difficult patriarchal world. To give men a sense of responsibility because women might find themselves unable to manage the economic needs of the family due to pregnancy or other personal reasons, is in fact a favor conceded to women. In the current legal language, the Qur'an displays positive discrimination towards women.[10]*

To absolve the Qur'an of misogyny, Lamrabet provides a misogynistic interpretation. Assuming that in certain cases and at particular stages of pregnancy certain women might not be able to provide for their families, how often are Muslim women incapacitated by pregnancy and how often are they pregnant, especially in light of fertility rate declines in Muslim-majority countries? More importantly, should pregnancy or any other "personal reasons" justify an economic discrimination against women and girls that has disastrous ramifications on their ability to build wealth? Contexts and interpretations do indeed matter. To be convincing, however, one needs more than mere claims that an injustice "is in fact a favor conceded to women." Those who grew up in Muslim-majority countries and attended primary school in these countries have already heard most of the "feminist" apologies in defense of religion. If they were not convincing then, in plain everyday language addressed to children, why would they be any more convincing now in academic language?

To be sure, not all feminists from North Africa and the Middle East approach scriptures with the same deference or defensiveness. One example is Egyptian feminist Nawal El Saadawi, who had a more ambivalent relationship with Islam. She openly criticized laws and practices that discriminate against women. In a 2001 interview, El Saadawi suggested a need for a reform in Islamic law of inheritance: "We have to rethink about the inheritance law because we have 30 percent of families in Egypt where the mother is working and paying for the family and the husband is not working. It is the mother who is the provider for the family, so why do women inherit only half?"[11]

Unequal inheritance was only one of El Saadawi's concerns. She was also critical of the veil, child marriage, female genital mutilation, and the pilgrimage to Mecca (hajj), which, she insisted, had pagan roots that preceded Islam. Her writings and commentaries forced her into four years of exile (1993–1997), which she spent at Duke University after Islamist groups in Egypt declared her a heretic and called for her killing. Her dissent also earned her the title "the new Salman Rushdie." In June 2001, El Saadawi appeared in court accused of apostasy. The lawyer who brought the case against her explained: "What she said about the pilgrimage and the laws of inheritance is atrocious. She has offended the feelings of Muslims . . . she should keep her opinions to herself, because they are against Islam. These opinions are poison to Muslims." The lawsuit also called for her divorce since as an apostate she could no longer remain married to a Muslim spouse.[12]

A few exceptions notwithstanding, overall, it is challenging to find examples of Muslim feminist scholars who openly denounce scriptural sources as foundational texts for misogyny and misogynists in Muslim-majority societies. Even El Saadawi at times tones down her condemnations of messages of inequality in Islamic sources by dismissing them as injustices inherited from other cultures and civilizations. The reluctance among most feminists to entertain the possibility that the "true" message of scriptural sources is inherently biased against women could be a pragmatic approach to feminist reform. Islamic feminists, particularly those who chose to live most of their lives in a Muslim-majority society, such as El Saadawi and Moroccan sociologist Fatima Mernissi, are well aware that most men and women in their societies have an unwavering allegiance to religion. A direct condemnation would be counterproductive and is, therefore, unlikely to produce any change for women and girls who live in these societies.

Ultimately, regardless of how feminists make sense of misogyny in Muslim-majority societies, and regardless of the genealogies they pursue or reject, the reality is that academic positions have very little relevance to shaping perceptions of women in Muslim societies. No matter the linguistic acrobatics that seek to turn a call for violence into an embrace of justice, the reality in North Africa and the Middle East is that medieval texts are understood in their simplest and most direct significance.

WOMEN AND PUBLIC SPACE IN MEDIEVAL SOURCES

It is not coincidental that much Islamic feminist scholarship focuses mainly on the domestic sphere, as the house in Islamic tradition is often seen as a Muslim woman's "natural" space. This focus, however, offers a limited understanding of women's representation in medieval sources, most of which are more concerned with women's relationship with public space. As Fatima Mernissi explains, Muslim societies are sexually segregated: the "domestic universe" is designated as women's space while the "public universe" is regarded as exclusively men's domain.[13] This sexual segregation is supported by the long tradition of scriptural sources. For example, in the Qur'anic verses 4:34 and 33:33, men are designated as "the protectors and maintainers of women," while women, on the other hand, are asked to remain home. In the hadith, the woman is established as "a ruler over the house of her husband and his children." The man, on the other hand, is seen as "a ruler over the people of his house" giving him legal and moral authority over his wife, daughter, and other women in his household (Sahih Bukhari 3.733). According to a *hadith* narrated by Ibn 'Abbas (d. 687/688), Prophet Muhammad stated that a woman has two shelters (*sitran*), her husband's house and her grave.[14] It is reported that when Fatima, the daughter of Prophet Muhammad, was asked: "who is the best of women?" she responded, "the ones who neither see men nor do men see them."[15] The message is clear: Muslim women ought to avoid nonsegregated public spaces.

Even when it comes to religious duties such as prayer, while women were not forbidden from going to the mosque, it was preferable for them to pray in their homes. According to an authentic hadith narrated by the Persian jurist Abu Dawud (d. 889), the Prophet said: "Prevent not the slave-girls of Allah from going to the mosques (to attend the prayer in congregation), even though it is better for them (to offer prayer in) their houses."[16] Free women, too, are encouraged to pray in the home. In his *Musnad*, a collection of hadith, the Iraqi jurist Ahmad Ibn Hanbal (d. 855) narrates a hadith according to which the Prophet stated, "The best place for a woman to pray is in the innermost part of her home."[17] It is important to point out that when it comes to men's prayer, it is recommended, at times even compulsory, that they congregate at the mosque and pray as a group. Indeed, even today for many Muslim men prayer at the mosque is an essential part of their Islamic practice, even if it were to expose them to danger. For example, one of the most challenging tasks for authorities in Muslim-majority countries during the COVID-19 pandemic, particularly during the early pandemic period, was to reinforce the ban on congregational prayers for men at mosques.[18]

Men going to the mosque and occupying public spaces in general while women are chased out of them is part of the social order in North Africa and the Middle East and, in order to maintain it, women and men must respect the spatial boundaries. This is the point Mernissi's father makes in *Dreams of Trespass*: "When Allah created the earth, said Father, he separated men from women, and put the sea between Muslims and Christians for a reason. Harmony exists when each group respects the prescribed limits of the other; trespassing leads only to sorrow and unhappiness."[19] When boundaries are crossed, women pay a price for their transgressions. It is said that a woman asked Prophet Muhammad: "What is the right of the husband over the woman?" He responded that in addition to obeying him, guarding his finances, and making herself available to him sexually, a woman must obtain her husband's permission before leaving the house. If she leaves without his permission, "she will be cursed by the angels of heaven, the angels of earth, the angels of wrath, and the angels of mercy until she returns to her house."[20] Islamic jurists are divided about what is meant by obtaining permission. There are those who argue that a woman must ask for and receive permission before she leaves. Others, on the other hand, believe that a woman does not need permission every time she wants to step out of the house as long as her husband does not explicitly forbid her from going out.[21]

To further dissuade women from being in public space, they are made vulnerable to the accusation of adultery (*zina*). According to a hadith, the woman on the street whose perfume can be detected by a gathering of men is likened to an adulteress.[22] In another hadith it is said that the prayers of the woman who wears a scent to the mosque will not be accepted until "she takes bath like that she takes to get clean from the state of *Janabah*." The *janabah* is "a state of impurity" resulting from sexual intercourse. *Ghusl* (bathing) *al-janabah* is therefore the required washing following a sexual act. It involves the thorough cleaning of the genitals and the rest of the body.[23] Also on the theme of perfume, a different hadith states that if a woman wearing perfume walks by men "with the intention that they should enjoy it, she commits fornication (*fa hiyya zaniya*)."[24] Adultery (*zina*) in Islam is one of the worst crimes punishable by one of the most severe sentences: stoning until death if the offender is married and one hundred lashes if the offender is not. Therefore, the accusation of *zina* is no trivial matter, making it an effective patriarchal tactic to coerce women into avoiding public space all together.

Street harassment is another tactic through which women were discouraged from leaving their houses. Not even the Prophet Muhammad's wives were spared. Indeed, it is believed that the verse often taken as the justification for veiling in Islam was in response to the harassment the Prophet's wives endured in public space:

O Prophet! Tell your wives and your daughters and the women of the believers to draw their cloaks all over their bodies. That will be better that they should be known (as free respectable women) so as not to be annoyed. And Allah is Most Forgiving, Most Merciful. (33:59)

To be sure, street harassment was a practice that predated Islam in the Arabian Peninsula, as did misogyny in general. One of the cruelest misogynistic practices of the pre-Islamic period known in Islamic sources as the *jahiliyya*, literally "the age of ignorance," was the infanticide of newborn infant girls, as described in the Qur'an:

> *When of them is told of the birth of a female child, his face is overcast with gloom and he is deeply agitated. He seeks to hide himself from the people because of the ominous news he has had. Shall he preserve it despite the disgrace involved or bury it in the ground? (16:58–61).*

In the context of a society in which a man's honor is dependent upon women's chastity, a woman's transgression could bring shame and dishonor on the family, even the entire tribe. It was therefore "safer" to put an end to girls' lives before their much-feared transgressions materialized.

Islam vehemently condemned female infanticide. It is a fact that many children in North African and Middle Eastern schools learn from an early age as part of a curriculum that emphasizes Islam's message of justice for all, including women. Islam, it is repeated, has protected and empowered women through rights they were denied earlier in the so-called *jahiliyya* period. Nevertheless, while Islam did abolish female infanticide, not all scholars embrace uncritically the narrative of women's empowerment under Islam. For example, Leila Ahmed rejects the "simplistic" reading of Islamic sources that suggests that women's lives necessarily improved under the new religion. On the contrary, Ahmed argues that in many aspects women's lives deteriorated under Islam, insisting that, for example, in pre-Islamic Arabia women enjoyed "greater sexual autonomy." Moreover, women in the so-called *jahiliyya* were active participants in public space, even holding leadership positions in various areas of public life still contested today in North African and Middle Eastern societies such as religion and warfare.[25] As the Arabian society adopted Islam, women were subjected to further and new restrictions not only in domestic space, under the institution of marriage, for example, but also in public. Indeed, in the Qur'an Muslim women were advised to distinguish themselves from the pre-Islamic women by refraining from leaving their homes: "And stay in your houses, and do not display yourselves as people did in the times of ignorance" (33:33). This perhaps explains why the verse about the veil cited earlier recognizes that women, including the Prophet's wives, were harassed in public, yet, rather than condemn men's behavior as inappropriate, it is women who must make a concession by veiling whenever in public. It is yet another reminder that women's mere presence in public is a transgression. As Mernissi puts it, "The veil means that the woman is present in the men's world, but invisible; she has no right to be in the street."[26]

***

As Islamic urban centers expanded throughout the Middle Ages, so did the restrictions on women in public spaces. In his *Kitaab Ahkam An-Nisaa* (The book of rules for women), the Baghdad native Hanbali jurist Ibn al-Jawzi (d. 1200) insisted that women should refrain from leaving the house not only for their safety but also for the safety of others:

> *It is appropriate that a woman be warned from going out whatever the circumstance, even if she feels safe, as the people may not be safe from her. If it becomes absolutely necessary for her to go out, she must do so only with the permission of her husband, and with a decent appearance, and she must stay clear of busy streets and markets, taking care that her voice is not heard. She must walk along the side of the street and not the middle.*[27]

In the many chapters of his *Ahkam*, Ibn al-Jawzi elaborates on the various restrictions that should be imposed on women in public space such as the color of clothing, the choice of accessories, and the use of perfume. Moreover, he insists that women should be forbidden from going to public baths and from participating in funeral processions. To give legitimacy to his repeated calls for confining women, Ibn al-Jawzi uses the words of the Prophet, who, it is narrated, said: "Woman is something shameful and impure. If she goes out, the devil gazes at her."[28] According to Ibn al-Jawzi, women are dangerous because they are particularly vulnerable to the deceits of the devil, a point on which he elaborates in

Talbis Iblis (Iblis's deception). Indeed, the association of women with the devil is a recurring theme in Ibn al-Jawzi's misogynistic writing.[29] This is significant because, to a great extent, one is only Muslim in opposition to the devil. Muslims' faith, even identity, is only affirmed through their resistance to the ruses of an ever-innovative devil. By extension, a Muslim man's faith is measured by his alertness to the ruses women employ to lure men away from the right path. To be defiant of women and their bodies, therefore, is necessarily built into religious practice and identity.

Ibn al-Jawzi's prolific writings, around 250 texts, come out of a specific political context. Several Abbasid Caliphs charged him with enforcing "respect for orthodoxy and orthopraxy" particularly in the public sphere.[30] He opposed with zeal religious movements he considered heretical, among them Sufism and Shi'ism. This earned him labels such as "conservative." When it comes to women, however, it would be misleading to attribute his views to an exceptionally conservative or "extremist" understanding of scriptural texts. His views about confining women to the domestic sphere were shared by numerous other medieval scholars, as Latifa Lakhdar has shown in *Les femmes au miroire de l'orthodoxie islamique*. Moreover, the belief that women ought to be excluded from public space permeated different types of writings and genres.

One example is the treatise on *al-hisba* (the regulation and supervision of markets), by the twelfth-century Maliki jurist from Seville Ibn Abdun, in which he dedicates considerable attention to women's comportment in markets, public gardens, and riverbanks. In medieval Islamic literature, these spaces were perceived as particularly dangerous, because they allowed women and men to meet and interact. Among the many regulations, Ibn Abdun forbids women from doing "their washing in the gardens, for these are dens for fornication." Women should also be forbidden from sitting "by the river bank in the summer if men appear there." During festivals, "men and women shall not walk on the same path when they go to cross the river." Moreover, "empty places must be forbidden, because men go there to be alone with women." Muslim women had to be separated from non-Muslim men, too. They "shall be prevented from entering their [Christians'] abominable churches, for the priests are evil-doers, fornicators, and sodomites." Because of this obsession with sexual segregation, women were forbidden to exercise professions that put them in contact with men. For example, the "contractor of hostelries for traders and travelers should not be a woman, for this is indeed fornication."[31] Whether such rules were upheld and the extent to which they were reinforced is another story. What is certain is that they are grounded in legitimate Islamic texts and, as seen later in this chapter, they would have a long-lasting impact on relations of women and men in Muslim-majority societies.

No laws and regulations, however, were ever enough to appease suspicions about Muslim women's behavior and intentions outside the home. In the fourteenth century, the Egyptian theologian Mohammad 'Abdari, known as Ibn al-Hajj (d. 1336), mourned a Cairo in which men have lost their "Islamic jealousy" (*ghaira islamiyya*) allowing women to speak with male strangers and walk the streets in clothes he judged inappropriate.[32] As far as he was concerned, women should never leave the house but for three reasons: "Some of the pious elders (may God be pleased with them) have said that a woman should leave her house on three occasions only: when she is conducted to the house of her bridegroom, on the deaths of her parents, and when she goes to her own grave."[33] Writing centuries later, Edith Wharton was surprised to see in early twentieth-century Fez that the only women in the streets were slaves, servants, and women of lower socioeconomic status. As to "the women of the richer classes, mercantile or aristocratic, [they] never leave their harems except to be married or buried."[34] If this passage were introduced today in most university classrooms in the West, it would automatically be dismissed as orientalist. However, for all the critique against Western orientalists, many of their observations were indeed based in realities, albeit partial, of the societies they described.

For other medieval chroniclers, the subservient place prescribed for women as well as the role assigned to men as their guardians became not only a source of masculine pride but also a sign of one's superiority vis-à-vis other cultures and religions. This became particularly evident in historical moments of encounters with other religions, such as the Crusades. Usama Ibn Munqidh (1095–1188), a soldier and poet from the Shaizar dynasty in northern Syria, documented the observations he gathered from his encounters with the Franks (Christian crusaders), whom he characterized as "void of all zeal and jealousy." He described their behavior in public: "One of them may be walking along with his wife. He meets another man who takes the wife by the hand and steps aside to converse with her while the husband is standing on one side waiting for his wife to conclude the conversation. If she lingers too long for him, he leaves her alone with the conversant and goes away."[35] To Ibn Munqidh, such behavior would be unthinkable in a Muslim context, and it gets even worse. He heard the story of another Frank who was a wine seller in Nablus. One day he went home to find his wife in bed with another man. Astonished, the merchant asked the stranger why he was in his bed, to which the man responded that he was tired, he found a bed, and he slept in it. And the wife? "Well, the bed is hers. How could I therefore have prevented her from using her own bed?" The husband then warned him that if he were to catch him again, he "would have a quarrel." Ibn Munqidh concluded dismissively, "Such was for the Frank the entire expression of his disapproval and the limit of his jealousy."[36]

Capitalizing on the entertainment value of his anecdotes, some of Ibn Munqidh's tales about the relationship between women and men among the Franks get even more absurd. A public bath owner near Aleppo told him of an encounter with a Frank who wanted him to shave off his pubic hair because he liked how the bath owner looked, which he did. Pleased with the result, the Frank called on his wife and asked the bath owner to shave her pubic area as well, which he did: "So I shaved all that hair while the husband was sitting looking at me. At last, he thanked me and handed me the pay for my service."[37] It is doubtful he would have brought his wife into the men's bath, especially since there were public baths frequented by Muslim and non-Muslim women, where the Christian wife could have enquired about full-body depilation. So why would Ibn Munqidh indulge in such imaginary tales about the Franks?

For Ibn Munqidh, the point of these stories is not so much veracity but rather to establish women's honor as a measure of superiority vis-à-vis others. A few pages earlier, Ibn Munqidh tells a story about how his mother was ready to kill his sister to save her daughter's honor. While Ibn Munqidh and the other men of the family were away, his mother, fearing an enemy attack, asked her daughter to cover up before she led her to a balcony: "I have given her a seat at the balcony and sat behind her so that in case I found that the [enemy army] had reached us, I could push her and throw her into the valley, preferring to see her dead rather than to see her captive in the hands of the peasants and ravishers." Ibn Munqidh had nothing but praise for his mother: "Such solicitude for honor is indeed stronger that the solicitude of men." His sister, too, was grateful.[38] Thus, having established in other sections of his book the Franks' inferiority in various areas, including war strategy, medicine, and intellect, Ibn Munqidh adds women's bodies as another battle terrain on which Muslims are once again the incontestable victors.

To be sure, medieval Islamic societies were heterogeneous and so were medieval Muslim women, who differed in socioeconomic class, education, marital and familial status, sexual orientation, and other factors that influenced the impact of misogyny on them. Nevertheless, as I have argued in earlier work, misogyny did not spare wealthy and powerful women in medieval Islamic societies.[39] The pages of this current book make the same claim about misogyny today, which, I argue, does not spare women and girls, regardless of privilege. Another important point to keep in mind is that each of the texts mentioned above has its own unique historical, political, ideological, and social context. Nonetheless, in most of them, and the many more not included here and which readers are invited to explore, there is an agreement about the need for regulating women's bodies, particularly in public, because women were seen as the untrustworthy guardians of men's honor, hence rationalizing back then, and now still, male tutelage over women.

MISOGYNY FROM TEXT TO PRACTICE

To a few medieval scholars with political aspirations, it was not enough to express their male unease with women's bodies in writing alone. They physically intervened to secure women's subordination. This was the case of Ibn Tumart (d. 1130), a native of Masmuda in the Atlas Mountains and the spiritual leader of the Almohad movement (*al-Muwahhidun*). Ibn Tumart adhered to the scriptural injunction "to commend good and forbid evil" (*nahy 'an l'munkar, wal amr bil ma'ruf*). Indeed, wherever Ibn Tumart traveled, he accused his hosts of deviating from the true message of Islam and waged war on their local and indigenous customs. He did not hesitate to use physical violence such as beating women in public, breaking musical instruments and pouring wine containers into the streets. Predictably, he provoked the ire of his hosts and he was expelled from various cities including Mecca and Alexandria. Even while on the boat that was carrying him from Alexandria, he bothered the sailors so much about their drinking and lack of piety that they threw him overboard. He survived and eventually made it back to his native Maghrib, which was under the rule of the Almoravid (*al-Murabitun*).

Upon his return "home," just as his leadership ambitions were growing so was his focus on women and gender in general. In a historical novel about Ibn Tumart and women, *Ben Toumert ou les derniers jours des Voilés* (2021), Moroccan writer Mouna Hachim claims that misogyny was central to his politico-religious project. Much of Ibn Tumart's disenchantment with his society, Hachim argues, was triggered by what he perceived as the insolence of women related to circles of power such as Sura, the sister of the emir Ali Ibn Yusuf Ibn Tashafin, and the two sisters, Mimouna and Fannou, who were Almoravid princesses.[40] This instrumentalization of gender as political critique is most obvious in Ibn Tumart's *A'azz ma yutlab*, a compendium of his writings, in which he admonished the Almoravid women for resembling "their menfolk in uncovering themselves, their faces unveiled, not wearing any head covering whatsoever." At the same time, he reproached the Almoravid men for wearing "women's attire in that they cover their faces with a veil." Both practices, he insisted, were condemned in the scriptures:

> *Resemblance to the male gender is prohibited, according to what Ibn 'Abbas narrated on the authority of the Prophet, may the blessings and peace of God be upon him. He said: "The Messenger of God, may the blessings and peace of God be upon him, cursed the mutashabihun: women who dress like men and men who dress like women. The curse is applicable to all. All of that is forbidden and is unlawful."*[41]

As it was customary for Ibn Tumart, he did not hesitate to take matters into his own hands. While roaming the streets of Marrakesh, he used violence against the transgressors. He and his followers were known for carrying sticks that they used to beat women and men who mixed in public places. Not even the prince's sister was spared. Ibn Tumart allegedly attacked Sura for riding a horse around the city of Marrakesh without wearing the veil.[42]

For the most part, Ibn Tumart had remained largely marginalized outside academic scholarship about Islam and the Maghrib. This changed following the 9/11 attacks, as Ibn Tumart along with a few other medieval scholars gained more popularity. Ibn Tumart, in particular, came to epitomize a radical Islam incompatible with modern values. For example, in a series on *al-Andalus* (Iberia under Muslim rule) disseminated on YouTube, Amr Khaled, a native of Egypt who abandoned his job as an accountant for a far more lucrative career as televangelist, accuses Ibn Tumart of spreading "extreme violence" (*shiddat al-'unf*) and of having "devious ideas" (*afkar shaddha*) and "extremist ideas" (*afkar motatarrifa*).[43] For Khaled, Ibn Tumart serves as a contrast with his brand of the anti–Bin Laden moderate Muslim.

More recently, however, a different interpretation of Ibn Tumart gained popularity, this time among young people for whom 9/11 and Bin Laden do not carry the same significance, nor do they evoke the same allegiances as they do for many Muslims Khaled's age. Combing through online content about Ibn Tumart, particularly the YouTube videos made and disseminated in accessible dialects of Arabic and other European languages including English and even Bosnian, one realizes quickly that rather than reject Ibn Tumart as a medieval Bin Laden, young people from North Africa, the Middle East, and beyond, are intrigued by and even admire him. Many online find in him a source of identity pride. For example, for many Amazighi-identified Algerian and Moroccan YouTubers, Ibn Tumart was a free Amazighi Muslim man the likes of whom have been intentionally silenced in the Arabocentric official history of the region. More importantly, they find in him a commendable and outspoken model of masculinity as he never shied away from critiquing what he believed to be affronts to the patriarchal order. Indeed, Khaled's video on YouTube has more than two hundred comments, most of which are positive. One viewer asks in the comment section why the Moroccan state-run school curriculum does not incorporate historical figures such as Ibn Tumart, to which another YouTuber responds: "Because they fear the righteous advocates [of Islam]" (*al-du'at al-salihin*). To be sure, this so-called righteous advocate of Islam accomplished no small feat. He succeeded in bringing together numerous disciples (*al-talaba*) motivated by a mixture of misogynistic violence and self-righteous zeal backed with scriptural legitimacy. He eventually created a political, military, and religious movement, which gave rise in the twelfth and thirteenth centuries to the dynasty of the Almohad, literally meaning "the unifiers," which ruled parts of Africa and Iberia.

Living under conditions far removed from the past, young Muslim people today are nonetheless finding resonance, even inspiration, in the writings and stories of the Middle Ages. This cohabitation of the past and present has been greatly facilitated by technology that deinstitutionalized medieval theological narratives and made them widely accessible thanks to the proliferation of religious programs accessible through satellite television, and, later, with even greater impact, thanks to social media platforms, especially YouTube.[44] In a video in English published in April 2018 on YouTube titled "Emotional Story by Ibn Jawzi," a Youtuber repeats a story from Ibn Jawzi's *Dhamm al-hawa* (The censure of passion). He details the demise of a respected Baghdadi *muadhin* (the man who issues the call to prayer from the minaret) following his obsession with a young Christian woman. Because he looked at a woman, the Youtuber laments, the muadhin "lost his *deen* (religion)." A viewer responded in the comment section: "May ALLAH give us a good ending."[45]

To many scholars in the West who write and think about Islam and Muslim societies, Ibn al-Jawzi, Ibn Tumart, and other medieval Islamic scholars are mostly relevant in strictly academic discussions about religion and the Middle Ages. For many young Muslim men today, however, medieval teachings continue to be of great relevance to their everyday lives because they cater to their desire for a patriarchal order, whose disappearance they anxiously fear in light of what they perceive as women's and men's deviance from their religiously assigned gender roles. Put simply, in order to understand misogyny in Muslim societies today, even in its extreme manifestations, it is important to ground such inquiries in the medieval past, which serves both as a source of legitimacy and a guiding inspiration.

Political developments in the region, too, exposed the artificiality of the divide between the past and the present. Indeed, if by now the discussion of medieval texts and practices brings to mind the highly mediatized and politicized misogynist practices of groups such as the Taliban, it is intentional. For one of the goals is to call into question the apologetic and presentist analysis of terrorist movements that sees them as strictly twentieth- or twenty-first-century developments. As any medievalist of the region will tell you, there is far more continuity with the past than discontinuity. In an article published in *Foreign Policy*, "Is Afghanistan 'Medieval'?" Thomas Barfield explains that while "medieval" is often perceived as an insult, the religious and political struggles of the Middle Ages can help us understand contemporary Afghanistan, particularly when it comes to the central role religion plays under the Taliban.[46]

Barfield does not bring up women and gender, but the Taliban could be considered medieval in those aspects as well. Indeed, much of what has been written about women in Islamic medieval sources served as the basis for Taliban's laws and regulations applied to women. Like the Almohad movement, the Taliban emerged as a radical Islamic movement opposing what it perceived as deviations from Islam's true message, especially when it came to the place of women in public space. Taliban leaders, like Ibn Tumart, realized from early on that women and girls' bodies could be instrumentalized to form unity among the movement's followers. In addition to banning drinking, music, and other forms of entertainment that could bring together women and men, the Taliban theocracy was built on sexual segregation and the removal of women's bodies from public space.

The Revolutionary Association of the Women of Afghanistan (RAWA), whose founder Meena was assassinated in 1987 for her activism on behalf of Afghani women and girls, lists restrictions imposed in Afghanistan under Taliban rule that mimic Ibn Abdun's instructions discussed earlier in this chapter. For example, Afghani women were banned from "dealing with male shopkeepers" nor were they allowed to wash clothes "next to rivers or in a public place." Moreover, they were forbidden from "talking or shaking hands with non-*mahram* males."[47] Women under Taliban rule were also banned from working outside the home. This restriction applied to most professionals including teachers and engineers. The only exceptions were a few women medical doctors and nurses, who were allowed to continue to practice in Kabul hospitals. The plan, however, was to eventually eliminate the possibility of such professions for women for they instituted an educational ban that forbade women from studying formally at universities and other educational institutions.[48]

Women were only allowed to leave their home if in the company of a *mahram* (a guardian, usually a close male relative). Even then, women had to be careful not to attract the attention of other men by covering from head to toe in the literal sense. Not even women's ankles could be seen outside. Women were not allowed to wear what were regarded as "sexually attracting colors." They were also forbidden from using makeup, nail polish, perfume, and heels because "a man must not hear a woman's footsteps." Indeed, all sounds coming from women were forbidden. A woman could not be heard on the radio or on the street. Women could not laugh in public, for "no stranger should hear a woman's voice." Even when inside, women's interaction with the outside had to be monitored. There was a ban "on women appearing on the balconies of their apartments or houses," and all households were ordered to paint their windows so that "women cannot be seen from outside their homes."[49]

The discomfort with the female body extended to representations as well. No visual depictions of women were allowed in newspapers, television, books, or films. Even the word "woman" came to provoke disgust. All places that included the word "women" were renamed. "Women's Garden" became "Spring Garden." Gradually, women were erased from all spaces outside the confines of the home.[50]

To ensure women's compliance, severe punishment was inflicted on trangressors. "Whipping, beating and verbal abuse" were a few of the punishments for women who did not follow the dress code. Women who were found wearing nail polish had "fingers cut off." Even more severe punishments were reserved for women who committed sexual "crimes." For example, women who had sex outside marriage were stoned publicly, at times to death.[51]

In light of these human rights violations, one can understand why it could be tempting to idealize, even yearn for the "before." In *Overcoming Violence Against Women and Girls: The International Campaign to Eradicate a Worldwide Problem*, Michael Penn and Rahel Nardos write with nostalgia and lament about the time *before* and *after* 1996, the year in which Taliban established the Islamic Emirate of Afghanistan:

> *After the Taliban took power in Afghanistan in 1996, women were beaten and stoned in public for not wearing proper attire, prevented from working or going out in public without a male relative, and were forced from their jobs and confined largely to their homes. Because they were not allowed to work, those without male relatives or husbands were sometimes limited to begging. Few medical facilities existed for women, and as a result of such harsh treatment, suicide and depression appeared to increase rapidly. Prior to 1996, the women or Afghanistan enjoyed relative freedom to work and dress generally as they wanted; they were allowed to drive and to appear in public alone. The resurgence of Islamic fundamentalism deprived women of all of these basic human rights. In other parts of the world, religious fundamentalism poses a similar threat to basic freedoms.[52]*

While the situation under Taliban rule was certainly lamentable, the time *before* Taliban was far from ideal. According to RAWA, many of the deplorable limitations imposed on women under the Taliban regime had been put in place by the Rabbani-Massoud government when it was established in 1992. Women were forced to "cover the whole body." They were not allowed to wear clothes that were "too thin," "narrow and tight," "decorated and colorful," or clothes that "resemble men's clothes." Moreover, women were forbidden from wearing perfume for "if a perfumed woman passes by a crowd of men, she is considered to be an adulteress." They were required to seek their husband's permission before leaving their house. Once outside, they were asked "not to walk in the middle of streets," and were forbidden "to talk to strange men." "If it is necessary to talk," it should be done "in a low voice and without laughter."[53] In sum, this is what life *before* Taliban was like for Afghani women, and nothing about it merits nostalgia. Neither does life *after* the Taliban, for that matter. Violence against women and girls, though perhaps to a lesser extent, continued despite the various government initiatives, such as the reopening of schools, parliamentary quotas, and the 2009 Law on the Elimination of Violence against Women (EVAW law). Many of these reforms remained on paper, only.[54]

Life after the return of the Taliban is not promising either. Even before the full withdrawal of US troops from Afghanistan, Taliban forces had already started killing Afghani women, particularly women's rights advocates. By June 2021, the Taliban had captured more than one hundred districts, including the Balkh district in northern Afghanistan. Their first order of business was to restrict women's movement in public space by, among other things, forbidding women from leaving the home without a male guardian and reinstating the burqa. Videos from the region show "official" Taliban propaganda hanging in public spaces demonstrating the correct form of veiling. In a few mosques of the Taliban-captured areas, it was announced that sharia would be implemented.[55] The violence against women that followed was clear indication that they were not bluffing. In early August, Nazaneen, a twenty-one-year-old woman, was dragged out of a car and shot dead by Taliban militants. Her crime? She was caught in Balkh district not wearing a veil.[56] Simply put: the life of Afghani women was not good before Taliban. It was not good under the Taliban. It was not good after the Taliban, despite the modest legal gains. And things do not bode well for them with the return of the Taliban.

Yet many who are concerned with women's rights in the region, including feminists, rely on the *before* and *after* narratives as strategies for measuring women's well-being not only in Afghanistan but throughout North Africa and the Middle East. *Before* and *after* is useful for telling linear, clean, even triumphant stories and for constructing a semblance of progress. More importantly, the narratives of *before* and *after* are used as a strategy for making sense of the present. They give a convenient, albeit superficial, answer to the question: How did we get here? Unfortunately, the *before* and *after* narratives most often cater to and are in defense of ideological allegiances for which women and their bodies are merely instrumentalized for ends that have little, if any, concern for women's rights. Women's stories in the region, however, cannot fit in a clean linear narrative. To tell them, and to hear them, one must expect fragmented accounts without beginning or end, messy stories whose continuities expand over centuries. In reality, moving from the seventh, to the twelfth, to the fourteenth, to the twenty-first centuries indicates that when it comes to women in the region, rather than discontinuities and ruptures from the past, there is an attachment to the past and explicit persistence that is made even stronger thanks to twenty-first-century technologies.

At the core of this continuity is the fragility of the condition of Muslim women. Independent of the time or place, the texts discussed in this chapter show women whose presence was not welcome in the streets of Mecca, Cairo, Marrakesh, Baghdad, and Kabul. This rejection from public space is often documented and made visible when it is connected to a larger, male-dominated and instigated event such as, for example, the emergence of politico-religious movements. The harassment of women in the streets of Mecca is evoked in the context of the beginning of Islam. Violence against Sura and other women in eleventh-century Marrakesh is discussed in the context of the rise of the Almohad empire. The brutality against women in Afghanistan is connected to the birth and rebirth of the Taliban regime. Yet women's suffering in North Africa and the Middle East today is not strictly limited to turning points, major historical events, or conflict zones. The war on women today is the legacy of centuries of prejudice grounded in and legitimized by authoritative texts and practices from the Middle Ages. As a result, it has infiltrated every aspect of women's lives in the region, including the most banal. Therefore, "How did we get here?" is not necessarily a productive question since we are where we have been for centuries. Perhaps a more constructive question would be: Why are we still here?

Notes

1. Ira G. Zepp, *A Muslim Primer*, second edition (Fayetteville: University of Akansas Press, 2000), 127.
2. See Amina Wadud, "Towards a Qur'anic Hermeneutics of Social Justice: Race, Class and Gender," *Journal of Law and Religion* 12, no. 1 (1995–1996): 48.
3. Hibba Abugideiri, "Hagar: A Historical Model for 'Gender Jihad,'" in *Daughters of Abraham: Feminist Thought in Judaism, Christianity, and Islam*, eds. Yvonne Y. Haddad and John Esposito (Gainesville: University Press of Florida, 2001), 92.
4. Shadaab Rahemtulla, *Qur'an of the Oppressed: Liberation Theology and Gender Justice in Islam* (Oxford: Oxford University Press, 2017), 120.
5. Asma Barlas, *"Believing Women" in Islam: Unreading Patriarchal Interpretations of the Qur'an* (Austin: University of Texas Press, 2002), 26.
6. Ibid., 5.
7. Ibid., 268.
8. See Kecia Ali's discussion of this passage in *Sexual Ethics and Islam: Feminist Reflections on Qur'an, Hadith and Jurisprudence* (London: Oneworld Publications, 2006).
9. Asma Barlas, *"Believing Women" in Islam*, 6.
10. Asma Lamrabet, *Women in the Qur'an: An Emancipatory Reading*, trans. Myriam François-Cerrah (Leicestershire: Square View-Kube Publishing, 2016), 150.
11. Quoted in Siraj Sait and Hilary Lim, *Land, Law and Islam: Property and Human Rights in the Muslim World*, vol. 1 (London: Zed Books, 2006), 125.
12. "Egypt Apostasy Trial Adjourned," BBC News, July 9, 2001, http://news.bbc.co.uk/2/hi/middle_east/1430497.stm.
13. Fatima Mernissi, *Beyond the Veil: Male-Female Dynamics in Modern Muslim Society*, revised edition (Bloomington: Indiana University Press, 1987), 138.
14. Muhammed Irshad Ahmed Qasmi, *Women of Paradise*, trans. Abdur-Rahim Qudwaee (Beyrouth: Dar al-Kotob al-ilmiyah, 2012), 101.
15. Muhammad ibn 'Abdallah al-khatib al-Tabrizi, *Mishkat al-Masabih*, trans. Muhammed Mahdi al-Sharif (Beyrouth: Dar al-Kotob al-ilmiyah, 2012), 48.
16. Ibid., 376.
17. There are variations of the same hadith. According to Imam Ghazli, the Prophet said, "The woman is nearest to her Lodr's Face when she is in the innermost part of her home. Her prayer in the courtyard of her house is better than her prayer in the mosque, and her prayer in her home is better than her prayer in the courtyard of her house, and her prayer in her chamber is even better than her prayer in her home." Quoted in V. A. Mohamad Ashrof, *Islam and Gender Justice: Questions at the Interface* (Delhi: Kalpaz Publications, 2005), 211.
18. Al-khatib al-Tabrizi, *Mishkat al-Masabih*, 376.
19. Fatima Mernissi, *Dreams of Trespass: Tales of a Harem Girlhood* (New York: Addison-Wesley, 1994), 1–2.
20. Quoted in Sachiko Murata, *The Tao of Islam* (Albany: SUNY, 1992), 176.
21. Hammed Shahidian, *Women in Iran: Gender Politics in the Islamic Republic* (Westport: Greenwood Press, 2002), 51.

22. Al-khatib al-Tabrizi, *Mishkat al-Masabih*, 376.

23. Ibid., 182.

24. Muhammed Irshad Ahmed Qasmi, *Women of Paradise*, 102.

25. Leila Ahmed, *Women and Gender in Islam: Historical Roots of a Modern Debate* (New Haven, CT: Yale University Press, 1992), 42.

26. Mernissi, *Beyond the Veil*, 143.

27. Saleh Fauzan al-Fauzan, *Rulings Pertaining to Muslim Women* (Riyadh: Darussalam, 2003), 67.

28. Quoted in Fadwa Malti-Douglas, *Woman's Body, Woman's Word: Gender and Discourse in Arabo-Islamic Writing* (Princeton: Princeton University Press, 1991), 49.

29. For a detailed discussion of Ibn Jawzi's misogynistic project, see Latifa Lakhdar, *Les femmes au miroire de l'orthodoxie islamique*, trans. From Arabic by Hichem Abdessamad (La Tour d'Aigues: Editions de l'Aube, 2007).

30. Nabil Mouline, *The Clerics of Imam: Religious Authority and Political Power in Saudi Arabia* (New Haven: Yale University Press, 2014), 33.

31. "The Markets of Seville," trans. and ed. Bernard Lewis, *Islam from the Prophet Muhammad to the Capture of Constantinople*, vol. 2 (Oxford: Oxford University Press, 1987), 157–65.

32. Huda Lutfi, "Manners and Customs of Fourteenth-Century Cairene Women: Female Anarchy versus Male Shar'I Order in Muslim Perspective Treatises," in *Women in Middle Eastern History: Shifting Boundaries in Sex and Gender*, eds. Nikki Keddie and Beth Baron (New Haven, CT: Yale University Press, 1991), 115.

33. Ibn al-Hajj, cited in Albert Houarni, *A History of the Arab Peoples* (Cambridge: Harvard University Press, 2002), 120.

34. Edith Wharton, *In Morocco* (New York: Charles Scribner's Sons, 1920), 49.

35. Usamah Ibn Munqidh, trans. Philip Khuri Hitti, *An Arab-Syrian Gentleman and Warrior in the Period of the Crusades: Memoirs of Usamah Ibn-Muqidh* (Kitab al-I'tibar) (New York: Columbia University Press, 2000), 164.

36. Ibid. 164.

37. Ibid., 165–66.

38. Ibid., 154.

39. Ibtissam Bouachrine, *Women and Islam: Myths, Apologies, and the Limits of Feminist Critique* (Lanham, MD: Lexington Books, 2014).

40. Mouna Hachim, *Ben Toumert ou les derniers jours des Voilés* (Casablanca: La Croisee des Chemins, 2021).

41. H. T. Norris, "Ibn Tumart and the Almoravids: 'The Evil Deeds of the Mujassimun from Kakudam,' Selected Passages from Ibn Tumar's A'azz Ma Yutlab," *Journal of Qur'anic Studies* 13, no. 2 (2011): 161.

42. James Allen Fromherz, *The Near West: Medieval North Africa, Latin Europe and the Mediterranean in the Second Axial Age* (Edinburgh: Edinburgh University Press, 2016), 127.

43. BoniteMedia, "Qissat al-Andalus," YouTube video, 19:36, June 16, 2015, https://www.youtube.com/watch?v=gIXmXmhhQlg.

44. ZamZamAcademy, "Abdur-Rahman Ibn al-Jawzi of Baghdad," YouTube video, 2:23, November 4, 2015, https://www.youtube.com/watch?v=GExOunYW3j0.

45. Dar al-Quran wa Sunnah, "Emotional Story by Ibn Jawzi [. . .] Must Watch!" YouTube video, 3:10, April 28, 2018, https://www.youtube.com/watch?v=-S-ARlcL4pU.

46. Thomas Barfield, "Is Afghanistan 'Medieval'?" *Foreign Policy*, June 2, 2010.

47. RAWA, "Some of the Restrictions Imposed by Taliban on Women in Afghanistan."

48. Ibid.

49. Ibid.

50. Ibid.

51. Ibid.

52. Michael L Penn and Rahel Nardos, *Overcoming Violence Against Women and Girls: The International Campaign to Eradicate a Worldwide Problem* (Lanham, MD: Rowman & Littlefield Publishers, 2003), 164.

53. RAWA, "Some of the Restrictions Imposed by Taliban on Women in Afghanistan."

54. For more, see Valentine M. Moghadam, *Modernizing Women: Gender and Social Change in the Middle East* (Boulder, CO: Lynne Rienner Publishers, 2003).

55. VOA News, "Taliban Put Strict Curbs on Women, Media in Afghanistan's Balkh District," YouTube video, 1:46, July 7, 2021, https://www.youtube.com/watch?v=A4wsylqhEn4.

56. "21-year-old Girl Shot Dead by Taliban in Balkh," *Afghanistan Times*, August 4, 2021, http://www.afghanistantimes.af/21-year-old-girl-shot-dead-by-taliban-in-balkh/.

CHAPTER 3

Isolatory Narratives

ON FEBRUARY 10, 2020, THE RABAT COURT OF APPEAL SENTENCED Abdelwahed Bichri to the death penalty for the torture and murder of Hanan. The decision was celebrated by many as the inevitable triumph of justice over injustice. However, Moroccan lawyer and human rights activist Mohammed Ziyan could not get past the initial sentence given before the video of the crime surfaced. Why would the Public Prosecutor's Office send the case to the Court of First Instance (*al-mahkama al-ibtida'iya*)?[1] Indeed, how could the legal system have seen Abdelwahed's crime as a mere misdemeanor (*junha*)? One reason, as reports about gender-based violence in the region show, is that violence against women is so common it has become banal. Indeed, structural and systemic violence have been part of the quotidian existence of women and girls throughout North Africa and the Middle East for so long that even a sentence of a few years in prison for a gender-based crime can be contested as unjust. When the court handed down prison sentences to several of Abdelwahed's accomplices (twenty years in prison for the man who filmed the video and five each for eight other defendants for various crimes including not reporting the assailant to the authorities),[2] friends and family members of the defendants denounced the sentences as unfair. They insisted that Hanan was often seen in the streets in the company of men, with whom she "had many [sexual] relations."[3]

It is common for families and friends to rally to the defense of the criminal using the victim's alleged promiscuity as a justification for the violence she endured. Before Hanan, there was another highly publicized case from a small village in Morocco's interior involving a seventeen-year-old girl named Khadija. In August 2018, she and her family reported that a gang of men, ages eighteen to twenty-eight, abducted, raped, imprisoned, and trafficked her. To immortalize their violent acts, they allegedly inscribed her body with tattoos and cigarette burns. The families of the accused men, twelve of whom were arrested, were unapologetic in their condemnation of the teenager: Khadija was a promiscuous girl often seen around the village drinking alcohol, smoking cigarettes, and hanging out with men in public spaces.[4]

Before Khadija, there was the case of Zeinab, a twenty-four-year-old woman with a mental disability. In August 2017, four teenagers assaulted Zeinab on a public bus in Casablanca. Neither the bus driver nor the other passengers who witnessed the crime intervened. Soon after the video of the attack was leaked, the victim was "quickly branded a runaway with loose morals."[5] Young men who knew the perpetrators related that Zeinab was a willing participant and that she used to *tshemker* with them (from *shemkar*, an insult in Darija that designates homeless people, often young boys in large urban centers, who are commonly assumed to be drug addicts).[6] As to the assailants, their actions were excused as a mere uncontrollable act of youth under the influence of drugs.[7] "Why else would they film their crime and incriminate themselves?" asked one of the interviewees.[8]

While this kind of reaction may appear to be morally counterintuitive, it makes sense in the context of Zakia Daoud's analysis of the division of space in Moroccan society, which echoes Mernissi's argument about sexual segregation in Muslim-majority societies discussed in the previous chapter. Daoud argues that the Moroccan patriarchal order is "fondé sur une hiérarchie verticale Homme/Femme, et une segregation horizontale: Femmes dedans/Hommes dehors" (Moroccan patriarchal order is founded on a vertical hierarchy Man/Woman, and horizontal segregation: Women inside/Men outside).[9] Hanan, Khadija, and Zeinab are therefore perceived as the transgressors for trespassing the boundaries of the home repeatedly and indecently. The violence their bodies have endured is merely patriarchy operating through misogyny, which is, according to Kate Manne, "the law enforcement branch of a patriarchal order."[10] It is not coincidental that most of the crimes discussed throughout this book occurred during warmer months when women and girls tend to spend relatively more time outside the house wearing fewer layers of clothing. As a reaction to what they consider a defiance of patriarchal authority, men feel justified in violating women's bodies.

In what follows, and in line with the argument presented in the previous chapter, I explore violence against women today as the manifestation of misogynistic disapproval of women's bodies outside the private sphere, even when such violence is committed in a domestic context. The goal is to go against what I call "isolatory narratives," which are narratives that seek to frame violence against Muslim women as a series of isolated and disconnected events. Instead, this chapter and the rest of the book propose a shift in the discussion about violence in North Africa and the Middle East from a phenomenon/*dhahira* that affects a few exceptionally unfortunate women to a reality that accompanies every woman's existence/*wujud*. First, however, it is important to consider gender-based violence in the region by numbers to better understand how normalized it is. To be sure, not all violence against women is physical, nor is it always quantifiable. The first section, however, focuses intentionally on physical gender-based violence because of its visibility on the body, making it relatively easier to document and, therefore, quantify. Moreover, while the later sections rely primarily on content produced in the local dialects, in this section I have incorporated mainly sources that are readily available and easy to access in English. Anyone concerned with Muslim women's rights and condition should have access to these statistics, which give a clear idea about the overall deplorable state of women throughout North Africa and the Middle East.

Banalized Violence

For anyone familiar with the region, it is undeniable that violence against women and girls, or violence in general, has become routine and normalized. This violence begins at an early age. A 2018 UNICEF report provides alarming data about violence against children and adolescents, both male and female. For example, while only 7 percent of the world's adolescents live in North Africa and the Middle East, in 2015 more than 70 percent of adolescent deaths caused by "collective violence" occurred in the region. Most of these deaths happened in war-torn areas including Iraq and the Syrian Arab Republic.[11] Violence, however, is not restricted to any particular area of the Middle East. Of the region's children between the ages of two and fourteen, 85 percent have experienced violent discipline at home. Indeed, Egypt ranks number one worldwide. Tunisia is in second place. The State of Palestine is in fourth place, Jordan in seventh, and Morocco in tenth.[12] This violence takes the form of both physical (e.g., shaking, hitting, and slapping) and psychological (e.g., yelling, berating, and insulting). When it comes to "severe physical punishment," defined as "being hit on the head, ears or face or being hit hard and repeatedly," 30 percent of this type of violence occurs in North Africa and the Middle East. Egypt is the country with the highest percentage of severe corporal punishment, with 45 percent, and Tunisia is in third place, with 32 percent. It is important to note that Egypt and Tunisia are two of only four countries in the region where children and adolescents have legal protection. Along with Israel and the State of Palestine, they have put in place legislation that "fully prohibits the use of corporal punishment against children at home."[13] This is yet another indication that laws alone are not sufficient to produce significant change.

A more detailed report published in 2019 looks at the gender variance in receiving and administering punishment at home. Boys in the region are 1.3 times more likely to be subjected to physical violence than girls.[14] Moreover, mothers are at least 1.3 times more likely to administer severe physical punishment to children than fathers are.[15] One could object here to the limited definition of what constitutes physical violence. For example, in general, girls tend to receive less food and nutrition than boys. Girls are also excluded from sports and other physical activities that usually take place in the streets. In addition to being deprived of the health benefits of exercising outdoors, they are also denied the pleasure as well as the growth, both emotional and intellectual, that come with participating in group sports. Even if they were to play outside, closer to the home, girls are often forced to wear clothing with more fabric in order to cover more of their body, contrary to boys whose shorts give them greater freedom of movement. Play, however, cannot interfere with completing their chores as most girls are expected to participate in household work since an early age. Cleaning, cooking, and other work is physically demanding and should, therefore, be counted as physical abuse. This abuse increases exponentially around periods of religious celebrations. For example, at the end of last Ramadan, there was a trend on YouTube and Instagram showing girls in kitchens throughout the region hand-washing large numbers of dishes immediately after breaking the fast. Meanwhile, family members and guests gathered in the living room, eating more food, watching special Ramadan television shows, and having a good time. While most videos were tongue-in-cheek, this does not diminish the implications such "trivial" injustices could have on girls and women.

With age, girls in the region, and later women, become disproportionately targeted by gender-based violence, defined as "violence that is directed at an individual based on his or her biological sex OR gender identity." This violence "includes physical, sexual, verbal, emotional, and psychological abuse, threats, coercion, and economic or educational deprivation, whether occurring in public or private life."[16] The shift in violence is not necessarily dependent on age but typically begins around the time a girl comes to be viewed as sexually available, regardless of how she views her own body and sexuality. Many feminists from the region have documented this shift in perception as the moment in which they intuitively recognized injustice, eventually developing into a feminist consciousness. In *A Daughter of Isis: The Autobiography of Nawal El Saadawi*, El Saadawi writes about personal instances in which the body of a child becomes sexualized. A photograph taken in June 1935, at Chatby Beach in Alexandria, triggers the remembrance of one such moment. El Saadawi was four at the time:

> In the photograph I can see myself lying on the sand wearing the swimsuit with its bands of black and white. My mother is sitting next to me wearing a swimsuit also colored black and white. It covers her belly and her chest, with shoulder straps on either side. My

younger sister, Leila, is sitting between her legs and is wearing a swimsuit which is smaller, but is just like mine. My father is sitting a little distance away, his chest and belly are bare, his swimsuit has no shoulder straps, and next to him is my brother wearing a swimsuit which covers only a small part of his body below his navel and above his thighs.[17]

On the other side of North Africa, Fatima Mernissi describes a similar experience in which she was not prepared for her body to be perceived as sexual. She writes in *Doing Daily Battle: Interviews with Moroccan Women* about an episode that involved her father. She, too, was four years old:

My father adored me. He used to take me on his mule to the mosque for Friday prayers, and he kept me by his side during long hours of reading or discussions with his friends. The books that he loved and regularly pored over were histories of Muslim civilisation, which was his passion. Nevertheless, my father, who adored me, who was immersed in our heritage and impassioned by our civilisation, bought me a djellaba and tried to force the veil on me at the age of four. For him there was no contradiction between civilisation, refinement, and immuring alive, physically and mentally, a child of the female sex.[18]

Mernissi and El Saadawi's grievances could easily be dismissed as the preoccupations of a privileged elite—both women come from relatively wealthy families. While they were inconvenienced by the expectation of covering their bodies, it could be said, boys and girls their age lacked the minimum necessities for survival. Unfortunately, this is a common tactic even among academics to silence critique of human rights abuses in North Africa and the Middle East. Rather than address the abuses, the critique is turned against the ones initiating it by shaming them and questioning their agenda. Why does one bring up an injustice that affects only a small minority? Are they catering to Western expectations of Muslim women and girls' oppression?

What is certain is that being suddenly deprived of certain public spaces and being forced into vestimentary concessions to occupy others was experienced by both girls as an injustice impactful enough for them to recall it decades later as grown-up women. At any rate, there is not much to gain from the trap of hierarchizing suffering. Rather than obsessing about what constitutes legitimate suffering, perhaps a more inclusive feminist approach would take seriously all injustices, even the so-called banal ones that only concern a small minority. What is more, every small and banal injustice is eventually connected to a graver one. The sexualization of girls' bodies, for example, has grave implications for girls, one of which is child marriage. The Convention on the Rights of the Child defines child marriage as "any legal or customary union involving a boy or a girl below the age of eighteen."[19] It is estimated that 14 percent of Arab girls are married before they reach eighteen, though the prevalence of child marriage in North Africa and the Middle East varies significantly from one country to another. Moreover, while it is believed that the percentage of underage marriage has dropped, countries with political instability have seen a massive surge among the local and displaced populations. For example, child marriage in Iraq increased from 15 percent in 1997 to 24 percent in 2016. Child marriage rates among Syrian refugees are believed to be four times higher than in pre-civil war Syria.[20] In Yemen, where there is no legal minimum age of marriage, the percentage of girls married before the age of eighteen increased from 32 percent before the war to 72.5 percent in 2016, of whom 44.5 percent were under fifteen when they were married.[21] Even in countries where laws set a minimum age of marriage, child marriage continues as a practice. In both Morocco and Jordan, for instance, the minimum legal age at marriage was raised to eighteen for girls. However, younger girls can be legally married with judicial consent because of legal loopholes.[22] These marriages are often difficult to track, which should automatically raise doubts about official claims of child marriage decrease in North Africa and the Middle East.

Child marriage is but one of the many abuses that girls endure in the region as a result of their sexualization. Female genital mutilation (FGM) is another injustice. In half of the countries where FGM in its various forms is practiced, the genital cutting is carried out on girls under five years old. In the other half, girls are cut between the ages of five and fourteen.[23] In certain regions, such as the Luxor governorate in Egypt, for example, genital cutting is carried out soon after birth.[24] According to the World Health Organization, FGM carries no benefits from a health perspective. On the contrary, it is harmful to girls and women in the short term (e.g., pain, bleeding, infections, urinary complications, even death) as well as in the long term (e.g., painful menstruation, painful intercourse, vaginal infections, obstetric complications, increased risk of prenatal death).[25] Moreover, FGM increases women's risk of acquiring sexually transmitted diseases including HIV.[26] Psychologically, FGM can lead to chronic mental health conditions, including depression, anxiety, post-traumatic stress disorder (PTSD), and a greater risk of suicide.[27]

To be sure, FGM is less common in North Africa and the Middle East compared to other parts of Africa and Asia. Egypt, however, has one of the highest rates of FGM in the world. According to a 2014 study, 92 percent of Egyptian girls and women between the ages of fifteen and forty-nine have endured female genital mutilation.[28] Following a highly publicized case of a twelve-year-old girl (or ten or eleven, depending on the source), Badour Shaker, who died at the hands of the physician who was performing the mutilation, FGM was banned categorically in Egypt in 2008 and became a felony in 2016.[29] Law, however, is incapable of protecting girls and women from opportunistic misogyny. In June 2020, in the midst of the COVID-19 pandemic, an Egyptian father "tricked" his three daughters, all minors, into FGM. He took the girls to the doctor under the pretense of getting a COVID-19 vaccine, but instead the doctor cut their genitals.[30] It was the girls' mother who reported the crime to the police. The parents, it is important to add, are divorced, which raises a few questions: Would the mother have reported the crime had she been living in the same house as the father and therefore been at immediate risk of retaliation? Was the reporting itself in retaliation against the father for previous acts of violence against his wife? In other words, is the mother convinced that FGM is a crime? What is known is that in most FGM cases, the cutting is performed with the mother's consent, whether she believes in the practice or succumbs to peer pressure. According to a 2003 study conducted by the Egyptian Ministry of Health and Population, 69 percent of women who endured FGM agree with subjecting their daughters to it as well.[31]

FGM, therefore, like many of the injustices that girls and women undergo in the region, is not a question of men versus women, for women, too, are accomplices and at times are even necessary for carrying out and upholding such unjust practices. Several feminists in the West fear that addressing violence against women in Muslim-majority countries would perpetuate colonial feminism or, as Gayatri Spivak famously put it, "white men saving brown women from brown men."[32] Academics relished coming up with the various reconfigurations: "White women saving brown women from brown men";[33] and "Brown women saving brown women from brown men."[34] Misogyny, however, has no allegiances as long as the work gets done. A white man, a white woman, a brown man, and a brown woman, too, are very much capable of carrying out injustices. Rather than produce isolatory narratives of injustice that attribute extreme cases of injustice and cruelty to exceptionally evil individuals, it is far more productive to think about gender-based violence, and misogyny in general, in terms of relations of power. Indeed, one must assume the inevitability of the occurrence of injustice in any unequal relationship of power that is not governed by an already established and reliable system of checks and balances. Reliability is crucial, for creating laws against violent practices is not enough when such laws are not clear, categorical, or reinforced, and when there are no serious attempts to close legal loopholes that allow discrimination against women and girls to continue.

Even then, it is not possible to completely eliminate violent practices, especially those that have collective support that goes beyond the individual and her rights. A case in point is honor killing, a crime for which it is difficult to collect statistical data, because it is often unreported or misreported as "natural" or "accidental" death. For example, when twenty-one-year-old Israa Ghrayeb from a village near Bethlehem was killed in 2019 by her brother and brother in-law for posting a video or a photo (accounts vary), her family declared that the cause of death had been a heart attack.[35] As to her broken spine, an injury she had sustained when she fell from the balcony as she was trying to escape her family's torture, it was blamed on the demon that possessed her.[36]

Unfortunately, despite being overwhelmingly underreported, honor crimes are growing more pervasive in the region. It is believed that in Yemen, four hundred deaths a year are the result of honor killings. In Pakistan, more than 1,184 honor killings occurred in 2015. In Jordan, 25 percent of murders annually are honor killings. These are only a few examples of a practice that, as Robert Paul Churchill argues, "remains accepted even in countries such as Jordan and Turkey where there have been highly publicized national efforts to stiffen sentences."[37] For many in North Africa and the Middle East, the value of a man's honor far exceeds the value of a human life, which explains why brutal crimes are committed against women by those closest to them. In July 2020, a video filmed in Jordan surfaced online of a woman's screams as her father smashed her head with a brick. The neighbors, who captured the footage on their smartphones, later testified that when he succeeded in putting an end to his daughter's life, the father sat by the body, smoked his cigarette, and drank a cup of tea.[38]

Yet, once again, despite the severity of the crime, the father might have escaped punishment were it not for the video recording and social media. This is due, in part, to the fact that local laws throughout the region tend to be lenient with honor killings, in many instances even allowing the victim's family to pardon the perpetrator. This is the case of Article 99 of Jordan's Penal Code, which allows the sentence to be reduced in half if the victim's family forgives the criminal or chooses not to take legal action against him. Since the criminal and the victim are usually from the same family, not to mention that the victim's family often approves of the crime, it is not surprising that in many cases the crime goes unpunished.[39] This, it is important to note, is not unique to North Africa and the Middle East. Indeed, according to a 2010 UN report, of the approximately five thousand honor killings that happen every year around the world, in most cases the criminal goes unpunished.[40] To make matters worse, the perpetrator is often seen by his family and society at large as the epitome of masculinity.

This explains why top-down interventions, such as public awareness campaigns on domestic violence, and laws criminalizing gender-based violence, such as Morocco's 2018 Law 103–13 on the elimination of violence against women, are rendered almost useless. When Waseem Baloch drugged and killed his sister, twenty-five-year-old Fouzia Azeem, best known by her stage name Qandeel Baloch, he did not hide his pride. Known as "Pakistan's Kim Kardashian," Baloch regularly posted on social media videos and photos deemed controversial.[41] Right before her death, she posted photos and a video she shot with a selfie stick from a June 2016 meeting with Mufti Abdul Qavi, a Pakistani religious cleric. Soon after the video and photos were leaked, the mufti lost his position on one of Pakistan's religious committees. On July 15, 2016, Qandeel's brother drugged and strangled her to death. He had been keeping track of her long list of transgressions. He confessed that, unlike other girls, Qandeel refused "to stay home and follow traditions," thus bringing "dishonor" on their family. The last straw was the video with the cleric. "I am proud of what I did," he declared unapologetically and unremorsefully, knowing very well that, in the eyes of many, his murder has made him a hero.[42]

INSIDE/OUTSIDE VIOLENCE

Declarations such as the ones made by Qandeel's brother ought to be taken seriously, for they betray a collective sense of entitlement over women's bodies. When Israa, Qandeel, and the many other women like them are murdered, their deaths are thought to restore not only the killers' honor but also the collective's honor—the collective here refers to other family members, but could also include neighbors, even all men, thus blurring the divide between the domestic and non-domestic space. Indeed, this collective entitlement over women's bodies could explain why sever gender-based violence in North Africa and the Middle East is not limited to the domestic sphere. In 2017, the Thomson Reuters Foundation conducted a poll about gender-based violence and megacities (defined as cities housing more than ten million people). Among the factors considered were the risk of sexual violence and harassment, harmful cultural practices, and access to healthcare, education, and economic opportunities. Cairo was found to be the most dangerous megacity for women in the world. Istanbul was ranked tenth. According to *Forbes*'s 2017 list of "10 Most Dangerous Places for Women Travelers," Egypt ranked in first place, followed by Morocco in second. To "stay safe," women are told to consider wearing sunglasses because "eye contact can be considered flirting." Clothes, however, are the main focus. Women are advised to "stick with modest styles" and avoid "belly-bearing shirts, short-shorts, and strappy tank tops."[43] What if a woman were to decide that short-shorts paired with a tank top are the perfect attire for a stroll down Casablanca's Boulevard Mohammed V one warm summer afternoon? Should she be blamed if she were to be assaulted?

According to the findings of a 2017 UN study, the woman would, indeed, be blamed. In Egypt, 74 percent of the men interviewed believe that women who dress "provocatively" deserve to be harassed. In Morocco, 72 percent of the men agree.[44] The countless videos uploaded online seem to confirm this attitude. These videos depict women from various parts of North Africa and the Middle East being harassed for wearing "revealing" clothes. A ten-second video from 2017 shows a large crowd of young men in the Corniche of Tangier harassing a woman wearing a pair of jeans and a t-shirt. The police denied that a sexual aggression took place. Instead, they insisted that the crowd of men had just formed due to a spectacle.[45] A less ambiguous video, also from Tangier, depicts a crowd of men harassing a woman while she was carrying an infant in her arms. The woman was blamed for wearing clothes judged too tight and for allegedly "flirting" with the men. The police intervened to save her from the aggressors.[46]

Another video, this time from Egypt, depicts the assault of a young woman by dozens of young men. The aggression took place sometime in the final hours of 2019 as she was walking home with a friend, also a woman, following New Year's Eve celebrations. When a crowd of men began harassing them due to their festive outfits, short dresses and heels, the two women took refuge in a nearby store, but the shop owner, fearing retaliation, asked them to leave. CCTV footage taken inside shows passive men and women bystanders, indifferent as the terrorized women were forced to exit. It is unclear what happened to the other woman once they had left, as only one is seen surrounded by a mob of men. Eventually, a few men helped her get into a car, while others jumped on top of the vehicle with sticks in their hands.[47]

Men's honor, it turns out, is not tied exclusively to women and girls to whom one is related. Men in the region have appointed themselves as the unofficial guardians of all women, forcing the latter into hiding behind layers of cloth. In recent years in North Africa and the Middle East, particularly since the 2011 Arab uprising, most women in countries where the veil is not mandatory have adopted some form of veiling. For example, about 90 percent of women wear the veil in Egypt.[48] These measures, however, have not diminished the harassment in public spaces. Although not all countries in the region maintain official statistics, the data available shows that sexual harassment and other forms of gender-based violence in public space are pervasive throughout the region, though to varying degrees. In Egypt, 99 percent of women have experienced sexual harassment.[49] A 2010 study from Lebanon found that 22 percent of respondents reported having "been touched or pinched against their will" while in a public space, and 61 percent of women experienced sexual harassment in public.[50] A 2015 survey from Tunisia found that 54 percent of women had experienced gender-based violence in public spaces between 2011 and 2015. The most prevalent form of violence while in public was psychological (78 percent) followed by sexual violence (75 percent).[51]

Therefore, concessions to misogyny, such as veiling, for example, have not produced safer streets for women. This is also reflected in the harassment videos posted online from Egypt, Morocco, and elsewhere in North Africa and the Middle East, which depict victims wearing a veil with some kind of long dress and, in a few instances, the woman is wearing a *niqab*. Men of all ages are seen touching or even masturbating behind the unsuspecting women. Women and girls are particularly vulnerable during religious and cultural celebrations that bring together large groups of people in unsegregated public spaces. Women are also vulnerable in public transportation. For example, videos filmed on Moroccan buses show women's *djellabas* covered with semen from the ejaculation of the men behind them. In most cases, the filming is done with the consent of the culprit. In other instances, the video documents the aggression without the knowledge of the assailant. In none of the cases is the filming done with the victim's consent or knowledge.[52]

Yet, no matter how many videos are posted online, and no matter how alarming the "official" statistics about public harassment are, it is safe to assume that the reality is much worse. Reporting incidents of gender-based violence in public is not common for many reasons. First, there is ambiguity about to whom to report. Once reported, the woman fears that she would not be believed. For example, the mother of Zeinab, the woman who was violated on the public bus in Casablanca, confessed that she did not believe that her daughter was raped until she saw the video. Even then, she claimed that initially she did not recognize her daughter but that others in the family did.[53] Moreover, as women and girls are often blamed for triggering men's behavior, even enjoying it, victims worry that reporting a crime would forever tarnish their honor and that of their families. In most cases, the victim and her family must endure continued violence and ostracism, as they are often too poor to move out of their neighborhood or town.

Finally, even if the woman is believed and the culprit or culprits are arrested, the punishment could be too lenient to merit the "scandal," which deters other victims from reporting the sexual crimes. In July 2016, a seventeen-year-old girl from Marrakesh set herself on fire and died after the prosecutor granted provisional release to the eight men who abducted her and took turns raping her when she was sixteen. Once free, the men threatened to publish the videos of the rape. The autopsy showed that she was pregnant.[54] Less than a year later, in May 2017, sixteen-year-old Nassima al Horr finally succeeded in killing herself by hanging. She had tried twice before, once by jumping off a building and the other by taking poison, but she failed both times. At fifteen, she had been abducted and raped repeatedly by four men, ages twenty to twenty-three. The girl's mother filed a complaint with the police. After preliminary investigation, the assailants were charged with, among other things, "violently raping a minor." When the offenders appeared before the judge at Marrakech's Primary Court, he allegedly declared all four offenders innocent.[55]

FEMALE FACIAL MUTILATION

Justice is not even guaranteed when proof of violence is written on a woman's face. In March 2014, a new trend known as *tshermil* emerged in Morocco, first in Casablanca then it spread to other cities. The term comes from Darija and refers to the culinary act of marinating meat in spices. *Mshermlin* (those performing acts of *tshermil*) came to refer to groups of young men known for posing for pictures with butcher knives, meat cleavers, and swords.[56] The trend has been compared to urban youth gang subcultures in the United States and Latin America because of the members' distinctive fashion and lifestyle. The *mshermlin* usually wear big and flashy jewelry and prefer designer sneakers, particularly the coveted Nike Air Max "Cobra." They are also very particular about their hairstyles, often inspired by international soccer players such as Neymar. Moreover, the *mshermlin* are known for bragging about their prized possessions including fast bikes, stacks of cash, drugs, alcohol, and breeds of dogs that are, sadly and unjustly, accused of being inherently violent such as pit bulls and rottweilers. As a cultural movement, *tshermil* has developed its own music genre and a distinctive dance that the *mshermlin* perform, often with swords.

However, what brought *mshermlin* into prominence are their criminal activities, as they do more than just pose for selfies with swords and knives. Indeed, it is believed that the name could also come from the fact that in several cases of aggression, the knife is dipped in garlic because it is believed that it prevents the wounds from closing and healing properly. Both women and men have been targeted by the *mshermlin* to steal smartphones, cash, jewelry, and even clothes. However, while there are no assault statistics by gender available, the *mshermilin* are known for operating in areas where women are most vulnerable such as, for example, outside textile factories and other industries that draw primarily women workers from lower-income households.[57] These factories often employ women for night shifts and are usually located outside the city center in areas that are neither well-lit nor easily accessible by public transportation. Based on anecdotal evidence, the attacks are generally timed to coincide with the victims' pay date. In some cases of *tshermil*, the swords and knives are used to scare the victim. In other cases, however, the robberies are accompanied by devastating facial mutilations.

In the absence of official statistics, one must rely on the firsthand accounts gathered on social media platforms. Upon listening to and watching these testimonies, one is quickly reminded that violence against women is not a mere number. It is a tragedy that leaves a trail of other tragedies. In June 2018, during the month of Ramadan, a young woman was on her way to work when a man accosted her from behind and started cutting her face before asking for her handbag. She delivered her testimony on YouTube, bandages covering much of her face and arms, as most of the victims of *tshermil* sustain defensive injuries on their hands and arms in the process of protecting their faces. Her mother, who is ill and financially dependent on her daughter, sat next to her in disbelief: "If she were bad [*khayba*], she would have deserved this punishment," she explained, but not her daughter who always walked outside "her eyes to the ground" [*hadra 'iniha*].[58] Similarly, Bouchra, a mother of three children, was on her way home in the evening after earning 50 dirhams ($5) for cleaning the stairs of a residential building when she was attacked by a man she had never seen before. Despite handing him her phone and wallet, he broke her nose and teeth because he had suspected her of hiding money.[59]

While initially *tshermil* targeted women in public spaces with no relation to the criminal, the practice was soon adopted by men with grievances against current or past partners. Twenty-year-old Fatima Zahra stopped by the store on her way home to get milk and yoghurt for her daughter. Her husband, from whom she had been separated but not divorced, attacked her from behind with two razors, cutting both sides of her face, her lips, and ear. He was angry because he had been ordered by the court to pay child support.[60] A nineteen-year-old woman was attacked by her husband while she was staying at her mother's home. He inflicted a fifteen-centimeter-long cut on her right cheek. She had married him when she was fourteen.[61] Another woman, Kalthoum, was sleeping at her mother's house when her husband, the high school sweetheart she had married when she was fourteen, cut her face with a kitchen knife he had dipped in garlic. She needed fifty stitches. The assault took place three days before their divorce hearing.[62] Twenty-five-year-old Mona was attacked by a wealthy man whom she had dated in the past but decided not to marry because of his aggressive tendencies. One night, he caught her on her way home from dinner with friends. The cut he inflicted on her face necessitated twenty-five stitches.[63] Nabiha was attacked by a former boyfriend on her way to get breakfast. He cut her left cheek and hit multiple areas of her head.[64] Ilham was attacked by her husband of five years as retaliation for her request for a divorce, which he took as an insult to his masculinity since he was incapable of having intercourse with her. He targeted both sides of her face, which left her unable to eat solid food for a month.[65] An eighteen-year-old was attacked following news of her engagement. Her assailant had asked to marry her a year and half earlier, but her family refused. When he found out that she was about to marry another man, he cut both sides of her face, her forehead, and neck. Bandages covered most of her face. Her hands were adorned with fresh henna designs from her engagement celebration.[66] A woman was surprised by her husband in front of her daughters' school after she had dropped them off. He cut her left cheek from her lips to the ear. Having endured years of abuse and threats of *tshermil*, she finally asked for a divorce, which the husband rejected because he was not willing to pay alimony.[67] A minor was attacked by a twenty-six-year-old man, who saw her walking while he was at a coffee shop and asked for her phone number. She refused. Infuriated by the rejection, he smashed the girl over the head with a stone, leaving his victim with a scar, the need for several surgeries, the loss of the long hair that she cherished, and episodes of memory loss.[68] Hajar's husband raped her then slashed the left side of her face with glass. He was planning to cut the other side as well were it not for a passerby who intervened. Neither the assailant's mother nor his aunt tried to stop him.[69] Imane was attacked by a former boyfriend she had not seen in years. He inflicted multiple cuts on her face to punish her for communicating with men on Facebook and for having married another man.[70] A woman changed her mind about marrying a man she had been dating briefly. After a period of stalking, he surprised her on her way to work and cut her cheek with a knife. The injury was so deep it affected her teeth. The woman, like many, though not all, was too poor to afford adequate treatment.[71] A young woman was attacked by her husband, who cut her face with a butcher's knife and poured acid over her while repeating, "No man will look at you after this." He was triggered by old messages on his wife's phone from a man she used to date long before her marriage.[72] A woman announced to her husband that she was pregnant. He demanded she terminate the pregnancy, which she refused. He cut both sides of her face with a razor while repeating, "this is your face now." He had been verbally and physically abusive throughout the relationship, but her family advised her against leaving given the prejudice and discrimination she could face as a divorced woman.[73]

There are countless more stories online of *tshermil* victims. Survivors and their families usually agree to share their traumatic experiences when the criminal justice system has failed them either because they were not taken seriously, or because, as many victims insist, the aggressor and his family are too rich and too well connected to be punished. In the case of Bouchra, who is a poor and illiterate woman, she was unable to provide the court with the necessary documents. As a result, her assailant was given a one-year sentence for beating her, blinding her in one eye, breaking her nose and teeth, and stealing her money.[74] Sharing their stories of abuse with the online community could therefore help women and girls influence public opinion in order to receive justice that was initially denied.

There is yet another reason for documenting one's abuse and displaying the cuts on one's face through a YouTube video seen by thousands, even millions, of viewers online. With *tshermil*, came to prominence a plastic surgeon, Dr. El Hassane Tazi, who, due to his engagement against *tshermil* and on behalf of its victims, came to be known as "the doctor of the poor" (*tabib al-fuqara'*). Tazi is a leading plastic surgeon sought after by patients not only from Morocco but also from other countries in Africa, the Middle East, and Europe. However, in the age of *tshermil*, he added to rhinoplasties, abdominoplasty, liposuction, and gluteoplasty a new popular procedure, namely scar revision surgeries and laser treatments for the victims of *tshermil*. As a result, it has become common for the victim in her testimony to appeal to the doctor for help. The journalists conducting the interviews are at times heard consoling the victim by mentioning the doctor's name. Even the viewers online appeal to him in the comment section, including for cases outside Morocco.[75] Many of these appeals were successful. And while the medical intervention does not eliminate the scars completely, the surgery and laser treatments that follow usually succeed in minimizing their appearance.

Unfortunately, no matter how generous Tazi is, he would never be able to treat all the victims of *tshermil*. Moreover, in most instances, the initial stitches are performed in the context of a medical emergency without concern for scarring, thus making esthetic revisions even more challenging. Finally, even after the physical wounds have healed, the victims of *tshermil* are left with anxiety, thoughts of suicide, fear of leaving the home, fear of being alone, failure to trust others, stress, shame, depression, nightmares, and disbelief. The latter is due to the inability to make sense of the injustice endured. The survivors often repeat that they did not do anything to merit such punishment, which is made even more traumatic by the indifference of bystanders. Almost all the crimes mentioned occurred either in crowded city streets or inside apartments in popular neighborhoods with high residential density.

Nevertheless, as one reads and listens to the victims' stories, it is important not lose sight of misogyny as the larger context for the violence. There is a reason why *tshermil* has appealed to such a large number of men and boys. As with acid attacks and other aggressions that target a woman's face, *tshermil* is a crime that calls for a rethinking of the domestic/non-domestic violence distinction. Even when committed by a domestic partner, the violent act is meant for an audience outside the domestic sphere. The *mshermlin* are, after all, performers. However, their performance is not solely about entertaining others. More importantly, it is a performance through which the *mshermel* affirms his masculine identity. This is fitting in the context of what Moroccan sociologist Adessamad Dialmy has described as the shift of masculinity from biology to practice. Dialmy argues that, in Morocco, masculinity, *rujula*, is no longer understood as "a natural given" (*une donnée naturelle*). Instead, masculinity is perceived as "something that one does recurrently, and in interaction with others, both men and women" (*quelque chose que l'on fait, que l'on fait avec récurerrence, en interaction avec les autres, avec les hommes et les femmes*).[76] In other words, it is no longer enough for one to be born *rajl*; a man has to become one through practice. This shift in the understanding of *rujula* is also evident in everyday language. An accusation in Moroccan Darija that has become popular in recent years is that one is "biologically male but not a man" (*dhker mashi rajel*). It is often used as an insult to challenge a man to prove his masculinity beyond that with which he was born.

Dialmy reads the shift of masculinity from biology as an optimistic development in a patriarchal society. Since masculinity is not merely a "natural given," or as he puts it, "no longer falls from the sky" (*ne tombe plus du ciel*), then "being a man," he argues, "no longer means total domination of the woman merely for being a man" (*être homme ne signifie plus totalement dominer (la femme) par le seul fait d'être homme*).[77] However, Dialmy's findings also invite a pessimistic reading, for they do not challenge the supremacy of masculinity/*rujula* in society. While in the past *rujula* meant a specific code of conduct *because* one was born a man, the shift in *rujula* means that *to be a man* one must adopt certain practices. This model of masculinity, however, continues to be constructed within a binary framework, always in opposition to the woman's body against which and through which *rujula* is validated. If anything, this new understanding of *rujula*, which is always in progress, never complete, is even more dependent on the body of the woman as men are constantly called upon to manifest and re-manifest their masculinity, all while its existence is doubted through a combination of alarmist rhetoric and nostalgia for the past. Judging from the popular songs, memes, and other digital content, *rujula* is scarce and on the verge of extinction. Currently on Facebook, there are more than one hundred Arabic pages named "masculinity is in danger" (*al-rujula fi khatar*). This growing anxiety about the scarcity of *rujula* triggers even greater anxiety to manifest one's *rujula* publicly. Yet, since there is no specific set of values and practices that make this masculinity, *rujula* becomes a "slippery signifier," generous in its ability to accommodate various meanings and practices, including the most violent, such as *tshermil*, as long as it is made visible to other men next to whom one is constantly evaluated as *less* or *more rajl*. In other words, this new model of *rujula* is no longer merely content with eliminating women from public space by confining them through a "horizontal segregation." The new *rujula* must make visible the process of absentiating the woman's body from public space. With *tshermil*, this absentiation is archived forever on the victim's own face.

From Phenomenon/*Dhahira* to Existence/*Wujud*

Statistics and testimonies of violence against women leave no doubt as to its prevalence in North Africa and the Middle East, yet whenever violence is discussed, it is often described as a novelty and exception. The term *phenomenon* (*dhahira* in Arabic) appears regularly in the narrative constructions of gender-based violence. In the aftermath of the wide distribution of the video recording of Zeinab's rape on the bus, the artist and activist Zahra al-Faisawi told *Al-Arabiya News* that "we all should unite against these phenomena to suppress them out of society so as not to ruin and rotten the moral level of Moroccans."[78] The "phenomenon" of rape and torture is attributed to developments in society such as "the crisis of values and morals and the loss of state prestige."[79] In a report about gender-based violence Le Haut Commissariat au Plan (the Higher Planning Commission), a government statistical institution, refers to violence against women in Morocco as a phenomenon.[80] The language of exception has even infiltrated political speeches. In his 2020 address at the opening of the eighteenth national campaign to stop violence against women, Prime Minister Saadeddine Othmani called for solidarity in order to eradicate the phenomenon of violence against women.[81]

Similarly, the term "phenomenon" has dominated discussions about gender-based violence during the COVID-19 pandemic. In Morocco, like elsewhere, the COVID-19 pandemic disproportionately affected women and girls. Overall, gender-based violence during the period of confinement in 2020 has increased by 31.6 percent compared to the same period in 2019.[82] In particular, there was a significant increase in violence committed within the domestic sphere. Between May 16 and April 24, 2020, 91.7 percent of reported incidents of violence against women were committed by husbands, and 4.4 percent were administered by other members of the family.[83] Women and girls' vulnerability increased because they were forced into even greater physical isolation within the house. As women's rights activist Souad Taoussi has pointed out, during periods of mandatory confinement only one person per household was given an official permit to leave the home. In most cases, the permit was handed to the man in the household, thus further increasing women's segregation from the outside world, including other family members, which left them entirely at the mercy of their husbands, brothers, or fathers, without any outside protection.[84] From men's perspectives, the surge in domestic violence in Morocco has been attributed to the hardships imposed on men during the confinement, including loss of income, inability to engage in everyday activities such as socializing with friends in coffee shops and other public spaces because of the curfew, or even the difficulty to secure drugs and alcohol.

To be sure, COVID-19 changed the world in ways that perhaps no other virus had in recent human history, affecting many physically, emotionally, and financially. Nonetheless, it is erroneous to describe violence against women during the COVID-19 confinement as a phenomenon/*dhahira* even if such violence is linked to circumstances connected to the pandemic. Labeling acts of violence against women phenomenon/*dhahira* seeks to conveniently confine gender-based violence temporally and spatially by suggesting that violence has a beginning, an end, and a specific place. More importantly, phenomenon/*dhahira* intentionally constructs violence against a woman as an exceptional event directly linked to a trigger often arriving from the outside. COVID-19 is a "foreign" virus that allegedly forced men into a state of uncertainty, which drove them into violence. Drugs are a foreign substance that allegedly forces men into atypical behavior such as violence. Interestingly, even the source of drugs is constructed as foreign. For example, Morocco and Algeria constantly accuse each other of intentionally exporting drugs with the purpose of corrupting the youth on the other side of their shared border.[85] Even the act of violence itself, which, it is often argued, is foreign to religious principles, is believed to be a deviation from true and authentic Islamic values. The causes for such deviance are, predictably, foreign. It is the West, allegedly serving a Zionist agenda, which stands behind the corruption of Muslim youth and the dissolution of the

Muslim family. For example, when the Moroccan film *Marock* (2005) was released, the filmmaker, Laila Marrakchi, was accused of promoting a "Zionist lobby" propaganda.[86] In addition to depicting a love relationship between a Muslim girl and a Jewish boy, what bothered even more was the sexual relation between the protagonists. Indeed, in the region it is believed that seductive popular culture helped normalize sexual relations outside the institution of marriage, which, in turn, is responsible for the increase in violence against women since they are seen as deserving of punishment for giving themselves "easily" to men.

Yet, none of these justifications warrant the use of the term phenomenon/*dhahira*. On the contrary, these examples of violence are confirmation that when confronted with new and unpredictable events, such as a global pandemic, men revert to old and comfortable practices, namely making visible through violence their disapproval of the woman's body, a persistent malaise with roots firmly grounded in the medieval Islamic tradition discussed in the previous chapter. To be sure, limiting discussions of gender-based violence in North Africa and the Middle East to the examples provided in the earlier section, namely FGM and honor killings, or even *tshermil*, could also contribute to the phenomenalization of violence against women by suggesting that it is a problem for certain women in certain parts of North Africa and the Middle East. The reality of women and girls in the region is that violence targets them all, regardless of time or place. It is uninterrupted, inescapable, and indiscriminate. It is not new, foreign, nor is it an isolated phenomenon.

Consequently, it would be more accurate for the discourse about gender-based violence in North Africa and the Middle East to abandon framing violence as phenomenon/*dhahira* and, instead, to define women and girls in the region through violence. In other words, violence ought to be considered in the context of women's and girls' existence/*wujud*. Put simply, all women in the region, regardless of age, education, ability, or socioeconomic background are subjected to violence because they exist as women.

When the body of a woman enters public space, this connection between violence and a woman's existence/*wujud* is even more pronounced. For no matter the concessions a woman makes not to trigger men's condemnations, no matter how much of her body a woman covers not to awaken the male discomfort, no matter how briefly, purposefully, and infrequently a woman occupies public space, she is always on the verge of becoming the next victim of violence. As the sociologist Jamal Khalil explains: "On n'a pas encore réglé la question de la femme à l'extérieur de la maison. On est dans une culture où l'on estime qu'elle n'est pas bienvenue dans l'espace public et que si elle est aggressée, c'est quelque part sa faute. . . . Une fille, quand elle sort de sa maison, doit avoir un plan de route et il y a des choses qu'elle ne peut pas faire. Ce n'est évidemment pas le cas pour les hommes." (We have not come to terms yet with the question of women outside the home. We are in a culture that assumes that [the woman] is not welcome in public space and that if she is assaulted, it is somehow her fault. When a girl leaves her house, she must have a road plan and there are things she cannot do. This is obviously not the case for men.)[87] Another sociologist, Soumaya Guessous, is even more direct: "Une femme est toujours considérée comme une prostituée dans la rue, même si elle porte le foulard." (A woman is always considered a prostitute in the street, even if she wears the veil.)[88] In the context of the region, a prostitute is the most degrading state for a woman. Her existence on the streets renders her a public property of all men, who are free to violate her as they wish.

This perception of women is also present in everyday expressions that attach women's moral worth to their absence from public space. Indeed, another expression in Moroccan Darija for prostitute is "girl of the street" (*bent zenqa*). On the opposite end, one finds *bent darhom*, literally meaning "girl of her home." It is one of the highest praises bestowed on a daughter, a sister, and most importantly, a wife. Expectedly, it is a common expression found in matrimonial ads. For example, a June 2016 matrimonial ad written in Darija using Latin script and numbers to represent Arabic sounds was titled "Bent darhom." The ad was posted by a forty-eight-year-old man who is "responsible" (*qad 3la mas'ouliya*) and financially stable (*ma ghadi yekhassak 7ta khir*). Other than age (he is looking for a woman between ages twenty-four and three-four), he has one condition: she must be *bent darhom*.[89] Despite being widely used, however, it is difficult to define what *bent darhom* means exactly, as seen on a thread posted on the forum section of *Yabiladi*, a website that caters to Moroccans living within Morocco and in the diaspora. The title of the thread is "Fille de leur maison?" (Girl of their home?). The question generated many comments and attempts at defining the expression. One forum user composed the following definition: "BENT DARHOM [est] differente de BENT ZENQA . . . , donc fille respectable et respectueuse bien éduquée, ne sort pas ou sort pour de vraies raisons travail, paperasse, courses" (*Bent darhom* is different from *bent zenqa*, therefore [she is] respectable and respectful, well educated, does not go out or goes out for real reasons [such as] work, paperwork, errands.)[90] Thus, the difference between the two is primarily spatial. The domain of *bent darhom* is the home (*dar*), within which her body and sexuality are physically confined. If she leaves the house, it must be for valid reasons and she must not deviate from the path that connects her home and the legitimate destination. It is often said that *bent darhom* is "home to school, school to home" (*ddar lmedrassa, lmedrassa ddar*) or, if she works, then "home to work, work to home" (*ddar lkhedma, lkhedma ddar*). *Bent darhom*, in other words, is one who strictly adheres to the spatial limitations imposed on the body of all those born a woman.

What happens to a woman whose employment, such as in the informal sector, forces her to spend most of her time in public spaces including the street? Could she still be considered *bent darhom* or would her reputation be ruined? From the perspective of misogyny, such questions are not relevant because, as a system, misogyny is not concerned with providing fixed and complete definitions. Expressions such as *bent darhom* and *bent zenqa* are intentionally constructed as vague signifiers that can be used at any given time to praise one woman and admonish another. Rhetorically, such expressions seek to construct acts of violence against women within isolatory narratives invested in showing the singularity of the sequence of events that led to violence. Often, the victim's past is resuscitated (or invented) to show how her transgressive deviations from the patriarchal norms provoked the violent outcome. For example, when asked about the abuse to which Khadija was subjected, including the tattoos covering her body, one of her neighbors insisted that she had witnessed behavior from Khadija that confirmed that she was not *bent darhom*. Similarly, following the attack on Zeinab a rumor spread claiming that she was HIV positive, a biological proof that she was a *bent zenqa*.[91] Her uncle (Zeinab's father is deceased) denied these accusations. Instead, he insisted that his niece was a "hero" for fighting to "defend her honor" despite her disability.[92] Being "*bent zenqa*," it appears, is far graver than rape.

WOMEN ARE NOT THE PROBLEM

Unfortunately, the persistent use and popularity of such expressions, especially when read in the context of the writings of scholars of Muslim societies such as Guessous and Khalil, announce a negative future for women in North Africa and the Middle East. To be sure, this goes against the more hopeful vision of feminists, who believe that women are capable of defeating misogyny and forcing men into accepting them in public space. For example, in *Scheherazade Goes West: Different Cultures, Different Harems* (2001), Fatima Mernissi puts her hope in women's education and professional success. She writes: "The basis of misogyny in Islam is actually quite weak, resting only on the distribution of space. If women invade public space, male supremacy is seriously jeopardized. And in actuality, modern Muslim men have already lost their power base, as their monopoly over public space has been eroded with the massive entrance of women into scientific fields and the professions."[93]

Mernissi is correct in the sense that more women throughout the region are pursuing higher degrees and professions in many disciplines, including STEM fields. Indeed, as many publications from the *New York Times* to *Teen Vogue* are eager to tell us, women in Muslim-majority countries are closing the gender gap in STEM careers such as engineering and tech. The false assumption here is that academic or career accomplishments would be significant enough to counter the persistent misogynistic suppression of women's bodies in public space. Unfortunately, misogyny in the region is far too complex a system to offset with degrees and titles. In fact, as seen in the following chapters, misogyny is ever innovative, capable of adapting to new technologies and a changing world, including one in which women are more educated and professionally successful.

Furthermore, this false assumption is problematic for it holds women, once again, responsible for the violence they face. The implication is that there is something that women could do to avoid injustice. Indeed, to suggest that education or professional success would spare women misogyny is no different than insisting that wearing the veil would stop women's harassment. Should women wear the veil to escape violence? Should girls and women study hard and excel at school to earn acceptance in public space? The answer is that women are already forced into too many concessions, whether it is veiling or the pursuit of higher education, without being spared the violence. Women and girls are already excelling in school, even surpassing boys and men including in some of the most challenging academic fields. For example, in the case of Morocco between 2000 and 2010, women's participation in higher degrees has increased in some of the country's most competitive schools such as the school of medicine, dentistry, and pharmacy where female graduates went from 51.8 percent to 63 percent. Women dominate certain medical fields by large margins. For example, 79.3 percent of graduates of odontology were women.[94] These numbers, however, do not translate into active participation and acceptance in public space. As Moroccan law scholar Fatna Sarhane has pointed out, unemployment among women, including those holding higher degrees, is almost double unemployment among men. Moreover, employment among women has been decreasing in the last decades. It went from 28.1 percent in 2000 to 22.4 percent in 2017. In 2016, 76.9 percent of Moroccan urban women were stay-at-home women. Sarhane attributes this "paradox" to enduring mentalities according to which the place of women is at home at the service of her husband and children.[95]

In sum, no matter their accomplishments, women with high degrees and impressive professional trajectories are just as unwelcome in society as any other women because deeply rooted beliefs around sexual segregation and their violent manifestations do not care about a woman's resume. This, once again, goes on to show that women are not the problem. Misogyny is. Moreover, while some Muslim women and girls' genius could be manifested through success in STEM fields, others' genius could be expressed through creative use of TikTok, Twitch, or other emerging new social media platforms. Except that the war on women and girls has spread online as well.

NOTES

1. Hibapress, "Al-hukm 'ala al-muttahamin fi qadiyyat Hanan," YouTube, February 14, 2020, https://www.youtube.com/watch?v=LN6o4UY7zxA.
2. Safaa Karaoui, "Moroccan Court Sentences Man to Death for Violent Rape, Murder," *Morocco World News*, February 11, 2020, https://www.moroccoworldnews.com /2020/02/293393/moroccan-court-sentences-man-to-death-for-violent-rape-murder/.
3. Sahifa24, "Lahadat mu'athira yahkiha 'anha adiqa' abdelali," YouTube video, 10:49, February 29, 2020, https://www.youtube.com/watch?v=VR4tvlk6TUk.
4. Soltana, "Khatir . . . 'ailat al-muttahamin bi'khtitaf Khadija," YouTube video, 5:58, August 26, 2018, https://www.youtube.com/watch?v=l-RFpFKQE1c&feature=emb_ title; Alyaoum24, "Haqa'ia mughayyaba fi qadiyyat Khadija . . . ," YouTube video, 13:06, August 31, 2018, https://www.youtube.com/watch?v=oSVG4tm-ioU.
5. Margaux Mazellier, "From Victim to Accused: Why Rape Victims in Morocco Suffer Double Trauma," *Middle East Eye*, September 17, 2018, https://www.middleeasteye.net/ fr/news/victim-accused-depressingly-familiar-story-moroccan-sexual-assault-14232945.
6. For more on the term *shemkar*, see Asmaa Bernichi, "Enfants de la rue de Casablanca: enfants et adolescents 'exilés dehors,'" *Adolescence* 31, no. 3 (2013): https://www .cairn.info/revue-adolescence-2013-3-page-531.htm.
7. Le360Live, "Bil-video: Hada ma qalaho sukkan al-ma'aquiz . . . ," YouTube video, 1:51, August 21, 2017, https://www.youtube.com/watch?v=gZ8MJaqZnAg&index =2112&list=UUGYE6-D0--78oXa4wDiOk6g.
8. Le360Live, "Viol dans un bus: la famille de la victime témoigne," YouTube video, 8:32, August 23, 2017, https://www.youtube.com/watch?v=ICb9VL5lq6g.
9. Zakia Daoud, *Féminisme et politique au Maghreb* (Casablanca: Eddif, 1993).
10. Kate Manne, "The Logic of Misogyny," *Boston Review*, July 11, 2016, http://boston- review.net/forum/kate-manne-logic-misogyny.
11. UNICEF MENA, *A Profile of Violence against Children and Adolescents in the Middle East and North Africa: Leaving No One Behind* (New York: UNICEF, 2018), 3, https:// www.unicef.org/mena/media/2826/file/VAC%20in%20MENA.pdf.
12. United Nations Children's Fund, *A Familiar Face: Violence in the Lives of Children and Adolescents* (New York: UNICEF, 2017), 22, file:///Users/ibouachr/Downloads/ EVAC-Booklet-FINAL-10_31_17-high-res.pdf.
13. Ibid., 4.
14. United Nations Children's Fund, *Violent Discipline in the Middle East and North Africa Region: A Statistical Analysis of household Survey Data* (New York: UNICEF, 2019), 18, https://www.unicef.org/mena/media/3561/file/Violent%20Discipline%20in %20the%20Middle%20East%20and%20North%20Africa%20Region.PDF.pdf.
15. Ibid., 61.

16. Megan Ott, "Series: What Does That Mean? Gender-based Violence," *Women for Women* (blog), November 21, 2017, https://www.womenforwomen.org/blogs/series-what-does-mean-gender-based-violence.

17. Nawal El Saadawi, *A Daughter of Isis: The Autobiography of Nawal El Saadawi* (New York: Zed Books, 1999), 56.

18. Fatima Mernissi, *Doing Daily Battle: Interviews with Moroccan Women*, trans. Mary Jo Lakeland (London: The Women's Press, 1988), 13.

19. UNICEF, "Child Marriage in the Middle East and North Africa" (New York: UNICEF, 2017), 27, https://www.unicef.org/mena/media/1786/file/MENA-ChildMarriageInMENA-Report.pdf.pdf.

20. UNFPA, "New Study Finds Child Marriage Rising Among Most Vulnerable Syrian Refugees," January 31, 2017, https://www.unfpa.org/news/new-study-finds-child-marriage-rising-among-most-vulnerable-syrian-refugees.

21. UNICEF, " Falling through the Cracks: The Children of Yemen" (New York: UNICEF, 2017), http://files.unicef.org/yemen/Yemen2Years-children_falling_through_the_cracks.pdf; Omer Karasapan and Sajjad Shah, "Forced Displacement and Child Marriage: A Growing Challenge in Mena," *Brookings Institution Future Developments* (blog), June 19, 2019, https://www.brookings.edu/blog/future-development/2019/06/19/forced-displacement-and-child-marriage-a-growing-challenge-in-mena/.

22. "Jordan," *Girls not Brides* (blog), https://www.girlsnotbrides.org/child-marriage/jordan/.

23. UNICEF, https://www.unicef.org/spanish/protection/files/00-FMGC_infographiclow-res.pdf.

24. World Health Organization, "Female Genital Mutilation and Other Harmful Practice," https://www.who.int/reproductivehealth/topics/fgm/fgm_prevalence_egypt/en/.

25. World Health Organization, "Female Genital Mutilation," February 3, 2020, https://www.who.int/en/news-room/fact-sheets/detail/female-genital-mutilation.

26. Laith J. Abu-Raddad, Francisca Ayodeji Akala, Iris Semini, Gabriele Riedner, David Wilson, and Ousama Tawil, *Characterizing the HIV/AIDS Epidemic in the Middle East and North Africa: Time for Strategic Action*. Middle East and North Africa HIV/AIDS Emidemiology Synthesis Project (Washington, DC: The World Bank Press, 2010), 74.

27. Serene Chung, "The Psychological Effects of Female Genital Mutilation," *28 Too Many* (blog), May 16, 2016, https://www.28toomany.org/blog/the-psychological-effects-of-female-genital-mutilation-research-blog-by-serene-chung/#:~:text=A%20study%20in%20practising%20African,(Keel%2C%202014%2C%20p.

28. UN Women, "Arab States: Facts and Figures, Ending Violence Against Women and Girls," *UN Women*, 2019, https://arabstates.unwomen.org/en/what-we-do/ending-violence-against-women/facts-and-figures.

29. For more details about the case, see Kestin Weigle, "Badour Shaker," *Cause of Death: Woman*, https://www.causeofdeathwoman.com/badour-shaker.

30. "Egyptian Girls Tricked into FGM with COVID-19 Vaccine," *Aljazeera*, June 5, 2020, https://www.aljazeera.com/news/2020/06/egyptian-girls-tricked-fgm-covid-19-vaccine-200605051857815.html.

31. World Health Organization, "Female Genital Mutilation and Other Harmful Practice," https://www.who.int/reproductivehealth/topics/fgm/fgm_prevalence_egypt/en/.

32. Gayatri Chakravorty Spivak, "Can the Subaltern Speak?" *Marxism and the Interpretation of Culture*, eds. Cary Nelson and Lawrence Grossberg (Basingtoke: Macmillan, 1988), 297.

33. Lila Abu-Lughod, "Introduction," in *Remaking Women: Feminism and Modernity in the Middle East*, ed. Lila Abu-Lughod (Princeton: Princeton University Press, 1988), 14.

34. Joseph Massad, *Islam in Liberalism* (Chicago: University of Chicago Press, 2015), 249.

35. Cassandra Gomes-Hochberg, "Honor Killings: Culture as Excuse for Killing Arab Women," *The Jerusalem Post*, September 20, 2019, https://www.jpost.com/magazine/honor-killings-culture-as-excuse-for-murdering-arab-women-602112.

36. Tom Bateman, "Israa Ghrayeb: Palestinian Woman's Death Prompts Sou-searching," BBC News, September 16, 2019, https://www.bbc.com/news/world-middle-east-49688920.

37. Robert Paul Churchill, *Women in the Crossfire: Understanding and Ending Honor Killing* (New York: Oxford University Press, 2018), 22–24.

38. Khitam al-Amir, "Father Kills Daughter and Drinks Tea Beside Her Body in Jordan," *Gulf News*, July 19, 2020, https://gulfnews.com/world/mena/father-kills-daughter-and-drinks-tea-beside-her-body-in-jordan-1.1595164364536.

39. Rothna Begum, "How to End 'Honor' Killings in Jordan," *The Jordanian Times*, April 1, 2017, http://www.jordantimes.com/opinion/rothna-begum/how-end-honour%E2%80%99-killings-jordan.

40. UNFPA, "Lives Together, Worlds Apart: Men and Women in a Time of Change," *State of World Populations 2000* (United Nations Population Fund, 2000), 29, https://www.unfpa.org/sites/default/files/pub-pdf/swp2000_eng.pdf.

41. "Viewpoint: Qandeel Baloch Was Killed for Making Lives 'Difficult,'" BBC News, September 30, 2019, https://www.bbc.com/news/world-asia-49874994.

42. Ibid.

43. Laura Begley Blook, "10 Most Dangerous Places for Women Travelers (And How to Stay Safe)," *Forbes*, July 28, 2017, https://www.forbes.com/sites/laurabegleybloom/2017/07/28/10-most-dangerous-places-for-women-travelers-and-how-to-stay-safe/#16eb17692448.

44. Interestingly, in both Egypt and Morocco more women share this attitude toward dress and harassment: 84 percent in Egypt and 78 percent in Morocco. UN Women/Promundo, *Understanding Masculinities: Results from the International Men and Gender Equality Study (IMAGES)—Middle East and North Africa*, available at https://docs.google.com/viewerng/viewer?url=http://promundoglobal.org/wp-content/uploads/2017/05/IMAGES-MENA-Multi-Country-Report-EN-16May2017-web.pdf.

45. Said Kadry, "Vidéo. Une Jeune Fille 'lynchée' par la foule à Tanger: ce qui s'est vraiment passé," *Le360*, August 1, 2017, https://fr.le360.ma/societe/video-une-jeune-fille-lynchee-par-la-foule-a-tanger-ce-qui-sest-vraiment-passe-129599.

46. Yassine Majdi, "Vidéo: Une mere agressée par une horde d'hommes à Tanger," *TelQuel*, July 28, 2015, https://telquel.ma/2015/07/28/video-mere-agressee-horde -dhommes-tanger_1457618.

47. Christy Cooney, "Savage Attack: Horrifying Video Shows Huge Mob Sexually Assaulting Screaming Woman During New Years' Celebrations in Egypt," *The Sun*, January 2, 2020, https://www.thesun.co.uk/news/10659730/video-mob-sexually-assaulting -woman-new-years-egypt/.

48. "Haughty about the Hijab: Women Campaign against Places that Ban the Veil," *The Economist*, August 7, 2015, https://www.economist.com/middle-east-and-africa/2015 /08/27/haughty-about-the-hijab.

49. Abdelkader Engy, "99.3 percent of Egyptian Women, Girls have Been Sexually Harassed," *Huffpost*, August 4, 2013, https://www.huffpost.com/entry/99-percent-of -egyptian-women-girls-have-been-sexually-harassed.

50. Banyan Global, International Center for Research on Women, Center of Arab Women for Training and Research, *Gender-based Violence in MENA Region: Context Analysis* (2016), 37. https://banyanglobal.com/wp-content/uploads/2018/02/MENA -Context-Analysis.pdf.

51. Ibid., 55.

52. These videos are widely available on YouTube and other platforms. I have decided not to refer to any specific examples.

53. Le360Live, "Viol dans un bus: la famille de la victime témoigne."

54. "Teenage Rape Victim Dies after Setting Herself on Fire in Morocco," *The Guardian*, August 5, 2016, https://www.theguardian.com/world/2016/aug/05/morocco -teenage-rape-victim-dies.

55. Ibid.

56. "Le phénomène marocain 'Tcharmil,' coup de frime ou vrai gang criminel?" *France 24*, April 18, 2014, https://web.archive.org/web/20190502122729/https://observers .france24.com/fr/20140418-phenomene-marocain-tcharmil-coup-frime-vrai-gang -criminel-maroc-casablanca-jeunes-police-delinquance.

57. "Insécurité: Agressions, Tcharmil, où va-t-on?" *Le Reporter*, April 9, 2014, https:// www.lereporter.ma/insecurite-agressions-tcharmil-ou-va-t-on/.

58. Chouftv, "Awal tasrih li-shabba lli shermelha sheffar..," YouTube video, 6:58, June 3, 2018, https://www.youtube.com/watch?v=JYlNUCeytmY.

59. LeSiteinfo, "Um l 3 atfal tata'arrad li-I'tida," YouTube video, 4:25, November 30, 2020, https://www.youtube.com/watch?v=E7W06c8nztM.

60. Flashinfo24, "Fatima al-zahra lli shermleha zawjeha . . . ," YouTube video, 6:54, March 11, 2015, https://www.youtube.com/watch?v=VxjkXJOX_Iw.

61. FebrayerTV, "Qissat al-jamila allati shawwaha zawjoha wajhaha . . . ," 2:44, April 22, 2016, https://www.youtube.com/watch?v=bdEAzXvqPZ4.

62. Chouftv, "ba'dama shermelha . . . ," YouTube video, 2:38, April 22, 2016, https:// www.youtube.com/watch?v=PO3ZpWTfCTU.

63. Hibapress, "Weld lefshosh yosharmil fatat . . . ," 4:18, June 30, 2017, https://www .youtube.com/watch?v=H8oIA6mN-RA.

64. Fez bel visa, "Tasrih qawiy men dahiyya Nabiha," YouTube video, 1:59, August 23, 2017, https://www.youtube.com/watch?v=65Y1-5_ADHs.

65. AlAyam24, "Video sadim . . . ," YoutTube video, 11:10, August 18, 2018, https://www.youtube.com/watch?v=y4ch1eQ9TU4.

66. https://www.youtube.com/watch?v=uGM5m9NRXew.

67. Chouftv, "Shabba jamila shermelha rajelha," YouTube video, 15:35, July 12, 2019, https://www.youtube.com/watch?v=g-1f2hTThOw.

68. Chouftv, "Qissa sadima wa fatat jamila jiddan," YouTube video, 10:05, October 10, 2019, https://www.youtube.com/watch?v=DaUiK4F3lH0.

69. LalaMoulati, "Al-qissa al-kamila li Hajar . . . ," YouTube video, 5:20, September 22, 2019, https://www.youtube.com/watch?v=2U5kW-8l4Z4.

70. LalaMoulati, "Awal tasrih lisshshaba Iman," YouTube video, 19:46, October 22, 2019, https://www.youtube.com/watch?v=rWo38h39bZA.

71. AlAyam24, "Jiran al-shabba al-yatima lli shermelha khatibha," YouTube video, 9:22, November 12, 2019, https://www.youtube.com/watch?v=wpZ2aAsqlYI.

72. Ihata TV, "Zawj bi murrakush shermel zawjeto . . . ," YouTube Video, 6:30, January 26, 2020, https://www.youtube.com/watch?v=_pFW4rUVfUg&t=26s.

73. AlAyam24, "tzewjat sirran dun 'ilm 'ailatiha," YouTube video, 6:20, July 1, 2020, https://www.youtube.com/watch?v=MXIhY-z5ba8.

74. Satv, "Tqeb liha al-'ayn . . . ," YouTube video, 14:37, January 2021, https://www.youtube.com/watch?v=mY-mvunO0P8&t=606s.

75. FACTS, "Li fat mat," YouTube video, 15:40, November 26, 2020, https://www.youtube.com/watch?v=PZD2OaqWFX4&t=4s.

76. Ibid., 33.

77. Abdessamad Dialmy, *Vers une nouvelle masculinité au Maroc*, 33.

78. "Update: Gang Rape of Woman on Public Bus Sends Shockwaves across Morocco," *Al Arabiya*, August 22, 2017, https://english.alarabiya.net/en/features/2017/08/21/Gang-rape-of-woman-on-public-bus-sends-shockwaves-across-Morocco.html.

79. Ibid.

80. Haut Commissariat au Plan (HCP), Enquête Nationale sur la Prévalence Enquête Nationale sur la Prévalence de la Violence à l'Egard des Femmes (Rabat: HCP, 2011), https://www.hcp.ma/Enquete-nationale-de-la-prevalence-de-la-violence-a-l-egard-des-femmes_a105.html.

81. A summary of the prime minister's intervention was published on November 25, 2020, at https://www.maroc.ma/fr/actualites/el-otmani-leradication-de-la-violence-legard-des-femmes-necessite-la-mobilisation-de-tous.

82. "Maroc: Les violences à l'égard des femmes s'accentuent de 31.6 percent Durant le confinement," *La VIEéco*, November 25, 2020, https://www.lavieeco.com/actualite-maroc/maroc-les-violences-a-legard-des-femmes-saccentuent-de-316-durant-le-confinement/.

83. "Munadhama maghribiyya tashifo hasilat al-'onf didda al-nisa' khilala al-hajr," *Maghreb Voices*, April 28, 2020, https://www.maghrebvoices.com/morocco/2020/04/28/.

84. 2MTV, "Ma wad' al-maghrib fima yakhosso moharabat dhahirat al-'onf didda al-mar'a," YouTube video, 14:01, November 30, 2020, https://www.youtube.com/watch?v=15zr1aYGMjk.
85. Safaa Kasraoui, "Algerian Official Accuses Morocco of 'Spreading Drug Scourge,'" *Morocco World News*, March 12, 2021, https://www.moroccoworldnews.com/2021/03/337174/algerian-official-accuses-morocco-of-spreading-drug-scourge.
86. Karim Boukhari, "*Marock*: Le film de tous les tabous," *Tel Quel online* 223 (2005), http://ykzxlck.telquel-online.com/archives/223/couverture_223_1.shtml.
87. Elsa Walter, "Analyse sociologique des agressions sexuelles: 'Une femmes est considérée comme une prostituée dans la rue."
88. Ibid.
89. "Cherche femme 3affifa bent darhom pour marriage," *Maroc Annonces*, https://www.marocannonces.com/categorie/353/Demande-en-mariage/annonce/5904262/Cherche-femme-3afifa-bent-darhom-pour-mariage.html.
90. "Fille de leur maison????" *Yabiladi*, September7, 2010, https://www.yabiladi.com/forum/fille-leur-maison-3-3916300-page=2.html.
91. Margaux Mazellier, "From Victim to Accused: Why Rape Victims in Morocco Suffer Double Trauma."
92. Le360Live, "Viol dans un bus: la famille de la victime témoigne," YouTube video, 8:32, August 23, 2017, https://www.youtube.com/watch?v=ICb9VL5lq6g.
93. Fatima Mernissi, *Scheherazade Goes West: Different Cultures, Different Harems* (New York: Washington Square Press, 2001), 192.
94. Abdellah El Ghazouani, *Les femmes dans l'espace public: le harcèlement sexuel* (Casablanca: Afrique Orient, 2015), 11.
95. Fatna Sarehane, "Le travail rénuméré en droit marocain: quels obstacles pour les femmes?" in *Las instituciones económicas y las mujeres en el mediterráneo en los albores del siglo XXI*, eds. María Teresa González Santos and Marie-Évelyne Le Poder (Madrid: Dykinson, 2020), 117–18.

CHAPTER 4

Misogyny Online

THE DISCUSSION SO FAR HAS FOCUSED ON SOCIAL MEDIA PLATFORMS AS tools through which violence against women and girls in the physical world is made audible and visible to a wider audience. In many cases, gender-based crimes would have never made it beyond the victim's family and local police precinct were it not for the leaked videos. This chapter turns to social media networks, YouTube in particular, as instruments of misogyny. Online misogyny is a global phenomenon that has been receiving increased scholarly attention in recent years, though most of the scholarship is concerned almost exclusively with Western societies.[1] A 2017 Pew Research Center survey about online harassment in the United States showed that although more men than women experience abuse in the form of offensive name-calling (30 percent versus 23 percent), women ages eighteen to twenty-nine are more likely than men in the same age-group to have been sexually harassed online (21 percent versus 9 percent).[2] In Europe, online violence and harassment against women escalated to the point that countries such as France and the UK implemented laws criminalizing certain forms of online violence.[3]

In the case of North Africa and the Middle East, there has not been any large-scale multicountry study about gender-based violence online. Instead, a few reports have been published by local organizations documenting the various forms of abuse that women in the region endure online including sextortion, blackmail, and hacking. According to a 2018 report by the Arab Center for the Advancement of Social Media, only

39.8 percent of Palestinian women feel safe posting photos and other personal information online.[4] According to a 2019 survey, 13.4 percent of women in Morocco said that they experienced cyberviolence, a number too low to be accurate in the context of a "culture of silence."[5]

In general, online violence against women in the region makes national and at times international headlines in exceptional cases only, usually when the victim is a public figure.[6] This is the case of Sarah Hegazy, a thirty-year-old Egyptian-born LGBTQ activist. Hegazy was detained in 2017, in Egypt, for "joining a banned group aimed at interfering with the constitution." Her real crime, though, was that she displayed a rainbow flag in Cairo in support of gay and trans rights during a concert for the Lebanese band Mashrou' Leila. Hegazy was detained for three months, during which the police allegedly subjected her to various forms of physical and emotional torture, including solitary confinement and electric shocks. Police also allegedly "incited other detainees to sexually assault and verbally abuse her."[7] Following her release, Hegazy moved to Canada, yet she continued to endure violence, this time online. As the Syrian feminist campaign Liberated T (*Ta' moharrara*) observed, "Although her body became safe in Canada, her soul is still suffering from what she was exposed to and the [online] bullying that continued."[8] When she could no longer tolerate the pain, she killed herself. In the suicide note, she asked her brothers and friends for forgiveness, but she forgave the world despite it having been "cruel to a great extent."[9]

The online world continues to be cruel to Hegazy. Months after her death, women and men persisted in publishing insults on various platforms, especially YouTube. One video, published on June 19, 2020, invites its viewers to "look at how Allah punished Sarah Hegazy" (*Shahid kayfa 'aqaba Allah Sarah Hegazy*). In less than a month, it accumulated close to one hundred thousand views.[10] When Nour Selim, a trans man and the son of the famous Egyptian actor Hisham Selim, posted a video on YouTube condemning Hegazy's treatment, two Egyptian lawyers filed a lawsuit against him for attempting "to spread homosexuality" in Egypt.[11]

The previous chapter argued against isolatory narratives of gender-based violence in the physical world. Cyberviolence, too, is far from being limited to isolated cases and events. Indeed, like physical violence offline, online violence has become part of women's existence/*wu-jud*. To illustrate this point, the current chapter explores how technology came to fuel what I term "expository misogyny," which is a strategy used by patriarchy to control, humiliate, and punish women by exposing them or threatening to expose them. One of the most violent manifestations of expository misogyny discussed in this chapter is "revenge porn." First, however, one needs to understand the larger context of the region's digital culture and how YouTube came to play such an important role in the daily lives of young women and men in North Africa and the Middle East. The digital overview that follows has two purposes: one is to shed light on the determination of the region's youth to participate actively and prolifically in the global, digital age, despite the many local limitations. The other goal is to show that misogyny online, as an extension of violence against women in the physical world, is intentional.

DIGITAL NATIVES

In 2018, the World Bank released a report about North Africa and the Middle East in which it identified a few of the factors that would facilitate economic growth in the region. One of them is the need to address the region's technology delay, which is caused by two main factors: a lagging infrastructure and state censorship. As far as the first is concerned, the digital infrastructure in North Africa and the Middle East falls behind that of many emerging economies including in East and Central Asia, resulting in relatively high prices and slow internet speed.[12] This lag in connectivity, the World Bank review shows, is due primarily to the fact that the region "has the most concentrated, least-competitive broadband markets in the world." For example, in the case of the countries of the Maghreb, midsized information technology companies, though allowed to exist, are not permitted to use their own infrastructure to provide the final client with high-speed internet. Instead, they must rely on "legacy infrastructure" from the "state-owned incumbent operators." This, the report concludes, deprives the region's youth of opportunities, including employment.[13] The fragile infrastructure was exposed even more during the COVID-19 pandemic, when people's daily lives and activities shifted from public physical spaces to digital networks.[14]

As far as censorship is concerned, state-imposed regulations/oversight, such as digital surveillance measures, impede connectivity and accessibility in North Africa and the Middle East.[15] In 2019, the US-based watchdog *Freedom House* published "Freedom on the Net," a study of internet freedom in sixty-five countries that were divided into three categories: free, partly free, and not free. Eleven North African and Middle Eastern countries were included. Tunisia, Morocco, Lebanon, Libya, and Jordan were designated as "partly free," while Bahrain, United Arab Emirates, Egypt, Saudi Arabia, Syria, and Iran were in the "not free" category.[16] Moreover, rankings can vary from one year to another. For example, following the 2011 uprisings, Egypt was upgraded from "not free" to "partly free." By 2013, it was back in the "not free" category. By 2015, its ranking was even lower within the "not free" category.[17]

Yet, there is more to digital culture in North Africa and the Middle East than a lagging infrastructure and state censorship. The region is home to one of the youngest populations in the world, with a median age of twenty-two years,[18] and one of the largest communities of "digital natives," defined as "a person born or brought up during the age of digital technology and therefore familiar with computers and the Internet from an early age."[19] Thus, despite the challenges and limitations, more than 90 percent of youth (between the ages of fifteen and twenty-nine) use internet regularly.[20] Even more interesting is the time spent daily online. In 2020, the daily average time spent online per capita in North Africa and the Middle East was approximately 384 minutes.[21] Globally, the daily average is 170 minutes.[22] The UAE is first in the region and fifth in the world, with an average of 474 minutes daily.[23] For the sake of comparison, the average daily screen time in the United States is 391 minutes.

Also telling is the nature of internet usage or the activities being conducted online. Studies about internet behavior in North Africa and the Middle East are still at their early stage and tend to be driven by inquiries into consumer behavior. What is available, however, indicates a trend throughout the region, which is not necessarily in accord with global tendencies. While considerably behind on global trends such as e-commerce and online banking, the region is ahead in the use of social media.[24] As of 2019, nine out of ten Arab youth use a minimum of one social media platform daily.[25] Moreover, throughout the region, average daily time spent on social media exceeds by far the time spent on other content online.[26] Until recently, the most popular platform has been Facebook. However, the number of YouTube users in the region, as in the rest of the world, is rapidly increasing, and mobile watch time of You-Tube in North Africa and the Middle East is one of the fastest growing in the world.[27] According to YouGov's BrandIndex Buzz 2019 brand perception survey, YouTube ranks third in Egypt, and sixth in both the UAE and Saudi Arabia.[28] The latter is "the biggest user of YouTube per capita in the world."[29]

Youth in the region are increasingly turning to social media platforms to watch films, listen to music (as discussed extensively in the following chapter), and follow the news. Indeed, the majority of young people in the region use social media as "their primary source of information to follow breaking news," and increasingly as the only source of news. Even more significant, a large number of them trust the information they read and hear on social media. Morocco ranks highest (77 percent) with respect to the percentage of people who trust the information available on social media platforms.[30]

Youth in North Africa and the Middle East, however, are not mere consumers of digital content. They are also among the most prolific pro-ducers of YouTube content in the world. According to *Arabian Business*, in 2018, the number of channels in North Africa and the Middle East increased by 160 percent, 200 of them had more than one million sub-scribers.[31] As of August 2020, North Africa alone had 476 channels with more than one million subscribers. There were 245 in Egypt,[32] followed by Morocco 144,[33] Algeria 64,[34] and Tunisia 23.[35] In the Gulf, Saudi Arabia alone had more than 250 YouTube channels with more than one million subscribers.[36] It is important to note that these numbers only account for YouTubers whose physical address is in the region and do not include YouTubers who produce content in local Arabic dialects but reside outside.

In addition to being home to one of the largest communities of digital natives, other factors have contributed to the success of digital platforms in the region, YouTube in particular. Among these factors is language. Although there is enormous diversity of dialects, many Arabic-speaking YouTubers use what is known as "white language," which is closer to Modern Standard Arabic, in an effort to make their speech intelligible to a wider audience throughout the Arabic-speaking region. Another, and perhaps even more significant factor behind YouTube's salience, is that despite being a relatively new technology (early 2005), it is compatible with the region's traditional forms of production and dissemination of knowledge. At its core, YouTube is a present-day form of oral tradition not that much different from old traditions of storytelling that preceded writing and reading in the conventional sense. In the specific context of Arab-African-Islamic cultures, oral transmission played a central role in the early years of Islam. Indeed, even before Islam, Arab and African societies have long used oral traditions to instill and reinforce salient values, among them misogynistic values. This is not meant to essentialize Arabs or Africans, nor is the goal to minimize the importance of reading and writing in these regions' history. It is merely an invitation to consider the success of digital platforms in the context of their compatibility with indigenous forms of knowledge in the region.

Regardless of the reasons, it is a fact that more women and men in North Africa and the Middle East are digitally literate, particularly among the digital natives and increasingly among the "digital immigrants," independent of their socioeconomic backgrounds and regardless of their non-digital literacy or educational levels.[37] Moreover, as more digital natives and immigrants produce, disseminate, and consume online content, the physical and virtual worlds are becoming increasingly intertwined: more people go online to find out "truth" about their world, a "truth" of which they are also the authors. This continuity of the online and offline realms goes against what is often perceived as a disconnect between the two or the idea that internet is an escape from reality. As a blogger put it, "The virtual world began as an escape from reality, then transformed into a mirror of current reality."[38] What follows indicates that with regard to misogyny, not only does the behavior online mirror the behavior offline but also, thanks to what is known as "online disinhibition effect," the internet has facilitated the manifestation of a more authentic hatred for women and their bodies.[39] If anything, analyzing behavior online exposes the intentionality of misogyny in the region as an attitude and behavior grounded in consciousness as opposed to being the mere consequence of exterior circumstances.

BEFORE AND AFTER

In 2019, it was estimated that 44.2 percent of women in the region had internet access compared to 58.5 percent for men, though gender disparities in internet usage vary greatly from one country to another.[40] For example, in Lebanon women and men are equal with respect to internet usage, while in Tunisia, Egypt, and Morocco, there is a gender gap.[41] Overall, however, the gender gap is narrowing considerably, especially in social media usage. Nonetheless, as with the physical world, the increase in women's participation in digital platforms has not made the virtual world any less unwelcoming to women. Some of the most popular genres of videos online are also some of the most misogynistic. One of such genres is known as the "before/after." These videos with hundreds of thousands, and at times millions, of views usually consist of a video montage of celebrity photos depicting singers and actresses before and after plastic surgery. The Lebanese singer Haifa Wehbe received a large share of attacks. In one video the viewer is invited to follow Wehbe's "transformation" step-by-step: first, the "original" Wehbe as a teenager, her weight loss and participation in a beauty pageant, then the lip injections, fillers, and nose jobs, all allegedly corroborated by plastic surgeons.[42] Another video, this time of Lebanese singer Nancy Ajram, titled "Nancy Ajram from the ages of 1 until 34. You will be shocked," shows photos of Ajram as a child before surgeries, and then as an adult post surgeries. The video's title was changed from Arabic to English, perhaps to attract more views.[43] "Ahlam before and after four plastic surgeries / you won't believe how she was," which targets the Emirati singer Ahlam, has gathered more than 1.5 million views in one year.[44] The comments on these videos are divided between those who like the transformation, and those who prefer the "original" version and reprimand the artist for tampering with "God's creation."

At times, the humiliating content is produced offline but disseminated and popularized online. This is the case of a video trend from 2016 and 2017, in which women were forced to take off their makeup in public. The trend was likely inspired by American singer Alicia Keys' "#NoMakeup" movement in 2016, when she declared that she would stop wearing makeup.[45] A video that gathered more than eleven million views in two years shows Tunisian celebrity Meriem Debbagh being asked, during a TV show, to take off her makeup. As she complies, the program host turns to other female guests and makes the same request.[46] On an Algerian show, a television host, this time a woman, challenges her guest, the winner of a beauty pageant competition for university students, to take off her makeup, which she does under the approving eyes of the show's host and her male guests. At the end, the woman is applauded and told repeatedly that she is more beautiful without makeup.[47] On an Iraqi television show, it is the host's turn to be asked by her own colleague and cohost to take off her makeup. As she wipes her face, the male cohost, giggling with excitement, reminds her of the eyebrow liner lest she forget.[48] On a Kuwaiti show, the host asks his guest, a fashion blogger and influencer, to take off her makeup. His point, he explains, is that a woman must be confident. "Perhaps she is even more beautiful without makeup," he remarks. As she pulls off her false lashes, the host comments that it's all "tricks" and that he worries her nose would come off next.[49]

Over and over again, women, usually young women, are subjected to the humiliating ritual of revealing their "true" faces to the public in the name of honesty and transparency. Ironically, according to Luiz Toledo, a Brazilian plastic surgeon who lives and practices in Dubai, women from the UAE, Saudi Arabia, Kuwait, Jordan, Iraq, Iran, and Egypt ask specifically for "small and upturned noses like Haifa Wehbe and Nancy Ajram."[50] Moreover, Wehbe is consistently ranked among the most beautiful Arab women. In 2017, she was ranked tenth on the list of "Top 10 Most Beautiful Women Over 40." The list includes Angelina Jolie, JLo, and Monica Bellucci.[51] Pointing out the contradictions, however, does not destabilize patriarchy. Misogyny tolerates contradictions because they allow for flexibility. One woman will be criticized for not "taking care of herself" through surgeries, while another will be mocked for deforming herself and changing the "image of God."

Whether the transformation is received with a "like" or "dislike," the point of the before-and-after videos is to expose the female celebrity as a fraud and stage her in a misogynistic spectacle through which she is subjected to public ridicule and humiliation. No matter how commendable are her talents and accomplishments, the artist is reduced to the object of violent critique. To be sure, unfair and defamatory critique has always accompanied celebrities in all fields, including art and politics since long before the emergence of digital media. However, as Ute Frevert has detailed in his study of humiliation in a Western context, shaming on the internet is different because of its "frequency and breadth of circulation." Another significant difference is that online humiliations are articulated in a language that "has become ever more brutal, particularly when they are directed against women." His study shows that online messages addressed to women celebrities by men include torture and rape fantasies.[52]

To these differences, one could add a key distinction in the misogyny that digital technologies have introduced. As a text, a misogynistic video published on platforms such as YouTube is never complete. The comment section below the video is an eternal invitation to add infinite insults and humiliations. Furthermore, parts of videos are regularly incorporated in the creation of new ones, forever recycling sexist content. Therefore, even if a celebrity has the funding to hire a tech and legal team to remove defamatory postings (and indeed there are celebrities who have succeeded, as several of the videos I have identified when I began working on this project in 2014 have since been removed from YouTube), the reality of the internet is that it is challenging to completely remove content once published online.

Fadi7a/ Scandal

As YouTube became more popular throughout North Africa and the Middle East, the "before/after" videos morphed into the even more popular genre of *fadiha*, or "fadi7a," to use the online spelling that replaces the Arabic "h" with "7." *Fadiha* in Arabic means scandal. How-ever, after viewing a few of these videos, one quickly realizes that what constitutes scandalous behavior is left conveniently vague. Moreover, there is no distinction between acts taking place in private or public spaces, with or without the consent of the women in the videos. The *fadi7a* of Moroccan actress Najat el Wafi is that she is seen dancing with friends and colleagues at a private party in a video filmed and published on YouTube without her consent.[53] The scandal of Moroccan TV host Nassima el Hor is that a video depicts her smoking a cigarette, using curse words, and having a good time while getting her hair done at a salon. "She was exposed" (*tfershat*), wrote one viewer in the comment sec-tion, while another insulted her using sexualized slang terms.[54] Another video, "Mona Fettou *fadiha* 2015," merely shows photos of the Moroccan actress Mona Fettou at various formal and public events. One commen-tator writes, "all we have is whores" (*qhab*), while another viewer blames men for not being "men" (*rjal*). In "Shireen drunk big scandal," Egyptian singer Shireen Abdel Wahhab is shown joking around and having a good time with friends as a guest at a private party.[55]

Exercising one's profession can also be a scandal. Many actresses are attacked for characters they have played in movies. For example, Sanaa Akroud is insulted for a kissing scene. A viewer even involved Akroud's husband, accusing him of not being a real man.[56] Similarly, a video that encourages its viewers to "watch before it's deleted," shows a one-minute scene between Egyptian actress Mona Zaki and a male actor. The scene suggests a sexual encounter but the only visible body parts are the actors' faces and feet. In a comment, a viewer asks if money earned from "this kind of acting" is halal, while another wonders how Zaki's husband and father, a famous actor himself, allowed her to be involved in such a film.[57] A scene posted on YouTube from an Algerian film depicting actresses in a hammam (Turkish bath) triggered close to two hundred comments insulting the actresses, the filmmaker, women in Algeria, and even French women of Maghrebi descent, using the pejorative term "beurettes."[58] As the titles and comments of these videos show, women are insulted for dressing up. They are insulted for dressing down. They are insulted for working. They are insulted for relaxing with friends. They are insulted for doing the most banal of human activities. In sum, they are insulted for existing as women.

A few celebrities became known for responding to online hate. For example, Akroud used to make videos "insulting back" her critics, which led to even more online attacks. She eventually stopped engaging directly with the viewers. For a while, she even closed her YouTube channel. Kaoutar "Kao" Boudarraja, a Moroccan fashion model and TV host, is also known for "talking back" to her online haters, which exposes her to significantly more harassment. In 2015, she was the target of a vicious online campaign in response to the outfits she wore during a photoshoot with the French magazine *Illi* for its September issue. Men and women online felt particularly offended by a photograph in which Boudarraja is seen wearing a backless red dress that displays a tattoo on her shoulder. She responded with a letter in French that she posted on her Facebook page. "Ladies and gentlemen," she wrote, "I do not represent nor do I wish to represent anyone." She explained that she would not wish her followers a "blessed Friday," nor would she "share Qur'anic verses in order to pick up 'likes.'" She declared that she would not "give birth to a child for the sake of selfies," nor would she use motherhood to improve her image. She insisted that she would not wear caftans to cover her body or as proof of her patriotism. Her message to her critics: "Fuck you! From all my heart, my body, and my soul . . . Fuck you! In jeans, in a skirt, and scantily clad. . . . Fuck you all NAKED!"[59] Even as the attacks continued, Bouadarraja never succumbed to the pressures to hide her body. She continues to wear and publish photos, participate in artistic projects, and make statements judged "inappropriate" for a woman in a Muslim society.

To be sure, not all responses to Boudarraja were negative. There were those who expressed their support, including celebrities. Radio personality Mohamed Bousfiha, known as Momo, published a photo of his naked back in solidarity with Boudarraja and to mock the absurdity of her attackers.[60] However, no matter the support, it could never be enough to counter the cyber-mob attacks on women celebrities online, which makes Akroud and Boudarraja the minority. Most celebrities deal with online harassment the way most women in the region deal with street harassment: they look the other way in the hope that their harasser will either give up or eventually move on to the next victim, for they are aware that defying the aggressors could potentially trigger their anger. This could have grave consequences, especially in the context of the region's large numbers of digital natives, many of whom possess relatively advanced digital skills that can be employed in technological attacks, which, in turn, can ruin a woman's reputation with long-lasting ramifications on the victim's life offline, including her personal relationships and professional career. The Moroccan-born Mariam Said, former TV presenter with the Saudi audiovisual group MBC, is well familiar with the devastating impact of cyberviolence. Following the leak of "compromising photos," she announced her "departure" from MBC at the peak of her success. According to *Dailymorocco*, she was allegedly fired because she "has tarnished the image of the group."[61] Moreover, her wedding was called off three days before the date. It was also rumored that her physical health, too, has been compromised by the continuous online harassment and the stressful events that followed. Nevertheless, the rumors could also be another facet of the misogynistic attacks. Illness is often seen as poetic justice, a well-deserved divine punishment for all women who defy the patriarchal order.

Regardless of the veracity of the rumors about Said's physical and possibly mental health, online misogyny succeeded in absentiating her body from the online public sphere. This withdrawal is predictable, as legal scholar Danielle Keats Citron has shown in the context of online misogyny in Western societies. As she writes, "To avoid further abuse, victims withdraw from online activities." Testimonies of victims of online harassment who were forced into hiding reveal that women were made to feel "like criminals."[62] This, once again, illustrates well the complexity of misogyny as a system that secures women's subordination by disciplining a few and deterring many more. In light of the severity of the punishment, it is safe to say that women would hesitate to consider a career similar to Said's.

Beyond the feeling of illegitimacy, withdrawal from social media has other ramifications such as loss of advertising revenue.[63] Many celebrities around the world, women and men, generate income through their active presence and participation via their various social media platforms. In fact, in many cases, celebrities' online revenue surpasses the income they generate from exercising their primary professions. A case in point is soccer players Lionel Messi and Cristiano Ronaldo, both of whom allegedly earn more annually from Instagram than their salaries as professional soccer players.[64] While Akroud, Boudarraja, and Said could never reach a number of followers comparable to that of Messi or Ronaldo, the loss of revenue for these female celebrities is far more impactful because employment in creative fields in North Africa and the Middle East is even more precarious than it is in many other regions. In many instances, celebrities rely on online activities to supplement their income, particularly in periods between contracts. These periods tend to be even longer for celebrities whose name has been attached to a scandal/*fadi7a*.

Unfortunately, despite its prevalence and gravity, online misogyny targeting high-profile women outside politics and a few professions such as journalism has not received the scholarly attention the topic merits. Perhaps such absence is due to the prevailing assumption, even in the West, that through their presentation (such as clothes and plastic surgeries) female celebrities are accomplices in an industry that objectifies women and therefore are to blame for the injustice they are forced to endure.[65] Feminist critique, however, does not benefit from using perceived privilege, or even actual privilege, to exclude groups of women from analysis for, as repeated throughout this book, misogyny does not spare any woman, including the most privileged.

REVENGE PORN

In light of the large population of digital natives, along with the democratization of technologies, online misogyny has moved beyond women celebrities to include all women and girls. In today's world any woman or girl could fall victim to online misogyny, which takes many forms including though not limited to insults, unwanted sexting, threats of physical harm, stalking, blackmailing, and technology attacks. The goal with online misogyny, as with offline, is to humiliate, punish, and, more importantly, to expose women for who or what they "really" are. "Revenge pornography," or "revenge porn," is an increasingly popular form of online misogyny seeking to expose women, in the literal sense. As with other forms of online violence, revenge porn is a gendered crime. According to data from the United States, 90 percent of the victims are women.[66] There is no equivalent study for North Africa and the Middle East, though it is safe to assume that the percentage of female victims could be even higher.[67]

Revenge porn is also one of the most devastating forms of online misogyny. In a study of US and Canadian adult female victims of revenge porn, Samantha Bates argues that the consequences of revenge porn are far from "trivial or ephemeral," and that women experience it as "a horrendous invasion of sexual privacy and personal space." The victims of revenge porn, Bates found out, suffer from a number of mental health issues including post-traumatic stress disorder, anxiety, and depression. Moreover, it has long-term impacts on the victims' relationships with others since their victimizer is usually "someone they loved and trusted."[68]

The material for revenge porn can be acquired in various ways. At times, explicit videos and images of women and girls are originally taken with the consent of the victim, for or by a lover. After a breakup or divorce, the man publishes the material as a form of revenge. In most cases, the pictures are taken and the videos are recorded without the woman's consent or knowledge. A large supply of revenge porn content comes from chat platforms popular throughout North Africa and the Middle East. As women and girls are generally unwelcome in public physical spaces, many join online sites to socialize and in the hope of meeting a partner, or what is known as "internet marriage." In many other instances, the content is accessed through technology attacks. A woman's phone or computer is hacked. The criminals then demand money or sexual favors and threaten to share the videos with the woman's family, friends, or place of work. Oftentimes, the hacker is also the victim's ex-partner.

Revenge porn has spread throughout North Africa and the Middle East. Moreover, judging from the victims' testimonies, it appears to be one of the most "inclusive" online crimes.[69] Indeed, it is the only crime against women for which there are considerable public testimonies from highly educated and well-off women. This does not mean that women with privilege are excluded from other forms of online violence, but instead it has to do with the socioeconomic background of women with greater online visibility. Digital technologies have not changed the fact that societies in North Africa and the Middle East continue to uphold what could be called "harem values," or the idea that women should not be seen in public spaces, whether online or offline. However, economic necessities have forced women online, at times with great reluctance as many express in the initial videos they publish on their YouTube channels. As a result, most women content producers in the region tend to be from less-privileged socioeconomic backgrounds. A case in point is Moroccan YouTube. The majority of Moroccan women active on YouTube as content creators are relatively economically disadvantaged. For many, YouTube is the only source of income not only for them but also for their entire family. Their online presence, in turn, exposes them to attacks from hackers, bullies, and stalkers.

Privileged women, on the other hand, can choose not to participate online as content creators, and, comparatively, very few do. Economic and other forms of privilege, however, do not give women any agency over a partner's or a hacker's actions and intentions, even if they themselves abstain from having an active online presence. If anything, their privilege, and at times ambitions, can expose them to more blackmail. For example, in 2018, several women election candidates in Iraq were blackmailed with revenge porn and sexual material to force them to drop out of the race. Intidhar Ahmed Jassim, a professor of economy and administration at al-Mustansiriya University in Baghdad, was forced to withdraw her candidacy for an Iraqi Parliament seat when an alleged sex tape surfaced.[70] Heshu Rebwar Ali, also a university professor with a PhD in economics, was running for office on the ticket of the ruling Kurdistan Democratic Party when her phone was hacked and a private video was leaked.

In other cases, financial privilege made women vulnerable to extortions. In 2017, *Ramallah Mix News* published the testimonies of Palestinian women whose intimate photos were used to blackmail them. One of the women "had a relationship" (*kanat laha 'alaqa*) with a man, who "promised to marry her." He later blackmailed her with intimate photos. She paid him 90,000 shekels to help with his university expenses, in addition to 64,000 dollars she paid to stop the blackmail. Another case involved a married woman who fell in love with a man she had met on Facebook. He later threatened her with pictures, forcing her to pay him 60,000 shekels and 300 grams of gold. The payoffs did not stop the extortions, and Palestinian police was eventually involved in both cases.[71] In 2019, *Middle East Monitor* published a two-minute video about "The rise of 'revenge porn' and 'sextortion' in Iraq." According to one victim, Hala, "some of them wanted money, some wanted a sexual relationship, even if it was just on the phone, others just wanted to bully [her] for no reason." Another woman had to pay her ex-boyfriend $200 every month not to publish her pictures.[72] Because of their social status, economically privileged women have more to lose from a scandal and are therefore less likely to report extortions, just as they are less likely to report domestic abuse. This silence makes them the ideal target for revenge porn.

The same is true for adolescent girls, who are the most vulnerable category of revenge porn victims. In the context of sex-negative societies in which virginity is sacred, girls and young women are the ideal targets for revenge porn since they are less likely to denounce the perpetrator. They cannot confide in their parents and usually lack a supportive network. Instead, as stories published online indicate, they go through fear, anxiety, and depression in isolation without ever seeking professional help through formal networks. A few seek support from online communities, though always anonymously because of the persistent fear of being stalked online. The Instagram page Mouvement.Dihafrassek (mind your own business movement), has published a few testimonies of victims, overwhelmingly minors, of revenge porn and sextortion in Morocco.[73] Some are written in "perfect" French, a clear indication of the victim's upper-class status. Others are written mostly in Darija. All express the devastating impact revenge porn has had on their mental health. One victim wrote:

> *Il y a quelques mois, suite à un malentendu avec mon mec, il a commencé à me menacer avec une video de nous deux dont j'ignorais l'existence. Il a bien profité de ma peur et frustration. 3ddebni mentalement et c'était la pire période de ma vie. Il me menaçait avec pour*

ne pas le quitter. Je n'ai pas pu deposer plainte par peur de lui, de ma famille. . . . J'ai tous les screens où il me menaçait. Je ne sais vraiment pas quoi faire, aidez-moi.

(a few months ago, after a disagreement with my boyfriend, he started threatening me with a video of us I didn't even know existed. He took full advantage of my fear and frustration. He tortured me mentally, and it was the worst time of my life. He threatened me so I don't leave him. I couldn't file a complaint for fear of him, my family . . . I have all the screenshots with his threats. I really don't know what to do. Help me.)

One reader in the comment section suggested that she should consult a lawyer. Most readers, however, advised her to go to the police station and file a complaint. Even victims of revenge porn later regret their silence. An eighteen-year-old victim describes the blackmail she endured from her ex-boyfriend four years earlier. To further humiliate her, he shared the photographs with his friends, who began to torment her also. The experience made her "very ill" (*mredt bezzaf*), "shameful" (*7chmana*), and forced her into silence for four years. She has never been able to speak about the traumatic experience with anyone (*maqdit n3awd l7ta chi wa7d ldaba*). However, she advises other victims not to follow her example and speak up (*Bghit ghir nqol lga3 lbnat li ki duzu mn hadchi bli makhasch iskto lf7al had nas kima drt ana*).[74]

Such statements, particularly when coming from victims, could reflect another facet of trauma as they continue to blame themselves for what happened and for how they reacted to what happened. The reality is that speaking up is not as easy, nor is it safe. For example, in Morocco, reporting online abuse such as revenge porn might lead to the victim's arrest and imprisonment under Article 490, which criminalizes sexual relationships outside marriage. This is what happened to a young Moroccan woman, Hanaa B., who was arrested in January 2021 following a leaked revenge porn video. She was sentenced to one month in prison and a fine of MAD 500 ($50).[75] Moreover, speaking up or reporting the blackmail could trigger further retaliation. A nine-minute audio documentary, *Catfishing in the Nile* (2018), looks at stories of women in Cairo who have been sextorted by men they trusted.[76] One of the protagonists is feminist activist Ghadeer Ahmed. When her ex-boyfriend threatened her with a video that she had shared with him when they were dating, she decided to file a complaint against him with the police. As a response, the ex-boyfriend went to the victim's father, showed him the video, and asked to marry her. It is important to point out that the video with which Ghadeer Ahmed was threatened is one in which she is fully clothed and dancing alone. In other words, the videos or images do not need to depict nudity or show the victim involved in a sexual act for them to serve as revenge porn.

Indeed, by now, most women and girls in the region are well aware of the consequences of producing "compromising" material, thus it is not as likely for them to make and send such material. Yet, revenge porn is increasing thanks, once again, to misogyny's innovativeness. Going through the many testimonies, one quickly realizes how easy it is for any woman or girl to fall victim to revenge porn. Photographs and videos of the victim do not even need to exist. A seventeen-year-old Moroccan girl described how an ex-boyfriend punished her for ending their relationship by spreading a rumor among her friends that she had sent him her naked photos even though she never did. The experience, she wrote, made her understand the feeling of injustice other blackmailed-girls suffer (*7ssit vraiment bl7gra liki7ssu biha douk lbnat likidiru lihoum chantage contre leurs photos*).[77] Another woman is still traumatized by the cyber abuse she had endured when she was fourteen. A boy in her school created a fake account with her name, posted pornographic pictures, and added all her friends to the page. Pretending to be her, he chatted with them about sex suggesting that she "would do anything [sexually]." She was left perplexed, unable to understand his behavior since they never had a relationship. A fifteen-year-old girl has been tortured for more than a year by someone who opened, under her name and using her picture, "an account" (she does not specify on which platform), where he has been publishing sexually explicit material. Her "entire school knows" (*mdrasti kamla sayqa lkhbar*), leaving her helpless and concerned about her reputation (*kicheweh ma reputation*). She concludes with a call for help: "Svp aidez-moi" (pls help me).[78]

Helplessness and despair eventually push women to becoming suicidal. Many of the girls who contacted Mouvement.Dihafrassek were considering suicide.[79] Chaimaa, a young woman from Bensergao in Morocco, was serious enough about committing suicide that her sister was forced to quit her job in order to take care of her on a full-time basis.[80] Chaimaa's life changed radically one morning when she woke up to accusations of having acted in pornographic films. It turned out that a man had published, under her name, a pornographic video of an actress whom she resembled. Since the video came out, Chaimaa became depressed because of the constant online threats and insults. She had been physically assaulted on the street, which left her in fear of leaving her parents' home. She was taken to a doctor who provided her family with a virginity certificate to prove that the woman seen in the video could not possibly have been Chaimaa. No proof, however, was strong enough to counter the certitude of what people had seen with their own eyes, and what they saw was a video with Chaimaa's name and face. With nothing left to lose, Chaimaa and her family posted a video on YouTube detailing their tragedy.[81]

There are many more stories online by women like Chaimaa, though it is safe to assume that there are many more victims of revenge porn who suffer in silence. Moreover, while most of the examples discussed in this chapter come from Morocco, revenge porn is so rampant throughout North Africa and the Middle East it has inspired many films and television shows. One example is a 2017 Egyptian series, *Haza al-masaa* (This evening), directed by Tamer Mohsen. It is one of the first in Arabic to examine in a detailed and critical manner cybercrimes against women in the context of a digital native society. The series exposes the sexual and emotional violence women endure at the hands of their blackmailers, who use their knowledge of technology to hack women's devices in order to stalk them and steal or fabricate intimate videos and photos, which are then used to force women into sexual slavery.

The entire series is available on YouTube. The first episode, alone, has collected more than two million views since it was uploaded in

May 2017.[82] The added advantage of watching episodes on YouTube is that they allow access to viewers' impressions, which are published in the comments section. Overall, the reviews have been favorable. One viewer, Malikat al-Ihsas, wrote that the series taught her to never click on a link sent to her phone. She is referring to the fact that one of the characters, Sonbol, sends links to women's phones, which then gives him access to the devices. The comment section also allows for different views, including disagreement, as in the example of an exchange (in Egyptian dialect) started by La Rose: "May god punish any coward who threatens a woman with her photos." Karim M responded: "Why does she take off [her clothes]?" Nour Hani replied to Karim M that she would do as she pleased with her phone, including taking photos of herself. Mohamed Helmy believes that a woman who goes to a man's apartment deserves whatever happens to her. Anna mijnmam wrote in a mix of Egyptian and Maghribi dialects that a true man (*lli rajel bsah*) would not behave like Sonbol. Khaled Gaming wishes God would punish "any girl who sells her honor, betrays her family, and shames them." Mohammed Ali agrees. He, too, wishes divine punishment on "any girl who does not protect her honor."

This exchange summarizes well society's division about revenge porn. Many believe that women deserve to be punished for their promiscuity, while others sympathize with the victims. All of them, however, are aware of its prevalence in their societies, and it shows no signs of disappearing any time soon. If anything, it is likely to increase, as it did during the COVID-19 pandemic. According to *L'orient Le Jour*, between February 21 and April 24, 2020, online sexual harassment and extortion, "à l'aide d'images à caractère sexuel," increased in Lebanon by 184 percent.[83] In Morocco, in August 2020, the authorities dismantled a criminal network specializing in sextortion and operating throughout Morocco's major cities.[84] The Instagram page Mouvement.Dihafrassek was launched in 2020 "to fight against dozens of 'revenge porn' accounts that appeared online during the country's coronavirus lockdown."[85] Western countries, including the United States and the UK, have experienced a similar surge during the pandemic.[86]

The rising incidence of revenge porn during lockdown has been attributed to many factors including social distancing, which forced sex-seekers into the virtual world. However, increase in digitally-assisted sexual activity does not need to translate into revenge porn. It is misogynists' inherent desire to humiliate and punish women that turns intimacy into revenge. This is an important distinction to make in order not to fall into the trap of isolatory narratives. Misogyny as a system invested in exposing women existed long before digital technologies. The latter, however, have been used as instruments at the service of misogyny. As technology evolves, it will continue to facilitate more abuse. A recent example is the development of so-called "deepfakes," which refers to "media generated and manipulated by AI."[87] Although initially discussed in the context of their political weaponization to spread fake news, deepfake technologies have been used mostly for misogynistic purposes. As of September 2019, 96 percent of deepfake videos were pornographic, 99 percent of which transposed the faces of women celebrities onto pornographic videos.[88] The morphing of the two faces produces realistic and believable videos that capture the celebrity's facial expressions. For now, I have found only one reference to a pornographic deepfake of a Moroccan female celebrity. It is inevitable, however, that in the near future, as deepfake applications become more accessible to non-experts, deepfake technology will be used to create revenge porn and terrorize celebrities and non-celebrities alike, including minors. Not only that, but in the not too distant future, any ex-partner or complete stranger could easily fabricate pornographic videos that cater to his most depraved fantasies, no matter how violent and degrading. The spread of this type of depictions could potentially normalize a graver degree of violence against women, such as the one suffered by Hanan.

Deepfakes, however, are not as bad as it will get. Perhaps even before this book comes out, there will already be new technologies that will make deepfake appear "harmless" in comparison. One can always count on misogyny to inspire and employ the latest innovations to intentionally cause women distress, depression, anxiety, and other mental and physical health issues; to intentionally cause women loss of their jobs and incomes; and, most importantly, to intentionally isolate women and girls and keep them out of public spaces, online and offline. In this sense, online violence, very much like offline violence, seeks to instill fear in women in order to deter them from full and equal participation in the online sphere. As Jessica Megarry puts it, "Equality online is dependent not only on the ability to occupy a space, but to be able to influence it and speak without fear of threat or harassment."[89] The traumatic stories of women and girls shared throughout this chapter indicate that, once again, the war on women does succeed in maintaining gender inequity, including online.

Yet, there is another side of online violence against women that has not been considered in this chapter, namely its authors. In *Empowered: Popular Feminism and Popular Misogyny*, Sarah Banet-Weiser agrees that the public shaming and humiliation of women online seeks to render them "unable to act, to disable their agency . . . : relationships are destroyed, jobs vanish, lives are lost." Nonetheless, Banet-Weiser argues, "engaging in humiliating women who have 'wronged' men (either as a culture or individually) is also about bolstering men's own sense of action or agency."[90] Indeed, as mentioned earlier, many of the comments published in response to YouTube videos depicting a woman's "scandalous" behavior wonder about the whereabouts of the father, brother, or husband. To these viewers, a man's indifference to "his" woman's transgressions is just as scandalous and as unforgivable as the woman's promiscuity. Next chapter will turn to men and their agency as they actively construct, through words and images, a world in which the only way to recuperate masculinity is by exorcising the feminine.

NOTES

1. See Kim Barker and Olga Jurasz, *Online Misogyny as Hate Crime: A Challenge for Legal Regulation?* (New York: Routledge, 2019); Debbie Ging and Eugenia Siapera, eds., *Gender Hate Online: Understanding the New Anti-Feminism* (Cham: Palgrave Macmillan, 2019); Karla Matilla, *Gender Trolling: How Misogyny Went Viral* (Santa Barbara: Praeger, 2015); Jacqueline Ryan Vickery and Tracy Everbach, eds., *Mediating Misogyny: Gender, Technology, and Harassment* (Cham: Palgrave Macmillan, 2018); and Anastasia Powell and Nicola Henry, *Sexual Violence in a Digital Age* (London: Palgrave Macmillan, 2017).

2. Maeve Duggan, "Online Harassment 2017," *Pew Research Center*, July 11, 2017, https://www.pewresearch.org/internet/2017/07/11/online-harassment-2017/.

3. European Institute for Gender Equality (EIGE), "Cyber Violence against Women and Girls," 2017, http://eige.europa.eu/rdc/eige-publications/cyber_violence_against _women_and_girls.pdf.

4. APC, "Online GBV in Palestine Means Losing Out on Women's Participation," genderIT.org, June 11, 2018, https://www.genderit.org/feminist-talk/online-gbv-palestine -means-losing-out-womens-participation#fn4.

5. For example, in the case of offline physical violence, only 6 percent of the victims of physical violence filed a formal complaint in 2019. See Safaa Kasraoui, "New Survey Shows High Rates of Violence Against Women in Morocco, May 15, 2019, https:// www.moroccoworldnews.com/2019/05/273120/survey-high-rates-violence-women -morocco/.

6. Olivia Cuthbert, "Arab Women Fight Against Online Sexual Harassment," *Al-Fanar Media*, September 25, 2019, https://www.al-fanarmedia.org/2019/09/arab-women-fight -back-against-online-sexual-harassment/.

7. Rasha Younes, "For Sarah Hegazy: In Rage, in Grief, in Exhaustion," *Human Rights Watch*, June 16, 2020, https://www.hrw.org/news/2020/06/16/sarah-hegazy-rage-grief -exhaustion.

8. Liberated T, "Hegazy ended her life yesterday at night," Facebook, June 14, 2020, https://www.facebook.com/LiberatedT.

9. Several online platforms have published Hegazy's note, including *Egyptian Streets*, https://egyptianstreets.com/2020/06/14/egyptian-lgbtqi-activist-sara-hegazy-dies-aged -30-in-canada/. For more on the case, see MEE Correspondent, "'Egypt failed Her': LGBT Activist Kills Herself in Canada after Suffering Post-prison Trauma," *Middle East Eye*, June 15, 2020, https://www.middleeasteye.net/news/egypt-lgbtq-activist-sarah -hegazi-suicide-trauma.

10. Hal tasma,' "Sarah Hegazy," YouTube video, June 19, 2020, https://www.youtube .com/watch?v=flr2XdYnr4k.

11. "Hisham Selim: A Lawsuit Accusing the Egyptian Actor's Son of Spreading 'Homosexuality' after His Sympathy for Sarah Hegazy," *Eg24 News*, June 24, 2020, https://www.eg24.news/2020/06/hisham-selim-a-lawsuit-accusing-the-egyptian-actors -son-of-spreading-homosexuality-after-his-sympathy-for-sarah-hegazy.html.

12. With the exception of the United Arab Emirates, which, as of July 2020, has the fastest mobile broadband in the world (110.90), followed by Qatar (88.78Mbps) and Saudi Arabia (71.73Mpbs) in fourth and fifth place respectively, he region overall has mobile and fixed broadband speeds inferior to the global average. See Speedtest, *Speedtex Global Index* (database), July 2020, https://www.speedtest.net/global-index; World Bank, *A New Economy for the Middle East and North Africa* (Washington, DC: Intersectional Bank for Reconstruction and Development/The World Bank, 2019), 45–46, http://documents1.worldbank.org/curated/en/331081537883965003/pdf /130143-WP-REVISED-PUBLIC.pdf. For Morocco, see Simon Kemp, "Digital 2020" Morocco," *DataReportal*, February 18, 2020, https://datareportal.com/reports/digital -2020-morocco.

13. World Bank, *A New Economy for the Middle East and North Africa*, 48–50.

14. Marolla Haddad and Suhail Shersad, "In the Middle East and North Africa, COVID-19 Puts Digital Infrastructure to the Test," *The World Bank Blogs* (blog), May 7, 2020, https://blogs.worldbank.org/digital-development/middle-east-and-north-africa -covid-19-puts-digital-infrastructure-test; Aziz Atamanov, Johannes Hoogeveen, and Laura Rodriguez, "Using Internet Surveys in the MENA Region During COVID-19: Will All Voices Be Heard?" *The World Bank Blogs* (blog), June 24, 2020, https://blogs .worldbank.org/arabvoices/using-internet-surveys-mena-region-during-covid-19-will -all-voices-be-heard.

15. To limit access online, several countries in the region rely on internet blocking programs to crack down on dissent and censor international critique of local practices, especially human rights abuses. See Jared Malsin, "Throughout Middle East, the Web Is Being walled Off," *Wall Street Journal*, July 18, 2018, https://www.wsj.com/articles/ throughout-middle-east-the-web-is-being-walled-off-1531915200; Samuel Woodhams, "Digital Authoritarianism Is Rising in the Middle East," *Foreign Policy in Focus*, August 20, 2019, https://fpif.org/digital-authoritarianism-is-rising-in-the-middle-east/; and Natasha Turak, "UAE Loosens some VoIP Restrictions as Residents in Lockdown Call for End to WhatsApp and Skype Ban," *CNBC*, March 26, 2020, https://www.cnbc.com /2020/03/26/coronavirus-lockdown-uae-residents-call-for-end-to-whatsapp-skype-ban .html. In more extreme, though increasingly frequent cases, some governments have resorted to shutting down the internet completely for hours or even days. See Nadine Dahan, "Internet, Interrupted: How Network Cuts Are Used to Quell Dissent in the Middle East," *Middle East Eye*, October 11, 2019, https://www.middleeasteye.net/news/ internet-interrupted-how-middle-east-countries-use-network-restrictions-clamp-down -dissent; Matt Liebowitz, "Internet Back On in Egypt After Five Days," NBC News, March 14, 2011, http://www.nbcnews.com/id/41387229/ns/technology_and_science -security/#.X1Q53WdKj6Y; "Libya Starts to Reconnect to Internet," BBC News, August 22, 2011, https://www.bbc.com/news/technology-14622279; Abdi Latif Dahir, "Algeria Has Blocked the Internet Days before Its Ailing President Files to Run for a Fifth Term," *Quartz Africa*, March 2, 2019, https://qz.com/africa/1563958/algeria-shuts -internet-amid-anti-bouteflika-election-protests/; "Post-election Internet Shutdown in Mauritania Following Widespread Mobile Disruptions," *Netblocks*, June 25, 2019, https://netblocks.org/reports/post-election-internet-shutdown-in-mauritania-following -widespread-mobile-disruptions-JA6zmeAQ.

16. Adrian Shahbaz and Allie Funk, Freedom on the Net 2019: The Crisis of Social Media, Freedom House, 2019, https://freedomhouse.org/sites/default/files/2019-11 /11042019_Report_FH_FOTN_2019_final_Public_Download.pdf.

17. Sherif Mansour, "Stifling the Public Sphere: Media and Civil Society in Egypt," *National Endowment for Democracy*, 2015, https://www.ned.org/wp-content/uploads /2015/10/Stifling-the-Public-Sphere-Media-Civil-Society-Egypt-Forum-NED.pdf.

18. Youthpolicy.org, "Middle East and North Africa: Youth Facts," https://www.youth-policy.org/mappings/regionalyouthscenes/mena/facts/.

19. Peter Radoll, "Information and Communication Technologies in the Classroom: Implications and considerations," in Kay Price ed. *Aboriginal and Torres Strait Islander*

Education: An Introduction for the Teaching Profession (Melbourne: Cambridge University Press, 2012).

20. Countries with the highest use of internet among youth include Lebanon (99 percent), Jordan (96 percent), Algeria (93 percent), Morocco (93 percent), and Tunisia (91 percent). These high percentages have a lot to do with the availability and affordability of mobile phones, which continue to be the leading tool used to access internet in the region. Arab Barometer, "Youth in the Middle East in North Africa," August 2019, https://www.arabbarometer.org/wp-content/uploads/ABV_Youth_Report_Public -Opinion_Middle-East-North-Africa_2019-1.pdf; Northwestern University in Qatar, "Media Use in the Middle East, 2017," http://www.mideastmedia.org/survey/2017/ chapter/internet-use/.

21. Statista, "Daily Time Spent on the Internet Per Capita in the Middle East and North Africa from 2012 to 2020," https://www.statista.com.

22. Statista, "Average Daily Time Spent Per Capita with the Internet Worldwide from 2011 to 2121," https://www.statista.com.

23. "Screen Time: UK vs US vs the Rest of the World Compared," *Business Fiber*, July 15, 2019, https://businessfibre.co.uk/screen-time/.

24. Cyrille Fabre, Anne-Laure Malauzat, Charbel Sarkis, Tanmay Dhall, and Josett Ghorra, "E-commerce in MENA: Opportunity Beyond the Hype," *Bain & Company*, February 19, 2019, https://www.bain.com/insights/ecommerce-in-MENA-opportunity -beyond-the-hype/.

25. Arab Barometer, "Youth in the Middle East in North Africa," 6.

26. Simon Kemp, "Digital 2020: Morocco."

27. Arab Barometer, "Youth in the Middle East in North Africa," 9; YouTube Series: The Rise of YouTube in Mena," *Think with Google*, April 2016, https://www.thinkwith-google.com/intl/en-145/perspectives/local-articles/youtube-series-rise-youtube-mena/.

28. YouGove BrandIndex, available at https://www.brandindex.com/ranking/2019-buzz.

29. Matt Smith, "Young Saudis Getting Creative on YouTube," *Reuters*, November 18, 2013, https://www.reuters.com/article/us-saudi-youtube/young-saudis-getting-creative -on-youtube-idUSBRE9AH0GY20131118#:~:text=With%20a%20population%20of %2028.3,2.33%20percent%20of%20all%20tweets.

30. Arab Barometer, "Youth in the Middle East in North Africa," 6–7.

31. "How YouTube Plans to Stay ahead in the Middle East," *Arabia Business*, July 15, 2018, https://www.arabianbusiness.com/media/400686-how-youtube-plans-to-stay -ahead-in-the-middle-east.

32. Social Blade, available at https://socialblade.com/youtube/top/country/eg/ mostsubscribed.

33. Social Blade, https://socialblade.com/youtube/top/country/ma/mostsubscribed.

34. Social Blade, https://socialblade.com/youtube/top/country/dz.

35. Social Blade, https://socialblade.com/youtube/top/country/tn.

36. Social Blade, https://socialblade.com/youtube/top/country/sa/mostsubscribed.

37. Mark Prensky calls "digital migrants" those of us "who were not born into the digital world but have, at some later point in our lives, become fascinated by and adopted many or most aspects of the new technology." Mark Prensky, "Digital Natives, Digital

Immigrants," 2001, https://www.marcprensky.com/writing/Prensky%20-%20Digital %20Natives,%20Digital%20Immigrants%20-%20Part1.pdf.

38. Sean Li, "Is the Virtual World Really an Escape from Reality?" *A Reasoner's Miscellany*, August 14, 2012, https://nargaque.com/2012/08/14/is-the-virtual-world-really-an -escape-from-reality/.

39. J. Suler, "The Online Disinhibition Effect," *Cyber-Psychology and Behavior* 7, no. 3 (2004): 321–26.

40. Statista, "Internet Usage Rate Worldwide in 2019, by Gender and Region," https:// www.statista.com/statistics/491387/gender-distribution-of-internet-users-region/.

41. Aziz Atamanov, Johannes Hoogeveen, and Laura Rodriguez, "Using Internet Surveys in the MENA Region During COVID-19: Will All Voices Be Heard?"

42. "Haifa Wehbe Ain't No Natural Beauty, According to Her Plastic Surgeon!" *Albawaba*, December 7, 2016, https://www.albawaba.com/entertainment/haifa-wehbe -aint-no-natural-beauty-according-her-plastic-surgeon-912800.

43. Iloula, "Nancy Ajram from 1 to 34 years old. Before and after plastic surgery," YouTube Video, 4:29, October 9, 2017, https://www.youtube.com/watch?v =ymVG1Dj9cTM.

44. The video was taken down (https://www.youtube.com/watch?v=tmSzBZM4964).

45. Jamie Feldman, "Alicia Keys Has Started a #NoMakeup Movement, and It's Amazing," *Huffpost*, June 3, 2016, https://www.huffpost.com/entry/alicia-keys-no-makeup_n _575175f3e4b0ed593f140fd8.

46. Attessia TV, "Meriem Debbagh taqbal tahaddi Amin wa tnhi l'makiyaj fil mubashi," YouTube Video, 3:31, January 6, 2018, https://www.youtube.com/watch?v =GBxLxZX36IM.

47. Video is no long available (https://www.youtube.com/watch?v=x03yF8QUmTY).

48. The video was taken offline.

49. AlArabiya, "Kuwaiti yamsah almakiyaj 'an wujuh al-mashahir," YouTube Video, 6:41, March 19, 2015, https://www.youtube.com/watch?v=ephksuwGV2w.

50. Asma Ali Zain and Nivriti Butalia, "Dubai: The Perfect Place to Stay Young and Beautiful," *Khaleej Times*, April 29, 2014, https://www.khaleejtimes.com/article /20140428/ARTICLE/304289902/1002.

51. "Haifa Wehbe among the World's Most Beautiful Women," *Arab News*, March 27, 2017, http://www.arabnews.com/node/1075116/offbeat.

52. Ute Frevert, *The Politics of Humiliation: A Modern History* (Oxford: Oxford University Press, 2020), 138.

53. The video is not included on purpose.

54. The video is not included on purpose.

55. The video was removed (https://www.youtube.com/watch?v=2tGB1yPhTpo).

56. Aldar.ma, "Sanaa Akroud: Lasto nadima 'ala film 'Ihki ya Shahrazad' wa lam atawassat li'okhti litadkhol al-majal al-I'lami," YouTube Video, 5:46, December 24, 2018, https://www.youtube.com/watch?v=coykkKhnaq8.

57. The video has been removed (https://www.youtube.com/watch?v=hbuCxuzjwlg).

58. Dz, "Film Algérien Vulgraire qui fait scandale en Algérie 2017," YouTube Video, 4:04, May 10, 2017, https://www.youtube.com/watch?v=asnq6Y67NJg.

59. "Kaoutar Boudarraja 'emmerde' les donneurs de leçons," *Bladi.net*, September 22, 2015, https://www.bladi.net/kaoutar-boudarraja-dos-nu,43099.html.

60. "Momo se moque de la polémique autour de la photo du dos de Kaoutar Boudarraja," *Femmes du Maroc*, https://femmesdumaroc.com/actualite/momo-se-moque-de-la-polemique-autour-de-la-photo-du-dos-de-kaoutar-boudarraja-3380.

61. "Mereiem Said Expelled from MBC," *Dailymorocco*, January 31, 2019, http://daily-morocco.com/meriem-said-expelled-from-mbc/.

62. Danielle Keats Citron, *Hate Crimes in Cyberspace* (Cambridge: Harvard University Press, 2014), 50.

63. Ibid., 8.

64. Niall McCarthy, "Highest Earners on Instagram," *Forbes*, October 28, 2019, https://www.forbes.com/sites/niallmccarthy/2019/10/28/the-highest-earners-on-instagram-infographic/?sh=6fd950ee1110.

65. See Deborah Jermyn and Su Holmes, eds. *Women, Celebrity and Cultures of Aging* (Hampshire: Palgrave Macmillan, 2015).

66. Alice Nutting, "Revenge Porn Is Vile Symptom of Modern Misogyny—But We Now Have a Chance to Stamp it out," *Independent*, November 16, 2014, https://www.independent.co.uk/voices/comment/revenge-porn-vile-symptom-misogynistic-modern-age-it-s-about-time-we-had-protection-law-9864101.html.

67. To be sure, not all the victims are women. One well-known case of sextortion from August 2020 involved an American citizen who was blackmailed by a person or criminal network residing in Morocco. After making close to fifty money transfers from the United States to Morocco, the victim, a man, finally resorted to the help of the Moroccan embassy in Washington, DC. In 2017, Oued Zem, a Moroccan town of ninety thousand, was dubbed "the sextortion capital of the world," when the police uncovered a network of three thousand criminals specializing in blackmailing men, usually foreigners, with compromising videos and pictures. See Maya Zidoune, "L'Ambassade du Maroc à Washington dénonce une affaire de sextorsion," *Le360*, August 13, 2020, https://fr.le360.ma/societe/lambassade-du-maroc-a-washington-denonce-une-affaire-de-sextorsion-221184; Julian Robinson, "The Village of the Sex Scammers: Moroccan Town Where Three Thousand People Earn Money by Duping Men into Performing Lewd Acts on Camera and then Blackmailing Them," *Daily Mail*, March 7, 2020, https://www.dailymail.co.uk/news/article-4289096/The-Moroccan-town-3-000-sex-scammers.html; and Manal Zainabi, "Maroc: Comment un coin perdu du royaume est devenu 'l'épicentre mondial de la sextorsion,'" *Sputnik*, August 20, 2020, https://fr.sputniknews.com/maghreb/202008201044284517-maroc-comment-un-coin-perdu-du-royaume-est-devenu-lepicentre-mondial-de-la-sextorsion/.

68. Samantha Bates, "Revenge Porn and Mental Health: A Qualitative Analysis of the Mental Health Effects of Revenge Porn on Female Survivors," *Feminist Criminology* 12, no. 1 (2017): 38.

69. It is important to note that the victimizers, too, are of all education levels and socioeconomic backgrounds. In a recent and highly publicized case, a highly educated and privileged Egyptian man was accused of sexually exploiting and blackmailing over fifty women. He often took pictures of the sexual encounters and later threatened to

share them with his victim's family and friends. "Egypt Student Accused of over 50 Sexual Crimes," *Middle East Monitor*, July 3, 2020, https://www.middleeastmonitor.com /20200703-egypt-student-accused-of-over-50-sexual-crimes/.

70. "Abadi's List Ends Woman's Candidacy Over Alleged Sex Tape," *Rudaw*, April 19, 2018, https://www.rudaw.net/english/middleeast/iraq/190420183.

71. "Qissat filistiniyya dafa'at 90 alf shekel wa 64 alf $ muqabal 'adam nashr sowariha 'ala al-internet," *Ramallah Mix*, August 8, 2017, http://www.rmix.ps/archives/106916.

72. "The Rise of 'Revenge Porn' and 'Sextortion' in Iraq," *Middle East Monitor*, November 28, 2019, https://www.middleeastmonitor.com/20191128-the-rise-of-revenge-porn -and-sextortion-in-iraq/.

73. The Instagram page of Mouvement.Dihafrassek can be accessed at https://www .instagram.com/mouvement.dihafrassek/?hl=en.

74. Ibid.

75. Khoulou Haskouri, "Revenge Porn Victim Hanaa B Appears before the Court of Appeals," *Morocco World News*, June 10, 2021, https://www.moroccoworldnews.com /2021/06/342844/revenge-porn-victim-hanaa-b-appears-before-the-court-of-appeals.

76. Aliah Salih, "'Catfishing in the Nile' Award-Winning Documentary Explores Online Blackmailing," *The American University of Cairo*, July 22, 2018, https://www .aucegypt.edu/news/stories/catfishing-nile-award-winning-documentary-explores -online-blackmailing.

77. Mouvement.Dihafrassek, https://www.instagram.com/mouvement.dihafrassek/?hl =en.

78. Ibid.

79. Sophie Davies, "Moroccan 'Revenge Porn' Victims Smash Taboos by Speaking Out," *Reuters*, July 14, 2020, https://www.reuters.com/article/morocco-women -revenge-porn/feature-moroccan-revenge-porn-victims-smash-taboos-by-speaking-out -idUSL5N2EL2OR.

80. Video has been removed (https://www.youtube.com/watch?v=9jx444ZTeoQ).

81. The video has been removed.

82. CBCDrama, "Haza al masaa," YouTube Video, 32:20, May 28, 2017, https://www .youtube.com/watch?v=gvKXAh3FSCg.

83. Claude Assaf, "Stimulé par le confinement, le chantage sexuel en ligne est en forte hausse," *L'Orient Le Jour*, May 6, 2020, https://www.lorientlejour.com/article/1216981/ stimule-par-le-confinement-le-chantage-sexuel-en-ligne-est-en-forte-hausse.html.

84. Hassan Benadad, "Sextorsion: Démantèlement d'un nouveau réseau, des responsables et des personalités parmi les victims," *Le 360*, August 5, 2020, https://fr.le360 .ma/societe/sextorsion-demantelement-dun-nouveau-reseau-des-responsables-et-des -personnalites-parmi-les-victimes-220686.

85. Sophie Davies, "Moroccan 'Revenge Porn' Victims Smash Taboos by Speaking Out."

86. Cristina Criddle, "'Revenge Porn New Normal' After Cases Surge in Lockdown," BBC News, September 17, 2020, https://www.bbc.com/news/technology-54149682; Stephen Dinan, "Extortion, COVID-style: 'Revenge Pron' Surges during Pandemic

Lockdown," *The Washington Times*, November 20, 2020, https://www.washingtontimes
.com/news/2020/nov/20/vengeance-served-covid-style-revenge-porn-surges-d/.

87. Karen Hao, "Deepfake Porn Is Ruining Women's Lives. Now the Law May Finally
Ban It," *MIT Technology Review*, February 12, 2021, https://www.technologyreview.com
/2021/02/12/1018222/deepfake-revenge-porn-coming-ban/.

88. Ian Sample, "What Are Deepfakes and How Can You Spot Them?" *The Guardian*,
January 13, 2020, https://www.theguardian.com/technology/2020/jan/13/what-are
-deepfakes-and-how-can-you-spot-them.

89. Jessica Megarry, "Online Incivility or Sexual Harassment? Conceptualising Women's
Experiences in the Digital Age," *Women's Study International Forum* 47 (2014): 46.

90. Sarah Banet-Weiser, *Empowered: Popular Feminism and Popular Misogyny* (Durham:
Duke University Press, 2018).

CHAPTER 5

Misogyny Speaks

ACCORDING TO ABDELWAHED, IT WAS A WORD THAT KILLED HANAN. She called him *zamel,* to which he responded, "You have been with me for about twenty years and you called me *zamel?*" The man recording the video, too, reproached her for using the word: "You sister Hanan, *Allah yehdik* (may Allah guide you). Sister Hanan [*sic*], is he *zamel* for you to call him *zamel?*" The derogatory term *zamel,* "passive homosexual," is meant to call into question a man's *rujula,* or masculinity, as penetrability, in a homophobic and misogynistic cultural context, places him at the same level of inferiority as a woman.[1] Abdelwahed, therefore, felt that his violent acts were justified. He had to reaffirm his masculinity, which he did through amplified penetration performed in front of a jury of men and recorded for others to bear witness to his virility.

In reality, a word did not kill Hanan. Abdelwahed did. Nonetheless, words do matter. This chapter turns to words and their connection with masculinity. It is motivated by the following questions: Does misogyny in North Africa and the Middle East speak? If it does, in what language, which medium does it use, and, more important, what does it say? Much of the focus in feminist studies, influenced as it has been by postcolonial scholarship, has been placed on women's ability to speak. The assumption, correctly, is that for centuries patriarchy has been invested in silencing women. This chapter shifts the focus to men's ability to speak and be heard, for, as discussed throughout this book, men, too, have been silenced in much of the feminist studies about Islam and Muslim societies in order to facilitate an unchallenged narrative of Muslim women's empow-erment. One way this silencing has been possible is by marginalizing men's languages and trivializing their forms of expression. For example, despite the region's relatively high illiteracy rates, feminists continue to privilege the written word in Modern Standard Arabic published by a few and read by even fewer. On the other hand, words spoken in various local dialects and disseminated to millions are disregarded. Convinced that all views, including those of misogynists, merit critical analysis, this chapter invokes the voices of young men "speaking their truth," repeti-tively and insistently, through hundreds of songs and music videos that as an aggregate have accumulated billions of views on YouTube.[2]

INNOVATIVE MISOGYNY

One of the unquantifiable outcomes of the so-called Arab Spring is its impact on the Arab male psyche. It gave men, especially among the youth, renewed confidence. They took down a few dictators and emerged with a newfound feeling of freedom that translated into various cultural trends and artistic expressions such as, for example, the abundance of street art in some of the region's metropolises.[3] Less discussed, however, is the impact of the "revolution" on men's construction of *rujula* and their desire to partake, at the level of visible symbols, in the globally dominant ideal of male aesthetic and masculinity. Driving through the streets, particularly in larger cities, one can't help but notice the proliferation of gyms and health clubs, along with clothing boutiques and high-end bar-bershops catering exclusively to the fashion needs of the new *rajel* (man).[4]

This aesthetic shift also came with a soundtrack. In recent years, a new musical genre of popular songs known as Moroccan Pop came to serve as an anthem for the new *rujula*. Produced primarily in Morocco and disseminated widely throughout North Africa and the Middle East, Moroccan Pop combines hip-hop, rap, and reggaeton with other African genres including chaabi, raï, and gnawa. Its main language is Darija mixed with European languages thanks in part to the influence of the Moroccan diaspora in Europe. The songs' simple lyrics and catchy beats have led to immediate success in the form of millions of views on YouTube, within hours of their release. These songs, as seen in the discussion that follows, testify to the innovativeness of misogyny: they mark a shift from the traditional patriarchal desire to confine Muslim women's bodies within walls and behind veils to an aesthetically appealing misogyny invested in publicly humiliating and punishing women, in preparation for exorcising them from private and public male life. Beyond their captivating beats, the appeal of these songs lies in their ability to liberate men in a way that allows them to participate freely in global trends and to take full advantage of certain aspects of modernity, yet without giving up on local allegiances to religion and tradition—a point I will elaborate further in the next chapter.

I began thinking "academically" about Moroccan popular songs quite accidentally. I am unable to concentrate in complete silence, perhaps because I was raised in Casablanca, one of Africa's noisiest cities. I need noise to think, and I need noise to write. When away from large cities, I developed the habit of listening to music while working. A few years ago, as I was making the final revisions on my first book, I listened regularly to a Moroccan radio station online that played the region's most popular hits. I liked these songs a great deal—along with millions more listeners in North Africa, the Middle East, and beyond. But as one song after another was released, each to great success, I came to realize that they had more in common than addictive beats and muscular singers dressed in the latest fashion. Many replicate the same storyline: a man exposes a woman for her emotional and financial abuse, leaving her ashamed and regretful while he emerges satisfied and happy.

Initially, I shared my "discovery" with my sister, who listens to the same music station, but whose pleasure yielded to chagrin once she began paying attention to the lyrics. I also delivered a few talks on the subject to audiences that were harder to convince. I played the videos and translated the lyrics, but my interlocutors consistently resisted "calling out" the misogyny in these songs. Almost inevitably, the discussion shifted to misogyny in popular music in the United States. "At least the music videos are not showing naked, objectified women," someone in the audience would retort, referring specifically to representations of women in US hip-hop and rap videos, as if this particular genre held exclusivity over misogyny. One might also ask whether covering women's bodies is less misogynistic than uncovering them. The issue, however, as it often is in exchanges of this kind, is not so much misogyny as it is establishing the dominance of the West in all matters concerning evil.

Initially, I focused on the leader of the musical trend, Saad Lamjarred, a young and charismatic singer who single-handedly revolutionized Arabic popular music. In the past, most Moroccan artists who aspired to make it big in Arabic music industry had to sing in other Arabic dialects, especially Egyptian, since most Arabic speakers used to find Moroccan Darija challenging because it is heavily influenced by several indigenous and European languages. Lamjarred made singing in Darija not only acceptable but also attractive. To be sure, he had an advantage going into the music industry. Born into a family of artists, he is the son of the well-known actress Nezha Regragui and the much-loved singer Bachir Abdou. In 2007, he was selected for, and, eventually, placed second in the fourth edition of the talent show *SuperStar*, the Arab version of the *Idols* franchise. Lamjarred's other advantage is his appearance. Moving away from the discreet male aesthetics to which Arab audiences had been accustomed, Lamjarred introduced onto the Arab stage a masculine body that was internationally readable as attractive. He was a candidate for "The 100 Most Handsome Faces of 2017," a list that included Brad Pitt and Leonardo DiCaprio.[5] Indeed, Lamjarred never hid his fascination with Western artists and fashion trends. He borrows their dance moves and cherishes the same luxury brands, all of which he carefully curates and shares with his over thirteen million followers on Instagram.

His dedication to his fans paid off. In 2017, Lamjarred was arrested in Paris on rape accusations and spent several months in detention before he was released on bail. Thanks to his fame and connections, he was represented by one of France's most distinguished lawyers, Éric Dupond-Moretti, who later withdrew from the case.[6] Some speculate that it was in response to Lamjarred's second rape accusation in France in 2018.[7] A short-lived social media campaign under the hashtag *#masaktach* (I [feminine] will not be silenced) succeeded in banning his songs from airing on many Moroccan radio stations. Yet despite it all, Lamjarred remained popular among his many fans who were convinced of his innocence. An on-air poll conducted by one of the most popular privately owned radio stations revealed that 68 percent of the audience wanted to continue listening to his music.[8] In any case, in this age of YouTube and other social media platforms, radio has lost its authority as the disseminator of music, especially for teens.[9] All Lamjarred's music is available on his private YouTube channel, giving his audience direct access to his old and new songs. Even while out on bail, Lamjarred continued to release new hits, both solo and in collaboration with other artists. In December 2019, he performed sold-out concerts in Dubai and Riyadh.

What is the secret behind this almost religious dedication to Lamjarred? The answer is found in his lyrics, which have acquired the status of an anthem, uniting men and boys in their hatred of and prejudice against women. In "Enty" (forty-three million views),[10] which earned him recognition outside Morocco, as well as numerous awards including the Lebanese music award Murex d'Or for "Best Arabic Song," the singer confronts a woman who wishes to emasculate and silence him. He accuses her of wanting someone who is "coldblooded" (*demo bared*) and does not "talk back" (*may3awedshi lhedra*), but he is no longer that man.[11] At the end of the confrontation, the male voice rejects the woman, ordering her to keep away.

In a second song, "Ghaltana" (Wrong [the noun is feminine]) (264 million views), the singer addresses a woman who returns to him full of regrets.[12] Again, using simple and repetitive lyrics, the song lists the woman's many transgressions: "you are wrong" (*ghaltana*) is repeated nineteen times in the music video, which is a little over five minutes. "You are regretful" (*nadmana*) is repeated nine times. "You became arrogant" (*tgharriti*) is mentioned four times, and the same for "you are greedy" (*temma3a*). In the end, the male speaker commands the woman to "get lost" (*di3i*).

Similarly, in "Let Go" (176 million views), the male voice mocks a naive woman who assumes that he would trust her again.[13] He gave her "everything" and, in return, she betrayed him. This time, the male turns to karmic justice, singing in English: "What goes around comes around, baby." Finally, in "Ana machi sahel" (I am not easy) (179 million views), the audience finds a "mean-hearted man" with respect to love (*fel 7ob qelbi qbi7*).[14] Following his mother's warning against being a "fool" (*ghafel*) and getting attached to "just any woman" (*mashi ay we7da*), this new *rajel* has opted for recycling his lovers seasonally. The music video shows fans of all ages, as well as celebrities, including the singer's own parents, lip-syncing in support of his transformation. It is the ultimate revenge against the cruel woman. Not only does the male voice emerge once again triumphant, but this time the male performer is visually surrounded by a large and supportive network of family, friends, and fans who join him in denouncing and mocking the woman, whom, we must assume, is the target of the video, and watches it alone, regretful, and sad.

Yet, out of all of Lamjarred's songs, the most direct anthem to *rujula* and misogyny is also his biggest hit, "Lm3allem" (The boss [a masculine noun]) (one billion views),[15] which received close to 23 million views on YouTube within three weeks of its release, earning Lamjarred a Guinness World Record.[16] *Lm3allem* is a term used throughout Arabic-speaking countries with variations in meaning. Overall, it refers to a man who has earned mastery in a craft, including music. This use has extended to represent the man who embodies the most idealized masculine qualities. In Moroccan jokes, *lm3allem* is used to signify "penis". As one might expect, if in "Enty" the male voice refuses to be silenced by a woman, in "Lm3allem" one chooses to "remain quiet" *(neskot wenta mawjud)*, for, in the presence of *lm3allem*, the most *rajel* of men, one does not speak. He "learns" (*mennek net3ellem*).

Rare was the Moroccan music critic who dared to address the misogyny in Lamjarred's lyrics. One exception is a blog entry published soon after the release of "Enty" in which the author, who self-identifies as male and writes under the pseudonym Zakmaf, asked, "Is Saad Lamjarred a misogynist singer?" (*Saad Lamjarred, chanteur misogyne?*) Zakmaf wrote that Lamjarred's "Enty" made him want to burn his radio (*j'avais envie de cramer ma radio*), and laments the fact that listeners, including feminists, have been enchanted by the song and its artist, oblivious to the message of the lyrics and the impact it would have on the already precarious state of women in Arab society.[17]

Yet, maybe Zakmaf has erred in taking away agency from Lamjarred's listeners? Perhaps "Enty," like Lamjarred's other songs, appeals to its millions of listeners not despite, but rather precisely because of the lyrics. When he released "*Lm3allem*" in 2015, Lamjarred could not have anticipated the extent to which he himself would turn into *lm3allem* to his fans, many of whom became artists who followed his aesthetics and lyrical model. Through his combination of love for fashion and hatred of women, he gave them license to participate in global trends available to them via Instagram, TikTok, YouTube, and other social media platforms without ever jeopardizing male supremacy over women. He has constructed for them a cool misogyny that allows them to take fashion risks, at times even transcending gender confines with layers of necklaces, earrings and hair dye, while holding on to a traditional *rujula* built on the mistrust of women.

Democratizing Misogyny

In 2019, on his thirty-fourth birthday, Lamjarred published on his Instagram a black-and-white photo of himself sitting confidently in a chair. The photo was interpreted as a message to his "haters" (*7aqdin*), announcing his return to "the throne of popular music" after the relatively brief interruption caused by the ongoing alleged rape accusations. Nevertheless, if he has been keeping up with the multitude of releases inspired by "Enty" and his other songs, Lamjarred would certainly know that the popular music scene of which he was a pioneer is no longer reserved for the privileged few. Technology has democratized and revolutionized all aspects of song making, from sound, to videos, to the dissemination of the music. Vocal tuning software such as AutoTune, which, as Gary Marshall put it, "fixes dodgy vocals," enabled a large number of men to become singers, including those whose voice would have previously disqualified them from such a career.[18]

Furthermore, technology helped lower significantly the cost of making and distributing songs. When all one needs to make a song is a laptop, artists are no longer dependent on recording studios. Nor do they need a budget and crew to film music videos, since most are made using a smartphone. Aymane Serhani is one of the first artists who popularized the "selfie clip" thanks to hits such as "Tonton" (Uncle) (97 million views),[19] "Nebghi Djini Bsurvet" (I want you to come to me in a tracksuit) (165 million views),[20] "Hayat" (131 million views),[21] and "La Beauté" (22 million views).[22] Most of Serhani's videos consist of scenes of the artist and his friends having a great time together, all filmed thanks to a smartphone and a selfie stick.

Finally, another and perhaps most significant change in the music industry has been the rise in the popularity of YouTube and other social media platforms in North Africa and the Middle East, especially since the so-called Arab Spring. To be sure, social media transformed global music making. For example, the internationally acclaimed French-Algerian artist DJ Snake explained in an interview that he owed at least part of his success to social media platforms, which "cut out the middle man" between performers and their fans.[23] In North Africa and the Middle East, social media, and YouTube in particular, since other music streaming platforms such as Spotify are not as accessible to the artists and listeners in the region, came to play a more crucial role. Almost all the music videos are published on the artists' personal YouTube channels, allowing them to monetize their content. This is especially important given the lack of clarity and enforcement of copyright laws in the region. For example, in Morocco there is a Bureau marocain des droits d'auteur (BMDA), yet artists are not remunerated when their songs are played on the radio. Thanks to YouTube ad revenue, however, many artists in the region have been able to make of music a reliable source of income.

MUTATING MISOGYNY

Unfortunately, as technology has democratized the music industry and opened it up as a potentially lucrative career for young men, regardless of socioeconomic status, family connections, or artistic abilities, it has also inadvertently democratized lyrics of misogyny. Inspired by the message and enabled by technology, numerous young men followed Lamjarred's example, except that with new songs the hate toward women grew stronger. Indeed, not to pathologize misogyny but revising this chapter during the COVID-19 quarantine it is hard to resist a comparison between misogyny and the virus, for the development that followed Lamjarred's success very much resembled the progression of a virus in its mutations. With every mutation, the insults became more widespread and the desire for revenge more pronounced. One of the earliest artists to adopt Lamjarred's musical style was Hatim Ammor.[24] In "Mchiti fiha" (You're a goner) (105 million views), which eventually surpassed the success of "Enty" in the number of views, Ammor addresses a woman who took advantage of his patience and betrayed him.[25] "You're a goner," he repeats. Dissimulated in the hurt is a promise of revenge, as he announces to the woman that he "used to have good intentions for her" (*kont nawi lik el khir*), meaning that he intended to marry her, which is something he must have promised her in order to seduce her into having sex with him.

To understand the significance of his words in their sociocultural context, one needs to realize how challenging it is in a Muslim-majority society to have sex outside marriage. First, one needs to find a place to have it. Young people in the region are generally expected to live with their parents or other family members until marriage, which is why they often turn to alternative spaces that can increase women's vulnerability and expose them to more abuse. From a religious standpoint, illicit sex, or *zina*, in Islam is in the category of offenses that are seen as crimes against God that violate his limits (*hudud al-Allah*). Finally, from a legal stand-point, in the context of Morocco, for example, the Penal Code Article 490 provides for a prison term of between one month and one year for a sexual relationship outside marriage. However, while the law and religion call for the punishment of both women and men, only women encounter stigma and blame because of the significance of women's virginity. To this day, women in the region are expected to bleed on their wedding night, which is taken as proof of virginity. This has pushed girls and women to resort to extreme practices such as hymenoplasty, or hymen reconstruc-tive surgery, the cost of which begins at around $200,[26] while those who do not have access to surgery or cannot afford it would, in some instances, resort to homemade inflammation-inducing substances that cause bleed-ing upon intercourse.

Women, accordingly, are generally reluctant to engage in sexual rela-tionships, at least until a promise of marriage. When the male character in Ammor's song threatens that he "used to have good intentions for her," it is his way of declaring publicly that he reneges on any promise he might have made her privately. Moreover, he renders any "deceiving" tactics such as a reconstruction of the hymen futile, for he has already exposed her to her family, neighborhood, and any man who could have been duped into marrying her thinking she was a virgin. It is for this reason that revenge lyrics like the revenge videos discussed in the previous chapter are particularly damaging in the context of North African and Middle Eastern societies, making them a popular method of women's punishment.

In Ayoub Africano's (Ayoub Azellal) "Tbeddelt" (I changed) (14 million views), the male protagonist, too, exposes his ex-lover for the sexual relationship she had with him.[27] When he finds out that she has been unfaithful to him with rich men in exchange for money, he abandons her, but not before sharing with his audience that he knew he "was not the first" (*Kont 3aref ana mashi lewlani*), to illustrate the degree of her promiscuity. But if he knew that she was not a virgin, and if a woman's virginity matters to him as it does to the society in general, then why did he have sex with her? The goal is to take back the claim of having been duped by a woman. He was disappointed, as the video shows, but by declaring that he knew, he turns from the one who has been tricked into the one who tricked the woman by exploiting her gullibility. In other words, unlike Ammor's character, he knew all along and never had any good intentions.

In "Feya9ni Lmessage" (The message woke me up) (31 million views), Mido Belahbib featuring LBenj (Zakaria Bennaji) plays on this narrative twist of the manipulator being manipulated. The woman messages him from fake social media accounts, calling him "baby" and "habibi."[28] He knows that she is a "materialist" obsessed with shopping, cars, and fast motorcycles, but he is playing along. He is explicit in his plan to exploit her sexually and move on (*wana gha 9adi gharadi*), but not before ruining any possibility of a life after him. He promises to expose her to her mother, father, and *lhouma*. In Darija, *lhouma* usually refers to a socioeconomically disadvantaged neighborhood. In many of these songs, however, *lhouma* appears not only as a space but also as an ally of men and misogyny. It is called upon to serve as an archive that documents and preserves women's and girls' every transgression.

This archive is especially oppressive to women since it forces them into a determinism that stifles their progress. Most often, the physical ties with *lhouma* last a lifetime, making any chance of radical reinvention almost impossible. *Lhouma* and its men will be there as a woman's historical memory to thwart her aspirations of social ascension or transformation. This is the storyline of Nouamane Belaiachi's "Bent Lhouma" (The girl from the neighborhood) (30 million views).[29] The song is about a man snubbed by a woman who dismissed him as "young kid" (*derri sghir*), meaning that he is incapable of providing for her financially. In the video, he is seen playing cards with his friends in the street, alluding to probable unemployment. In retaliation, he belittles her ambition using the Moroccan expression "you want to fly" (*bagha tirri*) and mocks her attempts at upward mobility, thinking that someone like her coming from *lhouma* would appear "classy" by wearing miniskirts. He wishes he could punish her but worries it is "shameful" (*hshouma*). In the video, however, the protagonist's friend, played by a Moroccan radio personality, is seen leading the woman inside a building. The obvious suggestion is that he would exploit her sexually in order to expose her promiscuity to his friend, and to *lhouma*. The male protagonist and the audience are also meant to get comedic relief from imagining the lies the equally unaccomplished friend must have told the ambitious woman to trick her into having sex with him.

The more songs are produced, the greater is the humiliation and punishment that women characters endure. Often, in the trajectory of the same artist one sees an evolution in the intensification of misogyny. Numerous are the examples of artists from the region who began their singing career with covers of songs about longing for the woman's love before embracing blatantly misogynistic representations in which a woman's love is not given but rather owed.

OWED LOVE

One of the most prolific entertainers in this genre of popular songs is Iliass, known by his artistic name Tiiw Tiiw. He made a career out of releasing songs in which women who dare to reject men are punished in different ways. "Maria dartha biyya" (Maria tricked me), featuring the artist Cravata (62 million views), tells the story of a man who endured "five years of suffering" (*khemss snin del hem*) with a woman only to find out that she was planning on marrying her cousin, a billionaire.[30] To make matters worse, her father is a "mafia boss" (*chef fel mafia*). Undeterred, the character of Tiiw Tiiw threatens that he would beat her (*reyyesh mmoha*). In the music video, a group of men led by Tiiw Tiiw and Cravata sneak into the wedding reception pretending to be performers in order to kidnap the bride. With the assistance of his devoted friends, the protagonist succeeds in recuperating what he is owed, though it is implied that he would eventually dispose of her once he has taken her virginity.

There are many variations on this male complicity, or what is summarized in American slang with the phrase "bros before hoes," meaning that the bond among male friends will always surpass in its honesty and longevity the relationship that a man could have with a woman. In these songs, participation in the punishment of a woman who has rejected the man's advances becomes the ultimate male bonding experience. In the video for Zouhair Bahaoui's "Décapotable" (Convertible) (364 million views), which was the hit of summer 2018, the character played by Bahaoui seeks revenge from a woman who has rejected him because she only goes out with men who drive sports cars so that she can show off a lavish lifestyle on Instagram.[31] Bahaoui's friend, played by Tiiw Tiiw, helps him steal a Mercedes convertible that he uses to trick the gold digger. When chased by the police, the driver abandons the car with the woman inside. The police arrive and handcuff her. Bahaoui celebrates his successful revenge with a jump in the air and satisfied grin on his face.

If the woman is physically out of reach, the violence is directed to her loved ones and material property. In "Hasta Luego" (ft. Tiiw Tiw) (253 million views), the man complains that he is "unlucky in love" (*ma3endi zher m3a l'amour*).[32] In the video, on the other hand, Bahaoui's character, with the help once again of Tiiw Tiiw, breaks into his wealthy girlfriend's family home, abducts her dog, and drives away in the family Ferrari.

These songs mark a significant departure from earlier ones in which a woman's abuse is detailed in order to then justify the punishment that follows. Songs such as "Décapotable" and "Hasta Luego" are not about revenge after a bitter breakup, since there was never a couple to begin with. Instead, the women are being punished for refusing a man's advances. To the protagonists of these songs, the idea that a woman is unavailable or unwilling to give herself to them unconditionally is unacceptable, even inconceivable. Rejection angers them as it puts a *rujula* built upon social endorsement of a man's superiority into crisis. How could the subordinate say no?

Such crises have brought many male characters to the verge of suicide.[33] As soon as they recover, however, they become consumed with a more sadistic agenda to punish women. In the last scene of "Dinero" (29 million views), a song about gold diggers, the character played by Bahaoui is seen punching a boxing bag out of which come bills.[34] In Tiiw Tiiw's "Poupia" (Doll) (ft. Naza and Blanka) (46 million views), the substitution of the woman's body is less ambiguous.[35] Filmed in a villa with a pool, the video depicts a dozen men playing with a life-size female mannequin. They change her clothes, remove her wig, detach her head and put it back, throw her in the pool, shake her, dance with her, and turn her around to expose her buttocks. Only a lack of imagination would permit *not* interpreting this video as a fantasy about gang rape.

Belaiachi's song misleadingly titled "Mi Amor" (My love) (38 million views), presents a glimpse into the extreme forms of punishment that await the woman who rejects and angers a man.[36] Within the popular music genre of the region, the video offers one of the most explicit depictions of physical violence against a woman. Although the lyrics say that the woman came to him, in the video, his friends of *lhouma* forcefully bring her to him. They attach her to a gate and revel in taunting and mocking her. The availability of the rope in the scene indicates that both the torture and the crime were premeditated. At one point, the character played by Belaiachi even brings another woman who also participates in the humiliation and whose role is to prove to the victim that he is capable of seducing better-looking women. When they are done, the woman is dragged to a car and attached to its roof. An aerial shot shows the car driving down a deserted road outside the city with the woman still tied down. The video ends leaving us to expect the obvious: torture, rape, and possibly murder, a fate eerily similar to that of the woman whose story opens this book, Hanan, who, too, failed to give a man his due.

"Mi Amor" is one of Belaiachi's most viewed videos. It has 243k likes, 19k dislikes, and 12k comments. The overwhelming majority is positive. A few commentators wish Belaiachi used his talent and voice to recite the Qur'an, while others repeat a line from the song with a sad emoji signaling to a shared experience of betrayal by a woman. One comment by a YouTuber named Hakim Taoumi stands as an exception: "We agree that this is kidnapping. A deep message (*risala 3amiqa*) is behind this video." Perhaps for the other thousands of viewers, the violence against the female character was not visible enough to merit a reaction.

Or perhaps, too, it was satisfyingly visible as the deserved punishment for women who reject men. The male characters in these songs and videos, like many of the men discussed throughout this book, feel that they are owed a woman's body and affection. Indeed, in their unchallenged male supremacy, they believe they are entitled to the devotion of women, all of whom ultimately fail to give a man what he deserves, with the exception of one: his mother.

MOTHERS/GOLD DIGGERS

Benevolent misogyny may seem like a contradiction, yet misogynists are capable of "loving" the few women they do not hate. Indeed, misogyny depends on these "exceptional" women to further justify the hate for and violence against the majority of women. The most loved woman in the songs studied in this chapter—and one could confidently say in North African and Middle Eastern societies overall—is the mother. Almost all the singers mentioned here have paid homage in one way or another to their mothers or to mothers in general. Lamjarred's mother, for one, is crucial to the public persona he has adopted. As mentioned earlier, both she and his father are featured in the video for "Ana Machi Sahel."

Moreover, in an interview in which all three participated, the interviewer asked about the characteristics of the woman Lamjarred would marry. His mother responded that she would want him to be with a woman that "would make him happy" and who would know his "mood and temperament." Lamjarred responded that his wife "must love his mother." It is "obligatory" (*darouri*), he repeats several times.[37] In 2016, Lamjarred released a song "L'Mima" (The mother), which, with barely 2 million views, is his least popular song on YouTube.[38] It is obvious, however, that he never imagined the song would be a commercial success, nor did he make a music video to promote it. Rather, a song about one's mother is one every artist from the region must include in his repertoire alongside a religious song. Lamjarred did both.

Not all songs about mothers are necessarily commercial failures. A case in point is Muslim's (Mohammed el-Hadi Mzouri) "Mama" (105 million views), which, even without a music video, has reached more than 100 million views, making it one of his most successful hits.[39] The use of *mama* as opposed to *l'mima*, *mmi*, or *lwalida* is noteworthy. In the Moroccan context, the first is usually reserved for young boys and would rarely be used by adult men, at least not in public, and certainly not in the company of other men, for it is considered "soft" or "feminine" in a culture that is, overall, homophobic. For Muslim to use *mama* is even more significant. Muslim's rap songs, such as "Dmo3 l7awma" (Tears of the neighborhood) (32 million views)[40] and "Zenqa" (The street) (23 million views), came to be considered somewhat of a blueprint of a *rujula* that adheres to a strict code of conduct: tough, straightforward, and unforgiving. Yet he was aware that his fans would not reproach him for being vulnerable given the subject matter: his mother. "I love you" (*kanbghik*) he tells her, which is just as unconventional as the use of "mama," for male expression of love is also viewed as a sign of weakness.

Even Tiiw Tiiw, whose many misogynistic songs are discussed here, has released a song "Te amo" (131 million views) about his mother, except that instead of singing directly to her as Muslim does, Tiiw Tiiw and the featured singers speak to an imaginary wife about their mother: "Sorry my wife" (*sem7i liya madamti*), the male sings, "I love my mommy" (*ana nebghi mmimti*).[41] He would give his mother a diamond, and for her he would be happy to "bring out the Kalashnikov" (*pour elle je sors la Kalashnikov*). He could even sacrifice his life for her. How could singers produce hateful lyrics toward women in general and venerate their mother at the same time? Isn't the mother, herself, a woman?

Yes, but in Muslim societies loving one's mother is a religious duty and act. Anyone raised in a Muslim family would be familiar with the hadith about the importance of the mother:

> *A man came to the Prophet and asked him "Who should I respect and obey?" The Prophet answered, "Your mother." Then he asked, "Who then?" The Prophet answered, "Your mother." Then he asked, "Who then?" The answer came, "Your mother." Then he asked, "Who then?" He answered "Your father. Thus, obedience comes three times to the mother before the father."*[42]

When the patriarchal system elevates a "woman," it must automatically trigger suspicion. One anonymous question posted on a website where Muslims are invited to express their concerns, alludes to this dilemma. Referring to the hadith according to which "Paradise is under the feet of mothers," the person asks: "Is this hadith valid for all mothers?" "Dear Brother/Sister," the answer begins, "the hadith does not mean that all mothers will go to Paradise." The author goes on to explain that one must respect and obey their mother. However, "according to Islam, a woman's place as a mother is one thing and her place as a person is another."[43] Probably what the author of the question had in mind was "bad mothers." Should one be obedient to them as well? But then what makes one a bad mother? Is a mother bad because she is a bad woman? The answer given does not provide much relief, since it does not point to a clear line of separation between a mother and a woman.

Representations of mothers in the region's visual culture, such as television series and films, deal with this dilemma by erasing the mother's femininity. Mothers' bodies are often camouflaged under layers of clothing as if, to be redeemable, a mother must give up on womanhood. Most often, especially when the mother's son is an adult, the figure of the father is eliminated or disabled. This is in part due to the usual age gap between spouses, and in part due to the intentional asexualization of the mother to liberate her, to dedicate all her affection, indeed her entire existence, to her son. She is there to serve and adore him unconditionally, which, in turn, makes it impossible for her to see any of his faults.

The status of motherhood comes with its benefits. After years of paying her dues to patriarchy as someone's daughter, sister, and wife, the mother finally receives respect, adoration, and a place at the gate of paradise. Moreover, she is finally welcomed into masculine spaces, even if it is just to serve food and give blessings to the son and his company. Motherhood, in this context, is, therefore, not only giving up on womanhood, it is also being released from it.

As far as the man is concerned, the mother serves to normativize his desire as she becomes the prescriptive model of a self-effacing womanhood. Indeed, this is key to understanding why the gold digger stands as the most hated woman in these songs. As a construct, the gold digger is everything the mother is not: she is selfish, her love is conditional, and, more important, contrary to the mother's irrational consecration to her adult son, the gold digger is rational in her choices. She evaluates every man based on what he can offer and has no qualms about rejecting those who have little. By putting a price tag on her body, affection, and time, she destabilizes *rujula*. A man being a man is no longer enough. He is owed nothing and must pay for everything. It is not coincidental that one of the things the singer in "Te Amo" admires most about his mother is that "her love has no price" (*son amour n'a pas de prix*).

To be sure, the gold digger stereotype as a trope is nearly universal, including in Western popular culture. However, it is important to examine the differences, as well as the similarities, one of the most important of which is the role that the gold digger plays in the "rags-to-riches" fable. In these song variations, the woman almost always stands as an obstacle to not only a man's mental but also his financial well-being. The woman is never an inspiration, but a hindrance to prospering. She is an evil from which men need purification, which can be achieved with the complicity of other men and through a ritual of publicly exposing women and denouncing them. Once the woman is exorcised out of a man's environment, the entire community of men achieves unlikely success.

Fnaïre's "Siri Siri," in which the woman is accused of wanting a villa and Ferrari, concludes with a scene inspired by the American franchise *Fast and Furious*, in which the male protagonist and his friends stand in front of a display of luxury race cars. In "Amoureux Tombé" (43 million views) by Lbenj, in which the woman is a "player" (*le3aba*) and materialist, the singers pose in front of expensive cars, including a Porsche Cayenne.[44] In "Tbedelt," discussed earlier, the man moves from driving a pizza delivery scooter to owning a collection of luxury cars and a Harley-Davidson. In Tiiw Tiiw's "Ki Kounti" (73 million views), in which the woman is shamed into remembering her modest origins, the man drives a Mercedes-Benz SLS AMG, a limited production sports car.[45]

The bottom line is that the most hated woman is imagined to have the same materialist dreams as men. Why then, do not their shared goals bring them closer together? The answer is that the gold digger is perceived to be an unfairly advantaged competitor. She uses her sexuality as a currency that enables her to too easily obtain that which a man could never reach with honest hard work. Their incompatibility is therefore a moral one as well. This is one of the messages of "Scénario" (51 million views) by DJ Hamida (ft. Aymane Serhani and Balti). The song begins, predictably, by mocking the gold digger who became accustomed to expensive taste: she likes Gucci, Ferraris, and prefers caviar to tagine. The plot, however, takes a turn when Balti intervenes with his lines. "The one spoiling her is an old man" (*lli mdellelha rajel 3jouz*), while young men are suffering (*chbab issouffri*) and risking their lives in an attempt to make it to Europe illegally (*l7arga*). Balti (Mohamed Salah Balti), a rapper from Tunisia, is one of the most prolific North African artists. He is known for his politically and socially engaged songs, highlighting young men's suffering because of poverty, addiction, religion, lack of freedom, and failed revolutions. Illegal immigration is a theme he has developed in several songs and collaborations such as "Clandestino" (Illegal) with Master Sina (79 million views).[46] It is not surprising that even when collaborating on the more commercial genre of songs discussed in this chapter, he would introduce *l7arga*. Yet what is surprising is that given his repertoire, he blames the gold digger for the circumstances that push young men into risking their lives on a boat, although one may also understand Balti's lines as a critique of the "old man" who is wasting his money on women while young men are dying. Either way, the woman is an accomplice for profiting from the corrupt system.

HIS TRUTH

At this point in the argument, one might introduce predictable "male anxiety." What these men fear is not so much women, but rather the fear of metaphorical "castration" that women's empowerment evokes in them. These young men, living at the intersection of so many fears including poverty, unemployment, and political oppression, respond to women's increasing participation in the workforce and higher education with misogynistic attitudes and actions. They hate women because they are anxious.[47] Nonetheless, the earlier chapters have made enough of a case to show how perverse it is to indulge in arguing anxiety, whose existence may also be validated, or invalidated, by checking the facts. According to a 2013 World Bank report, 75 percent of women in North Africa and the Middle East remain out of the labor force.[48] The numbers are more alarming for the age category targeted in these songs. Unemployment among young women actively seeking work is double that of male youth: 43.9 percent for female youth compared to 22.9 percent for young men.[49] Other factors, including the religious-based inheritance laws that are far more advantageous to men, mean men accumulate wealth and maintain it more easily than women. Statistically, it is far more likely that a man will acquire a Ferrari than a woman.

Even more perverse about evoking male anxiety in the North African and Middle Eastern context is the reality of violence and abuse among the demographic group portrayed in these songs. In Morocco, for example, while women of all ages can fall victim to domestic violence, those under the age of thirty are the most vulnerable. In 2016, 68 percent of violence targeted women between the ages of eighteen and thirty.[50] Further, if any type of couple violence were to occur among those the songs portray, whether physical, sexual, economic, or psychological, the abuser is much more likely to be the man.

Finally, the bigger problem with introducing "male anxiety" as an argument, as with any narrative that pathologizes misogyny, is that it eliminates key elements in misogyny, namely, awareness and intentionality. The misogyny "spoken of" in this chapter is not naïve, ignorant, or reactionary. On the contrary, it is calculated. Is this not why following the Paris rape accusation, Lamjarred took a hiatus from misogynist lyrics? The artist who made denigrating women cool and fashionable released a song about his lover's beauty "Ghazali" (My beauty) (182 million views),[51] followed by another one, "Casablanca" (178 million views), in which he tells the woman "I don't know who you are but the stars brought me to you" (*Je ne sais pas qui tu es/mais les étoiles m'ont mené à toi*).[52] Lamjarred, who usually refuses to speak French in interviews, sings the entire song in French. It is also his only song in French. He knew the French were listening, just as he also knew that singing to them in their language about an abusive gold digger would not sit well with the jury.

These singers, who have made a career out of reenacting and maintaining male supremacy, are even capable of appropriating a feminist narrative when needed. Heather Elise Nelson is a YouTuber who posts videos on cultural aspects of North Africa and the Middle East. One video presented on her series titled "British Girl Reacts" is "British Girl Reacts to Fnaïre Chayeb *My Mum's Choice*" on International Women's Day.[53] Nelson explains in the video's introduction that her mother, who "never had any interest in Arab culture," sent her a song asking her to film "a reaction," which is a genre of videos on YouTube that consists of filming oneself watching a music video for the first time and reacting to it. The song is Fnaïre's "Chayeb" (Old man) (33 million views).[54] "If my mom liked it," Nelson says, "it must be good." The song, which has English subtitles, is a condemnation of the marriage of young girls.

The Moroccan government, like many governments in the region, has sought to improve its poor record on child marriage, especially following the 2014 UN Child Rights Committee report, which reproached it for failing to remove girls from forced marriages. The committee also condemned the continuing practice of marrying girls as young as thirteen.[55] "Chayeb" could, therefore, be read as an example of the group aligning its songs with a political "feminist" agenda. This is not Fraïre's first of what could be labeled "commemoration" songs. In 2007, the group released a song "Yedd lhenna" (Hand with henna)[56] in response to the 2003 terrorist attack in Casablanca. In 2008, they came out with "Attarikh" (History),[57] to celebrate "1,200 years" of Moroccan history. In 2016, they released "Al Amir Nadif" (The clean prince) encouraging environmental awareness.[58] The song coincided with the United Nations Climate Change Conference organized in Marrakesh, Fnaïre's hometown.[59]

My intention here is not to question the artistic merit or appeal of "commemorative" art. It is, rather, to show that these musicians are aware of misogyny and its damaging impact on women and girls. It is also to show that, when necessary, misogynists are capable of commodifying feminist discourse to fit a national or personal agenda. Whether this type of state-centered feminist intervention is conducive to long-term change for women in the region is a point that is discussed more extensively in the next chapter.

Outside these commemorative concessions, however, Fnaïre, like the other artists, are their most authentic self when they are uninhibited in their lyrics and videos. That is when they speak their truth. In 2016, before the Paris rape accusation, Lamjarred had a twelve-minute interview with Liana Saleh, a journalist and culture editor at France 24. After a first part in which the journalist credits the artist with having revolutionized Arabic popular culture, the questions turn to the lyrics. Saleh asks Lamjarred about his relationship with women given his "harsh" lyrics, referring in particular to "Enty." Although Arab artists since Abdelhalim Hafed have been singing about women, the journalist explains, none have approached the subject the way he did. Lamjarred takes a deep breath and responds that he has intentionally departed from the Abdelhalim model, which, according to him, idealizes and positivizes love. Instead, the point of his songs, he insists, is to address lived experiences of today's real couples.[60] What Saleh sees as misogyny, Lamjarred sees as speaking the truth. He believes it, too, and so do the many other singers discussed here.

This chapter began with the question: Does misogyny in North Africa and the Middle East speak? The answer is that it does, loudly, clearly, and incessantly. It uses the latest technologies and the simplest lyrics. It speaks in local dialects, European languages, and images. Most importantly, it speaks its truth, rendering any fact-checking useless. Moreover, the words they speak in their songs are the same ones by which they live their private lives. With the exception of Ammor, who is often photographed with his wife, none of the artists discussed in this chapter have shown or intend to show their wives in public. When these male artists refer to their wives during media appearances, the answers are expectedly identical, collectively rehearsed in many settings. For example, Tiiw Tiiw said that his wife is his "jewel" (*ma femme est mon bijou*); he would never show her off.[61] Bahaoui's ideal wife would stay home, not that she would have much of a choice: "my wife, the house" (*mrati ddar*).[62] Lartiste, a French-Moroccan singer whose work is not addressed in this chapter, declared proudly during an interview that he has "never shown" his wife (*je ne l'ai jamais montrée*).[63] Lamjarred has no plans of hiding her, though he does not want her to be too beautiful. He is uncertain about how he would handle too many men looking at her.[64] For now, however, no one should hold their breath for it is unlikely for him to marry any time soon. His latest releases "Ensay" (Forget [feminine]) (235 million views),[65] a collaboration with the Egyptian singer Muhammad Ramadan, and "Asif Habibi" (Sorry my love) (41 million views),[66] a collaboration with Fnaïre, are both a celebration of the ecstasy generated by expelling women and sticking alone to the company of men.

These men speak their truth in their songs and in real life. Except that "their truth" is not just theirs, but that of their audiences, too. The democratization mentioned earlier gave voice not only to artists, but also to those who listen to them. When YouTube and social media platforms broke down the wall between the artist and the audience, they not only gave artists access to their fans, they also gave the fans access to their idol. This awarded decisive power to the audience. In the old days when music distribution went through state-owned television and radio stations, the listener had little if any agency. By contrast, in the YouTube age, no amount of privilege or family connections can purchase a robust, continuous following. Fans like what they like, and when they do not, they make it known. The artist's "vulnerability" has led, at times, to laughable concessions, for instance, when, not to anger viewers, scenes in music videos show an artist drinking coffee as he sits before a fully stocked alcoholic bar. The notable exception is the Tunisian artist Balti, who has never hesitated to show himself drinking alcohol in his videos—Tunisian "exceptionalism" is addressed in the next chapter.

Overall, the oral relationship that the artists of these songs cultivate with their audience is based on the articulation and repetition of a shared "spoken truth." The phrase "speaking one's truth" has been embraced by women and individuals from historically disenfranchised groups to make room for their voices and perspectives in spaces from which they have been systematically excluded. Nevertheless, speakers announcing that they will "speak their truth" is also a way of warning their interlocutor that their truth is not up for debate. It is in this way, too, that one must hear misogyny when it speaks its truth. And when it does, one must not silence or dismiss it. On the contrary, one must listen, even as it gets repetitive, boring, and predictable. One must take it seriously, especially feminists studying a region in which misogyny is spoken on loudspeakers through songs that are feeding an already overflowing reservoir of hatred. They must listen, not only because it is what critical rigor demands, listening to those with whom they agree, as well as disagree, and not only because they also listen when such misogyny speaks in the West. Feminists must also listen because what if a misogyny that speaks its "truth" were to inspire men to act, converting them into something far more than a music video in *lhouma*. And what if, guided by their truth, they were to establish a political state in which women are invisible and men are bonded under a single misogynous anthem? Or has that not already been done?

NOTES

1. In a study of sexual behavior among Moroccan youth, Moroccan sociologist Adessamad Dialmy explains that *zamel* refers to a sex worker paid to be penetrated. This is different from the *hassass* who pays men to penetrate him. A third category is the *louat* who is the man who penetrates but is never penetrated himself, whom Dialmy calls "doublement viril" for his ability to penetrate women and men. Abdessamad Dialmy, *Jeunesse, Sida et Islam au Maroc* (Casablanca: Eddif, 2000), 111.

2. The number of views listed in this chapter is based on the artists' official YouTube channel only. It does not include the views on other non-official YouTube channels that disseminate the songs.

3. See Basma Hamdy and Karl Stone, *Walls of Freedom: Street Art of the Egyptian Revolution* (Berlin: From Here to Fame, 2014); and Mia Gröndahl, *Revolution Graffiti: Street Art of the New Egypt* (Cairo: American University in Cairo Press, 2012).
4. In Morocco, for example, demand for upscale grooming services led a luxury barbershop, "The BarberShop Gentlmen Club," to open five salons catering not only to men, but also to boys five years and older and teenagers, to whom they teach "the basics of grooming." Farah Nadifi, "Barbershops: Où aller se faire tailler la barbe à Casablanca, Marrakech et Rabat?" *Shoe Lifer*, October 29, 2019, https://shoelifer.com/messieurs/grooming/barber-shops-aller-se-faire-tailler-barbe-a-casablanca-marrakech-rabat/.
5. TC Candler, "The 100 Most Handsome Faces of 2017," YouTube video, 10:53, December 27, 2017, https://www.youtube.com/watch?v=ojVQQBiwono.
6. In this chapter, the critique is concerned with Lamjarred's lyrics and the construction of his public persona. No assumptions are made about his guilt or innocence.
7. Safaa Kasraoui, "Lawyer Eric Dupond-Moretti Withdraws from Saad Lamjarred's Defense," *Morocco World News*, August 30, 2018, https://www.moroccoworldnews.com/2018/08/252827/lawyer-withdraws-lamjarreds-defense.
8. "Singer Lamjarred Case Reopens Morocco Violence Against Women Debate," *Arab News*, September 24, 2018, available at http://www.arabnews.com/node/1376776/offbeat.
9. Bobby Owsinski, *Music 4.1: A Survival Guide for Making Music in the Internet Age* (Milwakee: Hal Leonard Publishing, 2016), n.p.
10. Saad Lamjarred, "Enty," YouTube video, 3:58, May 6, 2015, https://www.youtube.com/watch?v=SyGI8TrrXx8.
11. Whenever possible, I have kept the same spelling used online.
12. Saad Lamjarred, "Ghaltana," YouTube video, 5:19, August 25, 2016, https://www.youtube.com/watch?v=ZulwKDO-6B4.
13. Saad Lamjarred, "Let Go," YouTube video, 4:57, August 8, 2017, https://www.youtube.com/watch?v=EvHW5vBSPjk.
14. Saad Lamjarred, "Ana Machi Sahel," YouTube video, 3:39, July 8, 2016, https://www.youtube.com/watch?v=ucNF2GHhk2k.
15. Saad Lamjarred, "Lm3allem," YouTube video, 4:14, May 2, 2015, https://www.youtube.com/watch?v=_Fwf45pIAtM.
16. As of February 5, 2018, it was ranked number one on the list of "the 25 most viewed Arabic songs on YouTube of all time." Eventually it became *the* single most viewed Arabic video on YouTube "The 25 Most Viewed Arabic Songs on YouTube of All Time," *Arabsound* February 5, 2018, available at https://www.arabsounds.net/top-25-most-viewed-arabic-songs-on-youtube-of-all-time/.
17. Zakmaf, "Saad Lamjarred, chanteur misogyne?" *Le Blog-Net Marocain* (blog), August 2, 2014, available at http://zakmaf.net/saad-lamjarred-chanteur-misogyne/.
18. Gary Marshall, *The Gut the Crap! Guide to Music Technology* (Buckinghamshire: Artemis Music Limited, 2003), n.p.
19. Ayman Serhani, "Tonton (Clip Selfie)," YouTube video, 3:16, March 26, 2017, https://www.youtube.com/watch?v=m2PSLf94j7M.

20. Ayman Serhani, "Nebghi Djini Bsurvet (Clip Selfie)" (ft. Harone Synthé), YouTube video, 3:20, July 9, 2017, https://www.youtube.com/watch?v=hUXU19SDXoA.

21. Ayman Serhani, "Hayat (Clip Selfie)" (ft. Safir), YouTube video, 3:02, November 19, 2017, https://www.youtube.com/watch?v=YTINAQoU4oo.

22. Ayman Serhani, "La Beauté (Clip Selfie)" (ft. Amine La Colombe), YouTube video, 3:14, February 4, 2018, https://www.youtube.com/watch?v=7K_SpSf4Mhk.

23. Clique TV, "Le Gros Journal de DJ Snake: le roi de la pop est français," YouTube video, 6:36, July 21, 2017, https://www.youtube.com/watch?v=htcU_sSjo9s.

24. The similarity is in part due to the fact that Ammor's hit "Mchiti fiha" was composed by Jalal Hamdaoui, who is behind many of Lamjarred's hits including "Salina Salina" and "Lm3allem."

25. Hatim Ammor, "Mchiti Fiha," YouTube video, 3:49, January 26, 2015, https://www.youtube.com/watch?v=La3_VmvLkPU.

26. Moroccan sociologist Abdesslam Dialmy has worked extensively on questions of sexuality in Islam in general, and in the Moroccan context in particular. See Abdessamad Dialmy, *Femmes et Sexualité au Maroc* (Casablanca: Éditions Maghrébines, 1985). For more on transgressive attitudes and practices toward virginity, see Soumaya Naamane-Guessous, *Au-Delà de Toute Pudeur: La Sexualité au Maroc* (Casablanca: Eddif, 1988).

27. Ayoub Africano, "Tbedelt," YouTube video, 3:26, October 26, 2018, https://www.youtube.com/watch?v=bxP6GFIoz8M.

28. Mido Belahbib, "Feya9ni Lmessage" (ft. Lbenj), YouTube Video, 3:24, December 2, 2017, https://www.youtube.com/watch?v=P2j7IN9doMQ.

29. Nouamane Belaiachi, "Bent Lhouma," YouTube video, 3:30, February 9, 2018, https://www.youtube.com/watch?v=G6HL3zW1of8.

30. Tiiw Tiiw, "Maria Dartha Bia" (ft. Cravata), YouTube video, 3:14, February 16, 2018, https://www.youtube.com/watch?v=3pD7QF3KDp0.

31. Zouhair Bahaoui, "Décapotable," YouTube video, 4:10, Aug 8, 2018, https://www.youtube.com/watch?v=Ph_tbASm31Y.

32. Zouhair Bahaoui, "Hasta Luego" (ft. Tiiw Tiiw and CHK), YouTube video, 3:20, July 1, 2017, https://www.youtube.com/watch?v=Mme9REVuidw.

33. In "Siri Siri" (Go away, go away) the male protagonist decides to commit suicide when he asked to marry a woman and she rejected him. His friends intervene and he ends up realizing that he is better off without her. Fnaïre, "Siri Siri," YouTube video, 4:50, April 10, 2018, https://www.youtube.com/watch?v=oY3XxNpRuu0.

34. Zouhair Bahaoui, "Dinero," YouTube video, 4:46, June 6, 2019, https://www.youtube.com/watch?v=7kqTzKTaofQ.

35. Tiiw Tiiw, "Poupia" (ft. Naza and Blanka), YouTube video, 3:49, August 10, 2018, https://www.youtube.com/watch?v=pYhypDoF_3k.

36. Nouamane Belaiachi, "Mi Amor," YouTube video, 3:21, July 6, 2018, https://www.youtube.com/watch?v=l74SQFu6Ms8.

37. CBC Live Stream, "Huna al-asima: Liqa' ma'a al-motrib Saad Lamjarred," YouTube, 31:38, December 26, 2015, https://www.youtube.com/watch?v=niunGAOvUIc.

38. Saad Lamjarred, "L'Mima," YouTube video, 3:55, March 21, 2016, https://www.youtube.com/watch?v=H2DJSTm5hQY.

39. Muslim, "Mama," YouTube video, 4:02, July 13, 2018, https://www.youtube.com/watch?v=RNRkJ0DksjU.

40. Muslim, "Dmou3 l7awma," YouTube video, 5:21, January 29, 2016, https://www.youtube.com/watch?v=14DFUnHqdAw.

41. Tiiw Tiiw, "Te Amo" (ft. Blanka and Sky), YouTube video, 3:43, September 4, 2016, https://www.youtube.com/watch?v=j9KKh215HTs.

42. Quoted in Yvonne Yazbeck Haddad, *Contemporary Islam and the Challenge of History* (Albany: State University of New York Press, 1982), 66.

43. "Paradise is under the feet of mothers." *Questions on Islam*, November 7, 2017, https://questionsonislam.com/question/paradise-under-feet-mothers-hadith-valid-all-mothers.

44. Lbenj, "Amoureux Tombé" (ft. Mounim Slimani and DJ Med), YouTube video, 3:34, September 27, 2018, https://www.youtube.com/watch?v=AN60XoWSo_0.

45. Tiiw Tiiw, "Ki Kounti" (ft. L'Algérino, Blanka, and Sky), YouTube video, 3:04, June 3, 2016, https://www.youtube.com/watch?v=keHEsFPBlTk.

46. Mater Sina, "Clandestino" (ft. Blati), YouTube video, 4:01, April 21, 2016, https://www.youtube.com/watch?v=keHEsFPBlTk.

47. For a reading of misogyny as a pathology, see David D. Gilmore, *Misogyny: The Male Malady* (Philadelphia: University of Pennsylvania Press, 2001).

48. The entire report *Jobs for Shared Prosperity: Time for Action in the Middle East and North Africa*, can be accessed at http://documents.worldbank.org/curated/en/540401468051871415/pdf/724690v40Full00Prosperity0full0book.pdf.

49. Maysa Jalbout, "Unlocking the Potential of Educated Arab Women," *Brookings*, March 12, 2015, available at https://www.brookings.edu/blog/education-plus-development/2015/03/12/unlocking-the-potential-of-educated-arab-women/.

50. Amira El-Masaiti, "Over 50 percent of Cases of Violence Against Women Committed by Spouses: Report," *Morocco World News*, December 18, 2017, available at https://www.moroccoworldnews.com/2017/12/236643/violence-women-spouses-morocco/.

51. Saad Lamjarred, "Ghazali," YouTube video, 3:56, March 9, 2018, https://www.youtube.com/watch?v=lhnmVSB-Rxc.

52. Saad Lamjarred, "Casablanca," YouTube video, 2:47, July 31, 2018, https://www.youtube.com/watch?v=ygHkJmTnmvo.

53. Heather Elise Nelson, "British Girl Reacts to Fraire Chayeb My Mum's Choice," YouTube video, 9:55, March 13, 2018, https://www.youtube.com/watch?v=H-bzlSZ9rd4&t=499s.

54. Fnaïre, "Chayeb," YouTube video, 4:59, January 31, 2016, https://www.youtube.com/watch?v=ZvvcQrmbggw.

55. The child marriage report on Morocco was published by Girls Not Brides, available at https://www.girlsnotbrides.org/child-marriage/morocco/.

56. Fnaïre, "Yed el Henna," YouTube video, 3:57, August 10, 2017, https://www.youtube.com/watch?v=b5WkB9ZW8kE.

57. Fnaïre, "Tarikh," YouTube video, 3:42, January 18, 2010, https://www.youtube.com/watch?v=BdUgo-pFsV8.

58. Fnaïre, "Al Amir Nadif," YouTube video, 3:40, October 31, 2016, https://www.youtube.com/watch?v=iAnifOd0sLw.

59. The decisions reached at the conference can be accessed on the UNFCC's COP22 website https://unfccc.int/process-and-meetings/conferences/past-conferences/marrakech-climate-change-conference-november-2016/decisions.

60. France 24 Arabic, "Saad Lamjarred: Uhawil Isal al-oghniya al-maghribiyya lil'alamiyya wa lil-'alam al-'arabi khososan," YouTube video, 12:20, October 7, 2016, https://www.youtube.com/watch?v=BhfLXEPm2f0.

61. CAP24TV, "Mrati jawhara wa lihadihi al-asbab arfodo dohoraha bijanibi," YouTube video, 3:26, June 30, 2018, https://www.youtube.com/watch?v=UKDkRn8Jv4g.

62. EchoroukTV, "Zouhair Bahaoui: ana ghayur we merti teq3ed feddar," YouTube video, 0:54, August 2, 2019, https://www.youtube.com/watch?v=l5cfDkP88_4.

63. Hit Radio, "Momo Morning Show-Lartiste," YouTube video, 1:41:58, June 26, 2019, https://www.youtube.com/watch?v=kalhUR3AjQk.

64. Radio Aswat, "Iktashif fatat Ahlam Saad Lamjarred," YouTube video, 6:49, October 20, 2016, https://www.youtube.com/watch?v=LvZNDBeSDtI.

65. Saad Lamjarred and Mohamed Ramadan, "Ensay," YouTube video, 7:46, July 17, 2019, https://www.youtube.com/watch?v=7iSJbEUuRnE.

66. Fnaïre "Asif Habibi" (ft. Saad Lamjarred), YouTube video, 4:01, February 23, 2020, https://www.youtube.com/watch?v=ssZ8vlY1rJU.

CHAPTER 6

Selective Modernity

In October 2001, the German magazine *Der Spiegel* published a document signed on April 11, 1996, in Hamburg titled "Death Certificate." It was the last will and testament of Mohamed Atta, the ringleader of the nineteen hijackers in the September 11, 2001, terrorist attacks. The document contains Atta's detailed instructions for his burial, three of which concern women directly:[1]

> 5. I don't want a pregnant woman or person who is not clean to come and say good-bye to me because I don't approve it.

> 6. I don't want women to come to my house to apologize for my death.

> 11. I don't want any women to go to my grave at all during my funeral or on any occasion thereafter.[2]

To those who knew him, such misogynistic statements would not have been surprising. Indeed, in addition to his hatred for the West, what stood out the most about Atta was his hatred for women. British journalist Jane Corbin claims that initially it was women, not men, who had suspicions about Atta. Immediately after the attack, and long before the names of the terrorists had been announced, a woman contacted the FBI to share her concerns. She knew Atta from the aviation school they both had attended and remembered that she had been alarmed by his contempt for women.[3] Indeed, Atta is said to have had a long history of "awkward" and at times threatening attitudes toward women. According to testimonies of friends and acquaintances, Atta left the room or closed his eyes whenever material he considered inappropriate, often involving a woman's body, was displayed on television. This discomfort with women intensified when he moved to Germany to pursue a graduate degree in urban planning.[4]

To make sense of his behavior, many have tried to pathologize Atta, diagnosing him posthumously with mental illness.[5] Yet, Atta's inconsistencies, like the inconsistencies of the Taliban discussed in chapter 2, are very much consistent with a broader culture in which deeply embedded misogyny intertwines with Western modernity, often perceived as unjustly empowering women and disempowering men.[6] Fouad Ajami, too, recognizes how *un-unique* Atta is in the larger context of today's Muslim-majority societies:

> *I almost know Mohamed Atta, the Egyptian who may have been at the controls of the jet that crashed into the north tower of the World Trade Center. I can almost make him out. I have known Egypt for nearly three decades, and so much of Atta's life falls neatly in place for me. I can make out the life of the 33-year-old man, one of a vast generation of younger Egyptians making their claims on a crowded land, picking their way through the cultural confusion that has settled upon the country in recent years.*[7]

Atta and the many young men like him throughout North Africa and the Middle East come out of a society in which Western modernity and tradition are forced into coexistence despite their fundamental incompatibility.[8] As Ajami puts it, youth in the region are caught between "the new liberties and the medieval theology side by side."[9] On the one hand, like many Muslim men their age, Atta and his companions were Western educated, used Western technologies, and were seduced by the freedom they encountered in the West. On the other hand, like many Muslim men his age, Atta was consumed with the inherited medieval orthodoxies discussed in chapter 2 that he used to dismiss any challenges to the dominant patriarchal order by equating them with the devil. This includes both women and the West.[10] Nevertheless, if Atta was indeed caught between modernity and medieval theology, his concluding messages and acts point clearly to the triumph of the latter. It is to medieval texts and traditions that the young man declared his final allegiance, albeit selectively and uncritically.

It is safe to say that most young Muslim men do not aspire to become terrorists. Nonetheless, most do share a similar uncritical allegiance to the past. Indeed, the previous chapters have examined how this allegiance provides a powerful framework for understanding misogyny and its persistence as an anthem uniting men in North Africa and the Middle East today. This chapter reads the persistence of misogyny in the context of the coexistence of the incompatible values of Western modernity and Islamic traditions. It argues that societies in the region have adopted a selective modernity without betraying their allegiance to the past, thus making it unlikely that genuine and lasting feminist reforms can be achieved if unsanctioned by religion and tradition. The first part of the chapter explores briefly the context of selective modernity and its legacy. The remaining sections illustrate the limits of selective modernity through two examples of top-down "modernist" reforms from countries usually seen as polar opposites with respect to women's rights: Tunisia and Saudi Arabia.

SELECTIVE MODERNITY

Growing up in an Arab-Muslim society, Atta and his companions must have heard the lament *al-taqlid al a'ma lilgharb* (being blind copycats of the West). Blind imitation here does not refer to Western science, technology, innovation, and other elements of Western modernity that Muslims are permitted to imitate. Instead, blind imitation concerns facets of Western civilization that allegedly promote debauchery and immorality, which are conveniently left vague in order to dismiss as "Western import" anything that challenges local orthodoxies. For example, a woman or girl wearing short-shorts, activists promoting the rights of sexual minorities, and advocacy for religious freedom as well as freedom from religion, all of which are criminalized in certain Muslim-majority countries, can be trivialized as blindly copying the West. Even banal acts such as participation in viral trends like the 2018 Drake-inspired Kiki dance challenge can earn online influencers the copycat label,[11] possibly exposing them to the accusation of promoting practices that are incompatible with tradition.[12]

This ambivalence toward Western modernity, Bernard Lewis argues, comes out of a specific moment in history in which "The peoples of the Middle East . . . became increasingly aware of Western superiority demonstrated on the battlefield and in the marketplace."[13] By the nineteenth century, as Western military superiority became indisputable, Muslim rulers and reformers embarked on a quest to uncover "the secret talisman of Western power."[14] At that moment, they faced a dilemma not dissimilar to that of Atta's and other Muslim youth today: which aspects of Western modernity to accept and which to reject. One example of the narratives that emerged out of this quest is Muhammad al-Saffar's (d. 1881) account of his visit to France between 1845 and 1846. Following the crushing defeat of the Moroccan army in the battle of Isly (1844) at the hands of a smaller French army, the Moroccan Sultan sent a diplomatic mission to France in the hope of understanding France's achievements and modernizing Moroccan military. Al-Saffar, who served as the ambassador's secretary in Paris, wrote a travel account in which he confirmed that French "mastery" in warfare was but one manifestation of "their marvelous organization" in all areas of life from war to the perfect alignment of trees in public spaces.[15]

Although the goal of the mission was primarily political and military, al-Saffar addressed in his report many aspects of French cultural modernity. Predictably, women, as the perceived guardians of tradition and men's honor, often come up in negotiations between Islamic tradition and Western modernity. The author wrote with praise, admiration, and, at times, perplexity about French women's beauty, revealing dresses, and slim waists, which, he found out, they "trained" with the use of corsets: "you could make a circle around the waist with your fingers, it is so slender and fragile."[16] Moreover, coming from a Moroccan-Muslim context in which making eye contact with a woman can be seen as an offense against a man's honor, al-Saffar was surprised to learn that to show good manners as a guest in "a man's house," one needs to acknowledge his wife by greeting her and exchanging "friendly speeches in a tone of modest gentility." The host, he writes, "will delight in that and his esteem and love for you will increase."[17] While attending a party, he noticed that women danced with other men in the presence of their husband. The king and his family, too, participated in such a custom: "I even saw the Sultan himself, his daughters, his sons, and their wives all dancing together and with others. He was laughing and enjoying himself immensely."[18] Yet what intrigued al-Saffar even more was Parisian women's talent in business: "The women [in Paris] are skilled in commerce just like the men, or even more so. The majority of people running shops are women."[19] Al-Saffar left his native Morocco to document French men's achievements but he encountered a modernity in which women were just as active participants.

It is tempting to read al-Saffar's positive evaluation of French society, and particularly his reluctance to judge the French for the freedoms enjoyed by women, as a possible embrace of the values of Western modernity. Nevertheless, it is important to remember that he is not willing to see the same reproduced in his native society. As a religious scholar and as a man from an upper-class Moroccan family in which women were veiled, often segregated in harems, and generally prohibited from participating in public life, al-Saffar remains attached to his indigenous religion and traditions. He concludes his account by reminding his readers that, their accomplishments notwithstanding, as infidels the French remain inferior to Muslims in what matters most: "They know well what is apparent in the life of this world, but are completely ignorant about the hereafter."[20] Perhaps al-Saffar did not feel the need to make more explicit his unease with Western modernity because French women's fashion and lifestyle were so far removed from the reality of women in his native Morocco, there was no risk of "contamination." Overly moralizing postures when there was no need for them would have taken away from the entertainment value of the tales he composed for the enjoyment of the Sultan and his small entourage.

When Egyptian intellectual Rifa'a Rafi' al-Tahtawi (1801–1873) visited France in 1826, he found himself in the context of an already familiar and threatening modernity, thus making it more challenging for him to refrain from judgment. Al-Tahtawi was part of one of the groups of students Muhammad Ali sent to Europe to study at European universities and acquire skills considered necessary for building Egypt as a modern nation. Though his role was initially as the group's *imam*, once in Paris, al-Tahtawi discovered the work of French intellectuals of the Enlightenment including Voltaire, Montesquieu, and Rousseau, and even translated some of their writings upon his return to Egypt in 1831.[21] In his memoir, al-Tahtawi, too, writes with admiration about French women's fashion: "very pretty" even if it is "immodest." Like al-Saffar, he was obsessed with French women's small waists: "so slim that one can hold it in both hands." However, unlike al-Saffar, al-Tahtawi seems more familiar with French fashion trends, such as wigs, which he had seen in Cairo already. "The strange thing," he writes, "is that the wearing of wigs has become a fashion in Egypt among women in Cairo."[22]

The point on which al-Tahtawi differs most from al-Saffar is his view of the freedom accorded to women in French society. He was disappointed to find out that French men, who have become "slaves" to French women, "do not have bad opinion of their women, despite their many faults." He further laments: "It has been said that Paris is a paradise for women, purgatory for men and hell for horses." Among the vices of French people, he cites "the small measure of chastity displayed by many of their women . . . and the absence of jealousy by their men with regard to things that arouse jealousy among Muslims."[23] Thus, despite his investment in Western modernity, al-Tahtawi remains concerned about what he sees as its pitfall: women are granted exaggerated power to the point of demasculinizing men. He borrows the words of a poem to warn his readers:

> Be disobedient to women, for this is rightly guided obedience
> The man who hands women his halter will not prevail
> They prevent him from developing many of his virtues
> Even if he were to strive towards knowledge for a thousand years![24]

Al-Tahtawi is more vocal than al-Saffar about his selective approach to modernity for one important reason: unlike the Sultan's diplomat, al-Tahtawi was personally invested in a political reform agenda. He was not merely recording facts about the life of the French, he was simultaneously envisioning which aspects of French society and civilization would translate into the context of a Muslim Egyptian modernity. Just as importantly, he sought to make visible aspects of Western modernity that he did not wish to adopt. French women's excessive freedom, it appears, is a particular point of contention for al-Tahtawi, because it challenges the continuity of gender hierarchy he wishes to preserve. His modernity, therefore, is one within which loss and untranslatability are embraced, even necessary, when it comes to some nonnegotiables such as the position women ought to occupy in a Muslim society.[25] This conditional and selective approach to modernity thus enabled him to engage with the Enlightenment project and its texts while maintaining his allegiance to the training he had received at al-Azhar religious seminary.

Al-Tahtawi and al-Saffar are far from unique in their ambivalence toward Western modernity. Other nineteenth-century Islamic thinkers, too, acknowledged Western accomplishments, yet to prevent "blind" imitation of the West, they called for a selective modernity, one that accommodates Islamic beliefs and traditions.[26] Nevertheless, in recent years, intellectuals from the region have been rethinking the legacy and persistence of such thought. Tunisian intellectual Mohamed Haddad, who was a student, at the Sorbonne, of the Franco-Algerian scholar of the Enlightenment and Islamic thought Mohammed Arkoun, describes people in North Africa and the Middle East today as living in what he calls a "suspended State" (*al-dawla al'aliqa*).[27] Haddad, who has compared democratic transitions in Eastern Europe with the Arab uprising, argues that despite having superficial elements of modernity, the region has failed to produce a modern state (*dawla haditha*). This failure, he explains, is due to an understanding of national belonging grounded in religion not citizenship. Rather than embrace "Islamic exceptionalism," Haddad instead calls for a separation of religion and politics. He claims that the pursuit of democracy without modernity creates a region incapable of accommodating plurality and difference, and always on the verge of chaos that threatens states' borders and sovereignty.[28] A recent example is the Islamic State in Iraq and Syria's (ISIS) attempt to reinstate the seventh-century institution of the caliphate, thus challenging the West-phalian system of modern states.[29]

Building on Haddad's arguments and concerns about Arab states and societies' "suspended" existence, Moroccan philosopher Ahmed Assid similarly insists on the need to separate religion from politics. He argues that Muslim-majority nations have never transitioned into "modernity" (*hadatha*). Instead, they adopted the "infrastructures of modernity" (*bin-yat al-dawla al-haditha*) without ever breaking away from "traditional infrastructures" (*binyat taqlidiyya*). This "double face" (*wajhayn*) gives the state greater flexibility allowing it to use the "tradition face" (*wajh al-taqlid*) to address its citizens and the "modernity face" (*wajh al-ha-datha*) when dealing with its international interlocutors. The individual experiences this authenticity/modernity (*assala/mu'assara*) binary differ-ently. Citizens, both women and men, are forced into a dual existence governed by two incompatible forces. On the one hand, there is "a legal façade" (*wajiha qanuniyya*) grounded in modernity. At the same time, the individual's "awareness and behavior" (*wa'y wa suluk*) within the various public and private institutions including education, the family, and the street are uncritically governed by allegiance to tradition.[30] This, Assid argues, has resulted in the production of individuals (and political parties) committed to the "superficial appearances associated with the technicalities of modern life" (*tiqniyyat al hayat al-'assriyya*), such as the possession of the latest technologies, without engaging with the values and philosophy of modernity.[31]

This selective approach to modernity, or what Assid describes as "retroactive modernity" (*hadatha bi-athar rij'i*), is most exposed when confronted with individual rights and the limits of the legitimacy of reli-gious authority.[32] If individual human rights are an essential principle of Western modernity, in the context of tradition the individual's rights and desires are annihilated in favor of conformity to the values and beliefs of the group. To address this point, Syrian-born political scientist Bassam Tibi draws on Jürgen Habermas's discussion of modernity and individual rights in *The Philosophical Discourse of Modernity* to conclude:

No unreformed, theocentric religion would ever share [the] under-
standing of human rights as individual entitlements vis-à-vis state
and society. The meaning of individual human rights is intrinsically
modern, as well as secular. It contradicts all forms of "historically pre-
existing law" (Habermas), primarily divine law, and hence also the
Islamic shari'a law. It follows that individual rights are among the
issue areas of Islam's predicament with cultural modernity.[33]

Religion's inability to accommodate universal human rights, Tibi insists, will result in what he dismisses as the "Islamic dream of semi-modernity," which adopts the material achievements of modernity while persisting in a "mindset of fatalism" that negates human agency and subjectivity.[34]

To be sure, with regard to modernity and Islam, there are divergent voices and different approaches to engaging modernity. Nevertheless, it is unfortunate that in Western academia one does not hear enough the voices of intellectuals from North Africa and the Middle East such as Haddad, Assid, and Tibi, especially since they are not invested in alternatives outside Western modernity. Although they disagree about the degree of incompatibility between Islam and Western modernity, and even the universality of Western modernity, these scholars agree that a bespoke modernity that enables Muslim societies to pick and choose which elements of modernity to keep and which to reject is ultimately a hindrance to the advancement of human rights in the region, particularly the rights of women and girls, who are among the most vulnerable in Muslim-majority societies. Their unapologetic rejection of an altered Western modernity to fit local sensibilities stems from awareness that the unwavering allegiance to tradition necessarily condemns reconciliatory concessions to one-sidedness. Assid gives the example of an imam preaching on a private Moroccan radio station, whose programs are also accessible online. The imam received a message from a man who confessed that "from time to time" he beat his wife and wanted to know if it was "legitimate" to do so. The imam responded that beating is part of educating one's wife and cited Islamic sources to justify his pronouncement. Ironically, the imam's statement coincided with a multimillion-dirham government-led campaign against gender-based violence. In light of the contradiction between his position on domestic violence and the national political agenda, the imam dismissed the campaign's slogan "No to violence against women" as "Western," insisting that it had nothing to do with Islamic culture.[35]

The anecdote shows once again that while tradition and superficial elements of Western modernity can and do coexist in Muslim-majority societies, the core values of Western modernity are condemned to failure when competing with medieval theology. Despite communicating via modern technologies, and despite being received through the most up-to-date devices—one imagines the audience listening to the imam on their smartphones or other gadgets—the message is identical to the one spoken in the seventh century. Unfortunately, the impossibility of discontinuity from the past not only threatens initiatives promoting the rights of women and girls, it also jeopardizes already obtained rights, particularly, as Haddad has pointed out, when these rights have been acquired through modernist reforms attached to the charisma of individuals rather than being grounded in a change of ideas and mentalities.[36] Tunisia, as Haddad recognizes, is a salient case in point.

ISIS AND THE LIMITS OF STATE FEMINISM

Of all states in the region, Tunisia is perhaps the most relevant to a discussion about the relation between Islam, modernity, and women, as it has been described as an anomaly regarding all three. "Tunisian exceptionalism" earned the group of civil society organizations known as the Tunisian National Dialogue Quartet the Peace Nobel Prize in 2015 for its contribution to building a modern democracy in Tunisia following the Arab Spring, which, it is important to note, also began in Tunisia in 2010.[37] It is also exceptional concerning the status of women and their rights, as its Code du Statut Personnel (CPS) "remains one of the most progressive family laws in the Arab world today."[38] Finally, Tunisia is exceptional in the region with regard to jihadism. The country exported the largest number of foreign fighters to the Islamic State of Iraq and Syria (ISIS).[39] Beyond a correlation, this section explores possible causal links among Tunisia's exceptionalisms. In other words, could the modernist-driven reforms that produced Tunisian women's unique status be responsible, at least in part, for the appeal of ISIS, an organization that sought to restore a global caliphate?

Following Tunisia's independence in 1956, the new government launched a modernization project, at the core of which were gender policies.[40] The first president of the Republic of Tunisia and charismatic leader Habib Bourguiba (1957–1987) implemented the CPS, which abolished polygamy and reformed custody and divorce.[41] State-driven feminist reforms continued into the 1960s as women were given access to state-subsidized contraceptives and abortion was legalized in 1965, making Tunisia the first Muslim-majority country to have legalized abortion for social as well as medical reasons.[42] Furthermore, women were encouraged to pursue greater participation in public life through education and work outside the home. To facilitate women's emancipation, Bourguiba openly opposed the practice of veiling, which he perceived as a hindrance to his national project of building a modern state.[43]

In many ways, these reforms have been a success. Tunisia continues to be the most progressive Arab country with respect to women's rights. Moreover, thanks to an active and organized women's movement, activists and politicians succeeded in securing additional rights.[44] However, Mounira Charrad calls for resisting the urge to label the 1950s reforms "feminist." As she explains, they were "prompted by a nationalist agenda to build a new sovereign nation equipped with a modern state."[45] Since they were state-imposed, the reforms did not reflect the convictions or desires of the majority. Charrad argues that the only reason the CPS was not met with significant opposition was because of the timing: "Defeated in factional conflicts during the anti-colonial struggle, the political groups that could have spoken for a conservative interpretation of Islamic law and blocked the reforms had lost all political leverage at that particular time."[46] Had Bourguiba waited, or had the opposition been stronger, it is likely that not all the reforms would have passed.

Tunisia's transition to democracy has further exposed the fragility of top-down feminism (and top-down modernity) in the context of a Muslim-majority society. Reports from the region indicate an increase in gender-based violence following the so-called Arab Spring.[47] As the journalist Cléo Fatoorehchi put it, the after-revolution has meant "less security" for many women, leading them to "regret" former president Zine El Abidine Ben Ali.[48] If anything, the democratic transition merely empowered misogynists to speak up publicly and unambiguously. In December 2020, during a plenary session at the Tunisian Parliament a deputy from the Islamist political party Al Karama (dignity) Coalition insisted, "single mothers are either sluts or raped women." He asserted that "the problems encountered by families and children today are the result of the freedoms advocated by defenders of women's rights."[49] The deputy, it is important to note, is a medical doctor born in 1981, more than twenty years after the CPS had been introduced. He was born into a Tunisia in which women had more rights than in any other Muslim-majority country. Yet as far as he is concerned, the CPS continues to be a Western import that accommodates promiscuous women and that does not conform to the provisions of Shari'a.[50]

As it turns out, Bourguiba's top-down feminism and modernity have produced resentment among some men who, until 2011, could only express their frustration within closed circles. Their dormant misogyny, however, was eventually awoken by the freedom that came with democracy, which finally liberated men to voice their grievances in public. Could these long-harbored misogynistic grievances then be the reason why ISIS, created only a few years after the uprising, disproportionately appealed to Tunisian men? According to testimonies from families whose sons joined the Islamic State, the first change they had noticed was the young men's physical distancing from the women in their environment. Like Mohamed Atta, many stopped shaking women's hands to avoid contact with the female body.[51] Could the accumulated resentment against what they perceived as an illegitimate emancipation of women, and what they experienced as an unjust affront to their *rujula* (masculinity) be the reason why so many Tunisian men joined ISIS?

These questions go against dominant assumptions about why men in general, not just Tunisians, enlisted with ISIS. Initially, it was argued that many of the fighters who fled to join ISIS, especially from North Africa and the Middle East, did so for economic reasons. The region had and continues to have high rates of unemployment among young people. The fighters were promised a salary and bonuses, all paid in cash.[52] However, subsequent studies about the link between ISIS foreign fighters and economic conditions have debunked this myth. Poverty and income inequality do not appear to be the determinant factors for joining ISIS.[53] A study by the World Bank corroborates these findings. The economic factor was not the root cause for joining ISIS, because the vast majority of foreign recruits had occupations in their native countries.[54] Moreover, the study debunks another myth about the profile of the ISIS recruit. Sixty-nine percent earned at least a secondary education. What is more, foreign recruits from North Africa, the Middle East, and South and East Asia were "significantly more educated than individuals from their cohort in their region of origin."[55] In other words, contrary to conjectures advanced by political analysts and others, ISIS foreign recruits were not driven primarily by economic gain, nor were they illiterates who were duped into joining.

Bangladeshi-Swedish feminist Taslima Nasrin, too, rejects the poverty argument. Instead, she believes that the fighters were driven by the desire to commit violence against women:

> *There is no point trying to confuse the issue by saying that poverty, frustration, lack of jobs and the absence of hope force people to become terrorists. It is, in fact, the other way around. The new terrorists are often rich and literate, highly qualified professionals, who have been seduced by fanaticism. They join ISIS because they know they will be at liberty to do whatever they wish to, and be given the sanction to rape, kill and torture at will.[56]*

To be sure, ISIS foreign fighters are a heterogeneous group with many goals and aspirations. But judging from the practices that took place in the territories under their control, it appears that the abuse and ownership of women and girls was a seductive incentive to many. As Iranian American scholar Haleh Esfandiari put it, to ISIS members "women are an inferior race, to be enjoyed for sex and be discarded, or to be sold off as slaves."[57] ISIS leadership, well aware of the desires of their audience, catered to the misogynistic fantasies and expectations of their recruits.

They used advanced digital technology to produce influential propaganda that constructed the caliphate as a misogynistic utopia where men were invited to act out their abuse, unconditionally, on thousands of women and girls, many of whom were in the most vulnerable of states: slavery. One of the ISIS question-answer pamphlets published online was about women and girl slaves. One question addresses whether it is "permissible to have intercourse with a female slave who has not reached puberty."[58] Even more persuasive were the propaganda slave videos. From its early days, ISIS disseminated videos of the slave markets where captured Yazidi women and girls were sold. In one of the most widely circulated videos, young men and boys are heard speaking in various Arabic dialects giddily awaiting the purchase of sex slaves.[59]

Like other ISIS fighters from the various nationalities, Tunisian men, too, participated in the slave trade, selling, buying, and owning women and girls. In *Your Sons Are at Your Service: Tunisia's Missionaries of Jihad*, Aaron Zelin claims that of all foreign fighters, Tunisians were "considered some of the most extreme jihadis in Syria."[60] Zelin reports that according to the chief of counterterrorism in Sanliurfa, the Islamic State "gave slaves to Tunisians to try and control them."[61] Indeed, Tunisian fighters come up in many testimonies, particularly of Yazidi women who had been enslaved by the Islamic State. Jihan Qassem is a Yazidi woman who was abducted at the age of thirteen. She was bought and sold by Tunisian militants. She was then forced to convert to Islam and marry one of the Tunisian fighters at the age of fifteen.[62] Nadia Murad, another Yazidi survivor, mentioned having been raped by Tunisian men.[63] Although most of the violence against Yazidi women went unpunished, there were instances in which Tunisian fighters were punished for crimes against "free" women. For example, in Iraq the locals stoned a Tunisian fighter to death for raping an Iraqi woman. Another one in Syria was strangled to death for the treatment of local women. In another town in Syria, there was a local demonstration against a Tunisian man who beat a woman for wearing a short coat.[64]

This is not to suggest that every misogynist has fantasies of joining ISIS or that misogyny is the only motive behind Islamic terrorism. Nor is it the case that Tunisian ISIS fighters were exceptionally and inherently more violent or more misogynistic than fighters from other nationalities. Indeed, Zelin attributes their reputation to the fact that many Tunisians came to occupy leadership positions in ISIS, which led to greater visibility.[65] Nevertheless, Tunisia's unique combination of "exceptionalisms" makes it a good illustration of how deep-rooted misogyny is in the region and how far reaching are its branches. Despite its long history of extensive modernist reforms, which gave women far more legal rights than their regional counterparts, Tunisian society also produced at least six thousand men who were lured into an organization which, like the Taliban regime discussed in chapter 2, was defined since its inception by strict gender policies, and where gender-based crimes were institutionalized and promoted. Democracy, employment, education, dignity, and infrastructure are all great, yet thousands of men escaped to a place without any of this, in the hope of belonging to a community that legitimized brutal punishment of women and girls including rape, flogging, burning, stoning, beheading, and shooting.[66]

This, alone, should invite feminists who still insist on minimizing the impact of misogyny in North African and the Middle East, or scholars in general who remain hopeful about the outcome of a selective modernity in the region, to reconsider their views. The case of Tunisia also calls into question the legacy of authoritarian state feminism. As feminist activist Amira Mhadhbi writes in an essay about women in postrevolutionary Tunisia, "The Tunisian experience with state feminism is a model to draw lessons from, especially for the Arab-Muslim countries whether governed by liberal autocratic regimes or Islamist regimes: whenever the regime talks in favor of women, read between the lines."[67] Unfortunately, states in the region continue to engage in feminist propaganda because Muslim women remain essential to the enactment of modernity. A case in point is Saudi Arabia's lifting of the ban on women driving, which, the next section argues, is symptomatic of a superficial modernity in which consumerism is mistaken for liberties and luxury is seen as emancipation.

Muslim Women and the Enactment of Modernity

Many Westerners view modest clothing as the ultimate sign of Muslim women's oppression. They assume that the concept of the veil, whether a headscarf or a full-body covering, is based on the outdated idea that women's bodies are overly sexual and must be hidden. The veil covers women, effaces them, signals that they are less valuable than men. According to this line of though, the veil is either forced on women by Muslim men or in an expression of an over-zealous form of piety. As a global phenomenon, it is regarded as the sign of a worrisome creep of Islam.[68]

To counter these assumptions about Muslim women and veiling, Elizabeth Bucar writes about her experience on a plane before its descent into Tehran airport: "I heard a slight rustling and looked over at the woman across the aisle from me. Thirty-something, dressed in skinny jeans and a Diane von Fustenberg patterned silk blouse. She caught me staring, smiled, and then winked. Out of her Louis Vuitton bag came an overcoat and a Gucci scarf." As Bucar is standing at passport control, she realizes that she is unfashionable compared to the Iranian women around her: "in my long black crepe overcoat and plain black scarf, surrounded by women in stylishly cut and colorful coats and tunics—I realized I had probably overcompensated and worn something too demure." She concludes, "Contrary to the assumptions of outsiders, women's dress in Iran continued to be enormously varied even after the legalization of mandatory *hijab.*"[69] There is something disconcerting about the surprise that Muslim women's fashion provokes. Is it assumed that the West is solely entitled to fashion?

Other scholars, too, have used Muslim women's fashion to confirm Islam's compatibility with Western modernity.[70] And while they are right to insist on the plurality of Muslim women's experiences, of which fashion and dress are manifestations, a romanticized tradition-modernity duality, however, does not constitute a counter narrative. Many in the West are already aware of the ability of Muslim women in Muslim-majority countries to engage with modernity as consumers of high-end luxury, particularly in Gulf countries. Pick any fashion influencer from the region and you will find that among her Instagram followers are women and men from around the world, including the West, lusting after her extensive collections of Birkins, Chanels, Louboutins, and stacks of Cartier, Van Cleef, and Chopard. The question is whether owning and displaying luxury goods equate to emancipation, and, just as importantly, whether combining practices of veiling with name-brand accessories is proof of the compatibility of tradition and modernity.

Like the many feminists who have written on the topic, the automobile industry, too, perceives consumerism as proof of modernity and even feminist consciousness. As soon as women were granted the right to drive in Saudi Arabia in 2018, ad campaigns were carefully prepared to lure Saudi women. Audi released a commercial on its Middle East YouTube channel under the title "Sometimes history is written. This time, it is driven."[71] The video, a little over a minute long, relies on elegant and simple aesthetics, the kind of simplicity it takes a fortune to pull off. A woman wearing a black abaya adjusts her scarf, exposing what looks like a Cartier watch on her wrist. She picks up her twenty-five-centimeter Hermès Emerald Kelly and leaves the room in the company of what can only be her husband, since the concept of *khulwa* makes it illegal for a Saudi woman to be in seclusion with a man who is not her *mahram*, or male guardian, usually her husband, brother, father, or son. When the couple approaches the gray Audi A8 parked outside, the man leans toward the door but the woman reaches first and opens it, cocking her head to tell him to get in. He complies. Next, she is seen inside the car, both hands on the wheel, her husband looking at her with an approving smile before she drives into city streets. The message is clear: Audi is selling an empowering object, and is particularly interested in the Saudi woman who carefully curates her luxury collection, picking the best brand for each of her possessions.

Nissan too wants to empower women through the latest automotive technologies, while at the same time upholding traditional local values. In January 2018, it launched a campaign under the theme #SheDrives, offering Saudi women their first driving lesson free.[72] The description under the video published on the Nissan Saudi Arabia YouTube channel states: "Driving can be stressful for many women in Saudi Arabia, to increase their confidence, we invited them to their first ever driving lesson, with an unexpected instructor." The unexpected instructor turns out to be the woman's father, brother, or husband. As each woman drives in the parking lot under the guidance of the male relative seated next to her, the camera shifts outside the car to catch the model, a Nissan Altima 3SSL, and the license plate: "2018 GRL" in both English and Arabic. The choice of "girl," *bnt* in Arabic, is significant since in many Arabic-speaking countries *bnt* is also a virginity status. To refer to an unmarried young woman as "woman" can be unacceptable, as it implies that she has lost her virginity through an illicit sexual relation. "GRL" as opposed to "WMN" is therefore a safer option, for, while Nissan wants to empower women with its cars, it does not want to disturb local patriarchy's notions about a woman's body and sexuality. Indeed, in the commercial's closing scene following the confessional model prevalent in reality television, the women are shown on a sofa speaking directly to the camera and expressing gratitude to their male relatives for their support.

Shell's commercial, too, tries to balance a feminist message of empowerment with deference to patriarchal expectations.[73] In May 2018, the company published a commercial in which five Saudi men (a hip-hop artist, an international in-line skater, a doctor, a TV personality, and an ex-navy officer) are each in the passenger seat being driven at night in the desert while reflecting on the question: "Are men ready for women drivers in Saudi Arabia?" The men first express concern, but eventually all five agree that despite the fears and possible difficulties, women are capable of driving. Once the car is parked, the driver exits, leaving behind the men to look at the photos of their women relatives projected on an open-air cinema screen. Each man is then surprised as his wife, sister, mother, or daughter enters the vehicle and sits next to him in the driver's seat. In the penultimate shot, the viewer reads "support her in her journey as she supported you in yours." Predictably, the last shot is of the product: Shell Helix Motor Oils.

There is nothing accidental about the choice of setting, namely the desert at nighttime and the music in the background. In Arabic literature and culture, even predating Islam, the desert has traditionally been constructed as an intimate space to reflect on intimate matters such as longing, love, and desire, as well as a stage to manifest culturally celebrated virtues including masculinity, hospitality, courage, nobility, and honor. Through its choice of a Saudi space as well as Saudi men, Shell claims authenticity for both the idea (women's driving) and the object being sold (Shell products). At the same time, it distances itself from other commercials such as the Audi video, for example, which was filmed at least in part in Casablanca, Morocco, and in which the role of the Saudi husband is played by Moroccan actor Fehd Benchemsi. Indeed, the Audi commercial was criticized for its inauthenticity.[74] The Shell commercial, on the other hand, was seen as more relatable, which, perhaps, accounts for its success in terms of views and number of comments.[75]

If it is relatable, then relatability does not necessarily mean support or approval. On the contrary, the Shell commercial was subjected to more scrutiny than the less relatable ones. To be sure, there were those who supported the message, notably several women who approve of lifting the ban. For example, a YouTuber by the name Fatima hopes to find a job and acquire her own car. Another woman, responding directly to the allegation that driving is only the beginning of debauchery, insists that driving does not equal taking off the veil and that she comes from a conservative family that supports women's driving. The majority of commentators, however, disapprove of women driving. There are those who question the practical aspect: "Right now the streets of Riyadh are crowded. What's going to happen when women start driving?" Another one seeks legitimacy for his dissent in a quote attributed to the late Prince Nayef bin Abdul-Aziz Al Saud, who allegedly said that those who call for liberating the Saudi woman are interested in the freedom to exploit her. Other viewers are more direct. One man states simply: "We do not want women to drive." Another one, reassured by his compatriots' unwavering allegiance to past traditions, responds, "There is still good in us."

The comments published in response to the Shell video offer a glimpse into the decades of debate about Saudi women's driving and, more generally, the clash of modernity and tradition. In 2011, a Saudi academic prepared a report for the Consultative Assembly (*majlis a-shura*), in which it was argued that allowing Saudi women to drive would lead to an avalanche of moral disasters, among which he named pornography, prostitution, and homosexuality. The report claimed, moreover, that within ten years of lifting the ban, there would be "no more virgins" in the country.[76] In several Western media outlets the report was mocked, comparing it to earlier connections between virginity and exercise, walking, and riding bikes.[77] Others diminished its significance by attributing it to an "ultra-conservative" and old guard, out of touch with the desires of the young population. Nevertheless, the anti-driving comments posted on YouTube and other social media platforms do not come from old men or disconnected Wahhabi clerics. On the contrary, online demographics indicate they most likely would have come from educated men between the ages of eighteen and thirty-four.[78]

It needs to be said, however, that a 2017 Arab News/YouGov poll shows that 71 percent of men and 82 percent of women agree with the decision to allow Saudi women to drive.[79] Therefore, there appears to be a discrepancy between the survey and the YouTube comments. One explanation for this discrepancy might be the distinction between the "idea" of women driving and the practice. Shell's ad introduces driving as an intimate practice involving one's wife, sister, daughter, and mother. Judging from the comments, Saudi men appear far more reluctant to see women closest to them behind the wheel. The poll, on the other hand, reflects support for the idea of driving, which is a way of safely engaging modernity without committing to change. Additionally, perhaps the men and women surveyed felt more comfortable agreeing with the idea because they were aware that thanks to the guardianship system, women's male guardians, who serve as the gatekeepers of religious tradition, would be the ones making the final decision about women's driving. In 2019, however, reforms to the male guardianship laws made it possible for women to obtain a driver's license without their guardian's approval. It would be interesting to see the results of a new poll about women's driving in light of these reforms.

Regardless of the reason behind the discrepancy, it is safe to say that lifting the ban on driving, like other gender-oriented reforms in Saudi Arabia, was not the result of a change in mentalities. It is also safe to say that these top-down reforms were not motivated by a feminist concern and an awareness of women's oppression in Saudi society. As Saudi-born British scholar Madawi al-Rasheed has pointed out, after 9/11 the state began to relax restrictions on women in response to international pressure and condemnation. "The masculine state," she writes, "needed women to dispel negative images of the country associated with Jihadi terrorism abroad and inside the country."[80] In 2016, women were yet again at the forefront of political discussion when Crown Prince Mohammad bin Salaman launched "Vision 2030," a plan to modernize the kingdom and promote economic growth.[81] It is in this context that, in September 2017, King Salman issued a royal decree authorizing women to drive starting in June 2018.[82]

Therefore, as has been the practice in the region including in Tunisia, Egypt, and Morocco, women in Saudi Arabia were called upon once more to serve as what Assid has termed the state's "modernity face." Nevertheless, it is a modernity on the regime's terms and according to its definition, or what Iranian American literary critic Kamran Talattof has termed "modernoid," to refer to "a society that resembles a modern one in some areas but lacks other essential modern structures."[83] Similarly, in *The Son King: Reform and Repression in Saudi Arabia*, al-Rasheed argues that the definition of "modernity and reform" in Saudi Arabia excludes "the basic, and fundamental, tenet of modernity: freedom to think, to debate all aspects of life, from the personal to the political and social, and to act on one's thoughts." Instead, al-Rasheed explains, "the modern" in Saudi Arabia "was limited to women driving cars, the introduction of the cinema and popular Western culture, and the transformation of a state capitalist rentier economy into an open liberal market."[84] Feminist reforms, therefore, are used as part of a political strategy to brand the state as modern, while at the same time continuing to disallow engagement with the values and practices of modernity.

Modernity, however, is not the only term to be called into question. Labeling Saudi state reforms feminist is also problematic, though not necessarily for the reasons Charrad describes in the case of Tunisia. In 2019, a little over a year after the ban on driving had been lifted, the Saudi state security agency declared feminism a Western import and a crime of "extremism" punishable by jail and flogging.[85] Other criminalized "extremist ideas" on the list include homosexuality and atheism. The agency eventually backtracked on equating feminism with a crime of extremism, though homosexuality and atheism, both of which are punishable by death under Saudi law, remain on the list.[86]

To be sure, the critique of selective state-sanctioned modernity and reforms is not meant to trivialize or minimize the work of feminists in Saudi Arabia who continue to pay a high price for their activism, including imprisonment and torture. In fact, the criminalization of feminism was in part intended to legitimize the imprisonment of dissenters, including Loujain al-Hathoul, who was instrumental to the campaign to legalize driving for women in Saudi Arabia.[87] Nor is this discussion meant to trivialize Saudi women's desire to acquire a car, drive it, and feel empowered by it. The goal is to call into question the automatic association between enactments of modernity and emancipation, between displaying luxury goods and the absence of oppression. The automotive industry's zeal to intentionally confuse the two is to be expected. In 2018, in Saudi Arabia alone, the luxury market reached a value of US$14.5 billion and, before the COVID-19 pandemic, was projected to reach a value of $22.2 billion in 2024.[88] Saudi women customers were expected to contribute to an increase in car sales from an annual average of 3 percent to 9 percent through 2025, and an increase in car leasing from 2 percent to 4 percent per annum.[89] But what do feminists stand to win from their endorsement?

***

Saudi Arabia and Tunisia are often constructed as brackets for the Arab-Muslim world regarding women's rights. They are described as the two extremes in between which fall the rest of the countries in the region. One is the "most modern state," "most secular," and is home to the most liberated Muslim women outside the West. The other is the birthplace of Wahabism, often regarded as one of the most conservative interpretations of Islam. It is also one of the most restrictive countries for women, particularly in public space. While these tropes can serve chauvinistic purposes on both sides, used to celebrate the progress of one or the authenticity of the other, they do not describe accurately the complex and conflicted relationship both societies have with religion and modernity. Nor do these tropes help advance women's rights in the region. There would be no solace to Tunisian women to know that they have had more rights than other women in Muslim-majority societies when many of their countrymen have been seduced by a misogynistic utopia. Moreover, while Saudi Arabia was, until recently, the only country where women were forbidden from driving, it remains true today that women and girls throughout North Africa and the Middle East are formally or informally prohibited from walking in public space without being subjected to concessions they must make merely for being women. Indeed, now that women everywhere are allowed to drive, perhaps the time has come to demand the right to walk!

Discussions of women's rights in the region, therefore, ought to move beyond superficial measures of modernity and religiosity and allow for the recognition of continuities along with discontinuities. Mohamed Atta could have come from any country. As a Tunisian, Saudi, Algerian, Moroccan, or Libyan man, it is likely he would have had the same selective approach toward Western modernity and a comparable allegiance to the past. To be sure, to live within what Iranian American philosopher Seyyed Hossein Nasr has described as "a polarized field of tension created by two contending world views and systems of values," cannot be easy, especially since, in general, Muslim societies do not foster a culture of doubt.[90] This, however, is not meant as a call for sympathy, for though the clash of values does not inspire most men to commit terrorist acts, allegiance to medieval theology, nevertheless, inspires and justifies misogyny, which impacts significantly the lives and existence of women and girls today as discussed throughout this book.

One of these women was Israa Ghrayeb, who, as mentioned in chapter 3, was murdered by men in her family for posting a photo of herself and a man at a café.[91] Like women and men her age, she too was captivated by selective elements of modernity including technology, fashion, and luxury brands. One of her online photographs shows her wearing a Gucci t-shirt. She even made of fashion and beauty her profession. As a makeup artist, she took great pride in publishing on social media platforms her various makeup looks and outfits of the day. Indeed, one of her last posts was about beauty. Despite the bandage on her forehead, she shared a smiling selfie accompanied by a message to her friends and clients who had previously booked appointments with her: "My spine is broken and I have a surgery today. If the surgery goes well, I will let you know and if not I will have to cancel everything." But Israa reportedly never made it out of the hospital alive. Male members of her family— allegedly two of her brothers, her brother-in-law, and father—beat her to death inside her hospital room, where they had joined her to complete the punishment that they had begun earlier at the family home.[92] A few days later, her body was buried according to tradition, and her story would have ended there were it not for the leaked hospital video recorded by a nurse in which Israa is heard screaming while being beaten.[93]

In the face of such injustice, one wonders if words, and more words, to explain contexts, to justify acts, and to understand motives, are mere strategies to intentionally obfuscate a simple reality. Misogyny in North Africa and the Middle East could not possibly be any clearer or more directly articulated through words, images, sounds, actions, and bodies. Yet, it is ignored, as too much scholarship is spent searching for reconciliations and compatibilities. To make matters worse, Muslim women are expected to be strong. One can sense the anger that the call for strength provoked in Israa as she was approaching her death. Awaiting a spinal cord surgery, she posted what was perhaps her last message on Instagram: "I'm strong and I have the will to live—if I didn't have this willpower, I would have died yesterday. Don't send me messages telling me to be strong, I am strong. May god be the judge of those who oppressed me and hurt me."[94] Having spent her entire life catering to others' expectations, it is understandable that in her painful state she did not wish to entertain any more demands.

What if feminists, activists, and policymakers were to honor Israa's last wish? What if the critical focus and demands were to shift to oppressors? What if Israa, and Muslim women and girls in general, came to be treated as ordinary beings without any special powers that miraculously make onlookers mistake their pain for strength? What if, to borrow Moghissi's words, instead of being "'more accepting' of practices which are unacceptable *here* but admissible *there*," we agree that what is not acceptable for women in the West should not be admissible for women and girls in Muslim-majority societies?

In a 2019 interview with journalist Rachid Hallaouy, Assid was asked about another Moroccan journalist who had just been jailed for having an abortion, which continues to be illegal. She was also charged with having a sexual relationship with her boyfriend outside marriage, which is also illegal. Without deference or concession, Assid was quick to point out that instead of engaging in long debates and endless justifications, the fundamental question is the human's right to "individual liberty." Assid did not qualify his statement. He did not introduce conditions, cautions, or caveats. He did not seek compatibility, consensus, or conformity. He did not acquiesce to the desires of the large audience that would later view his response once uploaded to YouTube, nor did it matter to him that he was speaking about a woman born, arbitrarily, *there*. As far as he was concerned, as a woman she could do whatever she pleased with her body, including having sex and an abortion.[95] Israa was owed to be treated as an individual, unconditionally. And so were Hanan, Ahlam, Zeinab, Khadija, Bouchra, Fatima-Zahra, Kalthoum, Mona, Nabiha, Hajar, Sarah, and Chaima. And so were the many girls and women whose last screams have never been heard, and whose last pain has never been seen.

NOTES

1. "Mohamed Atta's Last Will and Testament," PBS, https://www.pbs.org/wgbh/pages/frontline/shows/network/personal/attawill.html.
2. This is a direct reference to a hadith according to which "Allah curses those women who visit the graves." There are Islamic scholars, however, who have argued that the Qur'an does not forbid women from visiting graveyards, attributing such prohibitions to "radical" interpretations of Islam. See Faisal Devji, *Landscapes of Jihad: Militancy, Morality, Modernity* (Ithaca: Cornell University Press, 2005), 114.
3. Jane Corbin, "A Premonition of Evil," *The Guardian*, July 4, 2002, https://www.theguardian.com/world/2002/jul/05/gender.uk.
4. Paradoxically, while disdained on earth, women are also Atta's heavenly reward. When the FBI searched Atta's and other hijackers' luggage, they found a handwritten letter in Arabic containing spiritual and practical guidance for the hijackers. Once the terrorist attacks begin, Atta and his companions are instructed by the document's unknown author to "strike like champions who do not want to go back to this world."

What awaits them on the other side, they are told, is much better: "Know that the gardens of paradise are waiting for you in all their beauty, and the women of paradise are waiting, calling out, 'Come hither, friend of God.' They have dressed in their most beautiful clothing." "Instructions for the Last Night," PBS, https://www.pbs.org/wgbh/pages/frontline/shows/network/personal/instructions.html.

5. See J. Michael Mahoney, *Schizophrenia: The Bearded Lady Disease* (Bloomington: AuthorHouse, 2011), 302; Adam Lankford, *The Myth of Martyrdom: What Really Drives Suicide Bombers, Rampage Shooters, and Other Self-Destructive Killers* (New York: Palgrave Macmillan, 2013), 78. Others, however, disagree with the mental illness diagnosis. For example, Park Dietz, the head psychiatric consultant for the FBI, believes it is "unlikely that any of the terrorists suffered from a serious mental illness." Similarly, Harold Bursztajn, the co-director of the program in psychiatry and the law at Harvard Medical School, argues that Atta and the rest of the hijackers were not "suicidal," nor were they "depressed, hopeless, and helpless." Rather, they were motivated by "rage and a sense of self-righteousness." Andrew Giese, "The Mind of a Suicide Terrorist," ABC News, January 6, 2006, https://abcnews.go.com/Health/story?id=117233&page=1.

6. In this chapter, Western modernity is understood as defined by Kamran Talattof, "as any serious theoretical adaptation and manifestation of the Western discourse of modernity, enlightenment, reformism, and reason in different areas of life beyond industry and economy." Kamran Talattof, *Modernity, Sexuality, and Ideology in Iran: The Life and Legacy of Popular Iranian Female Artists* (New York: Syracuse University Press, 2011), 19.

7. Fouad Ajami, "The Way We Live Now: 10–07–01; Out of Egypt," *New York Times Magazine*, October 7, 2001, https://www.nytimes.com/2001/10/07/magazine/the-way-we-live-now-10-07-01-out-of-egypt.html.

8. For more on tradition and modernity, see Fouad Ajami, *The Arab Predicament: Arab Political Thought and Practice since 1967* (Cambridge: Cambridge University Press, 1993).

9. Fouad Ajami, "The Way We Live Now: 10–07–01; Out of Egypt."

10. For Atta, both women and the West are similar to the devil (or at times are the devil) in their untrustworthiness and inherent desire to make men deviate from the right path. The document found in Atta's luggage describes Muslims "who are fascinated with Western civilization, and have drank the love [of the West] like they drink water [unclear]" as the Devil's allies. See "Instructions for the Last Night," PBS, https://www.pbs.org/wgbh/pages/frontline/shows/network/personal/instructions.html.

11. The 2018 "Kiki dance challenge," which consisted of jumping out of a slow-moving car and dancing to Drake's song "In My Feelings," was among top Twitter trends in many Arab countries. It was mocked as yet another example of blind imitation of the West. Mohamed al-Wakil, "Video 'tahaddi kiki; ysh'il Twitter bil-khalij, was mugharridun: 'taqlid a'ma,'" *Masr al-Arabia*, July 20, 2018, https://m.masralarabia.net.

12. In the UAE, which banned the Kiki challenge, three social media influencers who participated in the challenge were detained "on charges of endangering their lives and the lives of others, and violating public morals using social networking sites to promote practices that are incompatible with the values and traditions of society." Egypt and Jordan, too, banned the challenge, citing public safety. See "UAE Detains 3 Social

Media Influencers over Kiki Dance Challenge," *Arab News*, July 24, 2018, https://www.arabnews.com/node/1344456/offbeat.

13. Bernard Lewis, "The West and the Middle East," *Foreign Affairs* 76, no. 1 (January/February 1997): 117.

14. Ibid., 123.

15. Muhammad As-Saffar, trans. Susan Gilson Miller, *Disorienting Encounters: Travels of a Moroccan Scholar in France in 1845–1846: The Voyage of Mushammad As-Saffar* (Berkeley: University of California Press, 1992), 193–94.

16. Ibid., 182.

17. Ibid., 161.

18. Ibid., 185–85.

19. Ibid., 157.

20. Ibid., 220.

21. Mona Abaza, *Debates on Islam and Knowledge in Malaysia and Egypt: Shifting Worlds* (London: Routledge, 2002), 155.

22. Rifa'a Rafi' al-Tahtawi, trans. Daniel L. Newman, *An Imam in Paris: Account of a Stay in France by an Egyptian Cleric, 1826–1831* (London: Saqi, 2004), 228.

23. Ibid., 182.

24. Ibid., 181.

25. A good example of al-Tahtawi's selective approach to modernity is his work on education, particularly girls' education, of which he was an advocate. See Rifa'a Rafi' al-Tahtawi, *Tahrir al-mar'a al-muslima: kitab al-murshid al-amin fi tarbiyat al-banat wa-al-banin*, ed. Yahya al-Shaykh (Beirut: Dar al-Buraq, 2000); and Kenneth M. Cuno, *Modernizing Marriage: Family, Ideology, and Law in Nineteenth-and Early Twentieth-Century Egypt* (Syracuse: Syracuse University Press, 2015).

26. See Mohamed Haddad, *Muslim Reformism—A Critical History: Is Islamic Religious Reform Possible?* (Cham: Springer, 2020).

27. Mohamed Haddad, *Al-dawla al-'aliqa: ma'ziq al-muwatana wal-hukm al-madani fil-mujtama'at al-islamiya* (Misr: Dar al-tanwir litiba'a wa al-nashr, 2018).

28. Hafida El Farsi, "Fi liqa' bimu'asasat abdel Aziz al-Saud li-dirasat al-islamiyya wa l'ulum al-insaniyya al-bahith al-tunusi Mohamed el-Haddad," *Al-ittihad al-ichtiraki*, November 5, 2018, http://alittihad.info.

29. See Glenn E. Robinson, *Global Jihad: A Brief History* (Stanford: Stanford University Press, 2021).

30. See Assid's oral intervention in Arabic about "The Problematic of Modernity in Moroccan Society," available at Tatsut Channel, "Ahmed Assid: ishkaliyyat al-hadatha fil mujtama' al-maghribi bayna al-mumarasa wal-turath," YouTube video, 28:02, December 21, 2019, https://www.youtube.com/watch?v=9Ty2u9qZ9d8&t=338s.

31. Ahmed Assid, "Al-hadatha bi athar rij'i," *Al-hiwar almutamaddin*, October 7, 2015, https://www.ahewar.org/debat/show.art.asp?aid=487680.

32. Ibid.

33. Bassam Tibi, *Islam's Predicament with Modernity: Religious Reform and Cultural Change* (New York: Routledge, 2009), 130–31.

34. Ibid., 33.

35. Hace Mess, "Ahmed Assid: Islam et modernités (Forsem, Lyon-France)," YouTube video, April 11, 2015, https://www.youtube.com/watch?v=9f-sYTqaAG4.

36. Hafida El Farsi, "Fi liqa' bimu'asasat abdel Aziz al-Saud li-dirasat al-islamiyya wa l'ulum al-insaniyya al-bahith al-tunusi Mohamed el-Haddad."

37. Noah Feldman, "A Peace Prize for Tunisia's Exceptionalism," Bloomberg, October 9, 2015, https://www.bloomberg.com/opinion/articles/2015-10-09/a-nobel-peace-prize-for-tunisia-s-exceptionalism.

38. Valentine M. Moghadam, "Women's Rights in the Middle East and North Africa—Tunisia," *Freedom House*, October 14, 2005, available at https://www.refworld.org/docid/47387b702f.html.

39. At the peak of its successes, it was estimated that it had 100,000 fighters. As of December 2015, 30,000 of the recruits were foreign fighters from more than eighty countries. The majority of recruits from non-Muslim majority countries came from Russian (2,400 fighters) and France (1,700). When considering the number of fighters per capita, Belgium is in first place supplying an estimated 470 militants, followed by Sweden with an estimated 300 fighters. It is estimated that Europe supplied over 5,000 militants. In Muslim-majority countries, outside Syria and Iraq, the majority of the fighters came from Tunisia with (6,000 official while the non-official number is 7,000), Saudi Arabia (with 2,5000), Turkey (2,100), Jordan (2,000 official and 2,500 non-official), and Morocco (1,200 official and 1,500 non-official). See Daveed Gartenstein-Ross, "How Many Fighters Does the Islamic State Really Have?" http://warontherocks.com/2015/02/how-many-fighters-does-the-islamic-state-really-have/; Jessica Stern, "ISIS and the Foreign Fighter Phenomenon," http://www.theatlantic.com/international/archive/2015/03/isis-and-the-foreign-fighter-problem/387166/; Efraim Benmelech and Esteban F. Klor, "What Explains the Flow of Foreign Fighters to ISIS?" Kellog School of Management, Northwestern University, April 2016, https://www.kellogg.northwestern.edu/faculty/benmelech/html/BenmelechPapers/ISIS_April_13_2016_Effi_final.pdf; and "Foreign Fighters in Iraq and Syria," https://www.rferl.org/a/foreign-fighters-syria-iraq-is-isis-isil-infographic/26584940.html.

40. For more on state feminism, see Lamia Ben Youssef Zayzafoon, "Home, Body, and Nation: The Production of the Muslim Woman in the Reformist Through of Tahar Haddad and Habib Bourguiba," in *The Production of the Muslim Woman: Negotiating Text, History and Ideology* (Lanham, MD: Lexington Books, 2005). For the aftermath of the uprising, see Lamia Ben Youssef Zayzafoon, "Is it the End of State Feminism? Tunisian Women during and after the Revolution," in *The Arab Revolution in Context: Civil Society and Democracy in a Changing Middle East*, eds, Benjamin Isakhan, Fethi Mansouri, and Shahram Akbarzadeh (Melbourne: Melbourne University Press, 2012), 43–62.

41. Mounira M. Charrad, *States and Women's Rights: The Making of Postcolonial Tunisia, Algeria, and Morocco* (Berkeley: University of California Press, 2001).

42. Colin Francome, *Unsafe Abortion and Women's Health* (New York: Routledge, 2016), 126.

43. For more on the positions on the veil in the Tunisian context, see Aili Mari Tripp, *Seeking Legitimacy: Whey Arab Autocracies Adopt Women's Rights* (Cambridge: Cambridge University Press, 2019).

44. See Hind Ahmed Zaki, "Why Did Women's Rights Expand in Post-Revolutionary Tunisia?" *Middle East Brief,* Brandeis University, Crown Center for Middle East Studies, October 2019, available at https://www.brandeis.edu/crown/publications/middle-east-briefs/pdfs/101-200/meb131.pdf. It is important to note, however, that not all calls for reform have been successful. A case in point is the resistance to changing the laws of inheritance to make it equal, despite the overwhelming evidence showing the economic abuse Tunisian women endure because of the current inheritance laws. See Victor Tanner, "Strengthening Women's Control Over Land: Inheritance Reform in Tunisia," *Developing Alternatives*, February 20, 2020, https://dai-global-developments.com/articles/strengthening-womens-control-over-land-inheritance-reform-in-tunisia.

45. Mounira M. Charrad, "Tunisia at the Forefront of the Arab World: Two Waves of Gender Legislation," in *Women in the Middle East and North Africa: Agents of Change*, eds. Fatima Sadiqi and Moha Ennaji (New York: Routledge, 2011), 108.

46. Ibid., 107.

47. A government study published in 2016 revealed that 53.5 percent of women have experienced violence in the public space in the period between 2011 and 2015, and that 78 percent of the women surveyed stated that they have suffered psychological violence. See Rikke Hostrup Haugbolle and Ahlam Chemlali, "Everyday Violence and Security in Tunisia," *Middle East Institute*, February 19, 2019, https://www.mei.edu/publications/everyday-violence-and-security-tunisia#_ftnref5.

48. Cléo Fatoorehchi, "Les femmes en Tunisie—Partie 1: L'après-revolution, plus de liberté pour moins de sécurié," *Opinion Internationale*, May 21, 2013, https://www.opinion-internationale.com/2013/05/21/les-femmes-en-tunisie-partie-1-lapres-revolution-plus-de-liberte-pour-moins-de-securite_17694.html.

49. "Violence Marks New Low in Tunisian Parliamentary Politics," *The Arab Weekly*, December 7, 2020, https://thearabweekly.com/violence-marks-new-low-tunisian-parliamentary-politics.

50. For the entire intervention, see Assemblée de representants du peuple, "Mohamed Affes," YouTube video, 6:31, December 2, 2020, https://www.youtube.com/watch?v=W2KCU4M_8hA.

51. See, for example, Journeyman Pictures, "Tunisian Jihadis: How the Islamic State Has Preyed on Tunisia's Youth," YouTube video, 15:07, May 19, 2017, https://www.youtube.com/watch?v=da8j33HO19Q.

52. For salaries and other financial incentives paid to the fighters and their recruiters, see "ISIS Pays Foreign Fighters $1,000 a month: Jordan King," NBC News, September 22, 2014, http://www.nbcnews.com/storyline/isis-terror/isis-pays-foreign-fighters-1-000-month-jordan-king-n209026; Jose Pagliery, "ISIS Cuts Its Fighters' Salaries by 50 percent," CNN, January 19, 2016, https://money.cnn.com/2016/01/19/news/world/isis-salary-cuts/index.html; "For an ISIS fighter, a paid honeymoon in Syria's Raqqa," *Al Arabiya*, May 27, 2015, http://english.alarabiya.net/en/perspective/features/2015/05/27/For-an-ISIS-fighter-a-paid-honeymoon-in-caliphate-s-heart.html.

53. In fact, the non-Muslim countries with the largest number of recruits per capita are Belgium, Sweden, and Finland, which are wealthy and highly equitable countries. See Efraim Benmelech and Esteban F. Klor, "What Explains the Flow of Foreign Fighters to ISIS?" 7.

54. To be sure, the study does not specify what type of jobs they held in their countries of origin. It is not uncommon for young people to settle for jobs when their education level exceeds by far the job requirements. World Bank, "Economic and Social Inclusion to Prevent Violent Extremism" (Washington, DC: The World Bank, 2016), 17, available at http://documents1.worldbank.org/curated/en/409591474983005625/pdf/108525 -REVISED-PUBLIC.pdf.

55. Ibid., 16–17.

56. Taslima Nasrin, *Exile: A Memoire* (Penguin Random House India, 2016).

57. Haleh Esfandiari, "ISIS's Cruelty Toward Women Gets Scant Attention," *The Wall Street Journal*, September 2, 2014, https://blogs.wsj.com/washwire/2014/09/02/isiss -cruelty-toward-women-gets-scant-attention/.

58. Kenneth Roth, "Slavery: The ISIS Rules," *New York Review of Books*, September 24, 2015, https://www.hrw.org/news/2015/09/05/slavery-isis-rules.

59. It is one of the earliest videos of the ISIS slave market. It was published on You-Tube in October 2014, depicting young men joking about Yaidi slaves' teeth, eye color, and the objects for which they are willing to exchange them. The video has since been removed but segments are available via other publications such as the *New York Times*, https://www.nytimes.com/video/world/middleeast/100000003226608/isis-slave-market -day.html.

60. Zelin argues that Tunisian fighters were involved in some of ISIS' most mediatized tortures and executions including the burning and killing of the Jordanian pilot Muadh al-Kasasbah. According to a former ISIS prisoner, "people from Tunisia were respon-sible for torturing." Aaron Y. Zelin, *Your Sons at Your Service: Tunisia's Missionaries of Jihad* (New York: Columbia University Press, 2020), 188 and 195.

61. Ibid., 196.

62. "Marking 5 Years Since IS Attack on Yazidis," VOA News, August 3, 2019, https: //www.voanews.com/middle-east/marking-5-years-attack-yazidis; "Agony of Yazidi Women Torn between Kids Fathered by ISIS Fighters and Returning Home," *The Straits Times*, July 14, 2019, https://www.straitstimes.com/world/middle-east/agony-of -yazidi-women-torn-between-kids-fathered-by-isis-fighters-or-return-home.

63. Anne-Marie O'Connor, "'Somebody Had to Tell These Stories': An Iraqi Wom-an's Ordeal as an ISIS Sex Slave," *The Washington Post*, November 23, 2017, https:// www.washingtonpost.com/world/middle_east/somebody-had-to-tell-these-stories-an -iraqi-womans-ordeal-as-an-isis-sex-slave/2017/11/22/4241145c-c8be-11e7-b506 -8a10ed11ecf5_story.html.

64. Aaron Y. Zelin, *Your Sons at Your Service: Tunisia's Missionaries of Jihad*, 188.

65. Ibid.

66. See Lisa Davis, "Reimagining Justice for Gender-Based Crimes at the Margins: New Legal Strategies for Prosecuting ISIS Crimes Against Women and LGBTIQ

Persons," *William & Mary Journal of Women and the Law* 24, no. 3 (May 2018): 513–58, https://scholarship.law.wm.edu/cgi/viewcontent.cgi?article=1478&context=wmjowl.

67. Amira Mhadhbi, "State Feminism in Tunisia: Reading between the Lines," *Open Democracy*, November 7, 2012, https://www.opendemocracy.net/en/5050/state-feminism-in-tunisia-reading-between-lines/.

68. Elizabeth Bucar, *Pious Fashion: How Muslim Women Dress* (Cambridge: Harvard University Press, 2017), 1.

69. Ibid., viii.

70. See Reina Lewis, *Muslim Fashion: Contemporary Style Culture* (Durham: Duke University Press, 2015). Lila Abu-Lughod, too, celebrated Muslim women's ability to reconcile modernity and tradition through fashion: "In the women I have known, I do not recognize 'the Muslim woman' of Hirsi Ali's books." She asks, "Is it . . . the fashion bloggers of Qatar featured in *Harper's Bazaar Arabia*? The glossy spread about them in 2010, titled 'Abaya Accessories,' reported on the young women who reach into their own closets for the latest designer wear about which to blog. Their elegant black abayas are set off by leopard platform heels by Christian Louboutin. Their Chanel sunglasses vie for attention with their Alexander McQueen rings and 'limited edition' Fendi two-tone python peekaboo bags. Are these the Muslim women Hirsi Ali implores her readers to think about when she pities 'the *others* . . . still locked in the world I have left behind'?" Lila Abu-Lughod, *Do Muslim Women Need Saving?* 73–74.

71. AudiMiddleEast, "Sometimes history is written. This time, it is driven." YouTube video, June 23, 2018, https://www.youtube.com/watch?v=llpjz-G69Lk.

72. Nissan Saudi Arabia, "Nissan Saudi Arabia Surprises Saudi Women," YouTube video, January 28, 2018, https://www.youtube.com/watch?v=NtLHigLmXNo.

73. Shell KSA, "Are Men Ready for Women Drivers in Saudi Arabia?" YouTube video, May 2, 2018, https://www.youtube.com/watch?v=pLM6s1mCgcY&t=24s.

74. One YouTube viewer mocked it for using an actor who does not know how to correctly wear the Saudi *shemagh*, or headdress. Another one wrote, "those are your women who act that way, not ours." A third viewer asked, "since when does the Arab-Muslim woman order her husband with a mere glance (*nadra min 3iniha*)?"

75. Of all the driving-related ads, Shell's video had the most views on YouTube (more than six million), and the largest number of comments (close to 7k), most of them in Arabic, specifically the Saudi dialect. It is also the video with the most comments by viewers who identify as Saudi. Moreover, of all the commercials discussed here, it is the one with the largest number of likes and an equal number of dislikes (12k each), though the viewers who have been monitoring the video since its release insist that the numbers are manipulated and that the likes are added while dislikes are erased.

76. Andy Bloxham, "Allowing Women Drivers in Saudi Arabia Will Be 'end of virginity,'" *The Telegraph*, December 2, 2011, https://www.telegraph.co.uk/motoring/news/8930168/Allowing-women-drivers-in-Saudi-Arabia-will-be-end-of-virginity.html.

77. Naomi McAuliffe, "Heard the One about the Saudi Cleric Who Said Driving Damages Ovaries?" *The Guardian*, September 30, 2013, https://www.theguardian.com/commentisfree/2013/sep/30/saudi-cleric-driving-damages-ovaries.

78. The age-group of twenty-five to thirty-four makes up 44.3 percent of Internet users, while the eighteen to twenty-four-year-olds make up 39.5 percent. See Lama, "Social Media Statistics in Saudi Arabia," *Talkwalker*, September 3, 2019, https://www.talk-walker.com/blog/social-media-statistics-saudi-arabia.

79. Nada Hameed, "Saudi Women Prefer Minivans to Larger SUVs," *Arab News*, January 15, 2018, https://www.arabnews.com/tags/saudiwomencandrivepoll.

80. Madawi al-Rasheed, *A Most Masculine State: Gender, Politics, and Religion in Saudi Arabia* (Cambridge: Cambridge University Press, 2013), 40.

81. An official summary of the 2030 vision is available at https://www.vision2030.gov.sa /v2030/leadership-message/.

82. Bloomberg Economics predicts that by 2030 women's driving could add $90 billion to economic output. See Zainab Fattah, "Saudi Arabia's $90 Billion Reason to Allow Women to Drive," Bloomberg, June 24, 2018, https://www.bloomberg.com/news/articles/2018-06-24/saudi-women-driving-is-seen-better-for-economy-than-aramco-ipo.

83. Kamran Talattof, *Modernity, Sexuality, and Ideology in Iran: The Life and Legacy of Popular Iranian Female Artists*, 21.

84. Madawi al-Rasheed, *The Son King: Reform and Repression in Saudi Arabia: Reform and Repression in Saudi Arabia* (Oxford: Oxford University Press, 2021), 90.

85. See Madawi al-Rasheed, "Will Feminism Be a Crime in bin Salman's Saudi Arabia?" *Middle East Eye*, November 15, 2019, https://www.middleeasteye.net/opinion/will -feminism-be-crime-new-saudi-arabia.

86. "Saudi Arabia: Categorizing Feminism, Atheism, Homosexuality as Crimes Exposes the Kingdom's Dangerous Intolerance," *Amnesty International*, November 12, 2019, https://www.amnesty.org/en/latest/press-release/2019/11/saudi-arabia-categorizing -feminism-atheism-homosexuality-as-crimes-exposes-the-kingdoms-dangerous-intoler-ance/; Patrick Kelleher, "Saudi Arabia U-turns on Declaring Feminism 'Extremism,'" *PinkNews*, November 13, 2019, https://www.pinknews.co.uk/2019/11/13/saudi-arabia -backtracks-feminism-extremism-homosexuality-crime-atheism/; Bill Bostock, "Saudi Arabia's Counter Terrorism Department Labels Feminism 'Extremism,'" YouTube video, 1:04, November 12, 2019, https://www.youtube.com/watch?v=MHbj3PN3RYw.

87. See Madawi al-Rasheed, "Will Feminism Be a Crime in bin Salman's Saudi Arabia?"

88. Research and Markets, "Saudi Arabia Luxury Market: Industry Trends, Share, Size, Growth, Opportunity and Forecast 2019–2024," April 2019. The entire report can be accessed through the website https://www.researchandmarkets.com/.

89. PWC, "Women Driving the Transformation of the KSA Automotive Market," March 2018, https://www.pwc.com/m1/en/publications/documents/women-driving-the -transformation-of-the-ksa-automotive-market.pdf.

90. Seyyed Hossein Nasr, *Islam and the Plight of Modern Man* (Cambridge: Islamic Texts Society, 2002), 27.

91. "Palestinian Woman Allegedly Killed after Posting Picture with Fiance," *Gulf News*, September 4, 2019, https://gulfnews.com/world/mena/palestinian-woman-allegedly -killed-after-posting-picture-with-fiance-1.66200478.

92. Tom Bateman, "Israa Ghrayeb: Palestinian Woman's Death Prompts Soul-searching," BBC News, September 16, 2019, https://www.bbc.com/news/world-middle-east-49688920; Maya Oppenheim, "Suspected Honour Killing of 21-year-old Woman Sparks Palestinian Protests," *Independent*, September 3, 2019, https://www.independent.co.uk/news/world/middle-east/israa-ghrayeb-palestine-honour-killing-protest-beit-sahour-a9089976.html; "Palestinian Woman Allegedly Killed after Posting Picture with Fiance," *Gulf News*, September 4, 2019, https://gulfnews.com/world/mena/palestinian-woman-allegedly-killed-after-posting-picture-with-fiance-1.66200478.

93. The video was initially posted by "Do You Know Him?" a Palestinian Facebook group dedicated to denouncing men who mistreat women. Tom Bateman, "Israa Ghrayeb: Palestinian Woman's Death Prompts Soul-searching."

94. Zachary Keyser, "Palestinians Protest in Bethlehem after Alleged 'Honor Killing' of 21-year-old Woman," *The Jerusalem Post*, September 3, 2019, https://www.jpost.com/middle-east/palestinians-protest-in-bethlehem-after-alleged-honor-killing-of-21-year-old-girl-600405.

95. Matin TV, "Ahmed Assid dans l'Info en Face," YouTube video, 49:37, September 10, 2019, https://www.youtube.com/watch?v=__FaR51qj4o.

Index

About the Author

Ibtissam Bouachrine is professor, department chair of Spanish and Portuguese, and former director of the Middle East Studies Program at Smith College, where she teaches courses on gender and sexuality, Islam and the West, Islamic Spain, and minorities in North Africa and the Middle East. Bouachrine's first book, *Women and Islam: Myths, Apologies, and Limits of Feminist Critique* (Lexington Books, 2014), examines the discourse on Muslim women from the Middle Ages to the post-9/11 era.

www.ingramcontent.com/pod-product-compliance
Lightning Source LLC
Chambersburg PA
CBHW022314280326
41932CB00010B/1102